P9-DKD-760

PROSPECTS OF SOVIET POWER IN THE 1980s

Prospects of Soviet Power in the 1980s

Edited by

CHRISTOPH BERTRAM

ARCHON BOOKS
1980

St. Philip's College Library

327.47
P966b

Chapters 1–13 © The International Institute for Strategic Studies 1979
Chapters 14–16 © The International Institute for Strategic Studies 1980

All rights reserved. No part of this publication may be
reproduced or transmitted, in any form or by any means,
without permission

First published 1980 in the U.K. by
THE MACMILLAN PRESS LTD
London and Basingstoke
and in the U.S.A. as an
ARCHON BOOK
an imprint of The Shoe String Press, Inc.
995 Sherman Avenue, Hamden, Connecticut 06514

Printed in Great Britain

Library of Congress Cataloging in Publication Data

Main entry under title:

Prospects of Soviet power in the 1980s

Based on the papers presented at the 20th annual
conference of the International Institute for Strategic
Studies, held in Sept. 1978 in Oxford, Eng.
  Includes index.
  1. Russia—Foreign relations—1975–   —Congresses.
2. Russia—Defenses—Congresses. 3. Russia—National
security—Congresses. I. Bertram, Christoph, 1937–
II. International Institute for Strategic Studies.
DK274.P73   1980   327.47   80–17058
ISBN 0–208–01885–9

CONTENTS

76061

Introduction

CHRISTOPH BERTRAM

Any exploration into the nature of Soviet policy and the rationality of Soviet behaviour is a risky affair if only because it is, inevitably, influenced by basic moral and emotional judgments. The Soviet Union is a subject which raises either passion or at least discomfort: hers is a political system alien to, and often opposed to, Western values. A polarization of political opinion in the Western debate is therefore both inevitable and bewildering, particularly since supposedly fundamental differences of view on principle usually melt down to marginal differences when it comes to practical policies. Perhaps it is the narrowness of differences which makes for the bitterness of the debate; because there is no basic dissent, marginal dissent can give rise to fierce argument. The nature of Soviet power has been the major problem of Western security for so long that it is no longer amenable to cool analysis. It has shaped our thinking, it continues to define our concerns. Moreover, Soviet policy and secrecy have tended to encourage pessimism and, sometimes, alarm, rather than confidence.

And yet, as we are approaching the 1980s, it is perhaps even more necessary than before to see Soviet power, strengths and weaknesses, ambitions and policies in perspective. It was one thing to live with Soviet power at a time of unquestioned American strategic superiority and internationalist determination – but quite another when the Soviet Union has reached parity in most of the major indicators of military power and the United States' military effort is impeded by the need to come to terms with pressing domestic problems; it is one thing to pursue security through detente and deterrence within the familiar and relatively well-defined boundaries of East–West relations in the North-ern Hemisphere (NATO–Warsaw Pact, SALT and European Security Conference) – but quite another when the rivalry extends to resource-rich yet volatile regions of the southern part of the globe. It is for this reason that the Institute made this the subject of its Twentieth Annual Conference, held in September 1978 in Oxford: to explore Soviet interests and power from the Soviet perspective. The papers published in Adelphi Papers Nos. 151 and 152 were given at the Conference and amended in light of its debate. Their purpose is to provide a basis for understanding and coping with this major issue of international security in the next decade.

Constraints on Soviet Power

What may be the primary contribution of these papers is that all point to the limits of Soviet power. The agenda of major problems for the Soviet leadership in the 1980s is indeed long. Georges Sokoloff analyses the stagnation of Soviet economic growth; the stagnation in the growth of the Russian population; and the limitations of an economic system that makes increases in productivity unlikely. The decline in Soviet hard currency earnings as a result of decreasing oil and energy exports is forecast and will limit the Soviet ability to offset costly imports from abroad. The success of Soviet policy in the Middle East and in other areas of the Third World is put in doubt and the achievements of Soviet detente policy are seen in perspective. The ideological challenges of China and Eurocommunism are emphasized. The tenuous nature of Soviet control over Eastern Europe is underlined. The record of the Brezhnev leadership team can scarcely be called an unqualified success of Soviet foreign policy. The problems facing the next generation

1

St. Philip's College Library

of leaders are indeed formidable: how to keep up massive spending on defence *and* satisfy consumer demands; how to maintain present forces in Europe *and* the Far East when the Russian population growth is declining; how to keep Eastern Europe calm *and* decrease its dependence on Western credits and resources; how to satisfy the growing demands of the various minorities in the Soviet Union; how to reconcile the new technocrats' desire for efficiency with the inefficiency of the party apparatus.

However formidable the problems facing the future Soviet leaders, they appear unlikely to produce any major changes in Soviet policy. Continuity remains the catchword: it will be seen in a nationalistic, even chauvinistic leadership, nevertheless cautious in its policy, not ready to take incalculable risks, continuing to depend on military strength and expecting to be able to cope with the pressures from within and pursue Soviet interests without. What may be major problems from a Western perspective could seem less disturbing from a Soviet one. It is in the nature of totalitarian regimes that they can measure their success by past achievements, not – as is the case with our impatient democracies – by their ability to cope with present and future challenges. And, as Robert Legvold reminds us in his paper, the USSR's achievements, even if compared to what was and not what could have been, are impressive. This in itself will create confidence about the future among those who follow Mr Brezhnev.

It is true that to make these problems more manageable, flexibility will be needed not only in practical politics but in Soviet ideology as well. The trend has rather been towards greater rigidity, an aversion to reform, a discouragement of new approaches. But the ideological rigidity may have resulted from insufficient pressure to adapt, since there is an element of dynamism in Soviet ideology. To put it more pragmatically: politicians will seek ways of avoiding dangerous deadlocks and will not permit ideology to stand in their way if they feel they have no alternative – and as with all abstract notions, Leninist ideology lends itself to being re-interpreted and re-justified.

Uncertain Projections
On this basis, it is plausible to predict continuity – of aims, military programmes, internal control –

within the Soviet Union and in Eastern Europe. Indeed, it is a safe bet in international politics that things will change but not all that much, and the traditional Soviet ability to control disturbing internal pressures by instilling resignation and submission in her subjects (if necessary by force) should grant a degree of permanence to the present structure and stability of the Soviet regime. And yet predictions depend for their accuracy on the reliability of the factors on which they are based, and one must be careful to choose the right ones. As William Hyland suggests, the continuity of Soviet military advantage, both for Europe and for certain aspects of the central strategic balance, is by no means assured; perhaps the Soviet Union will lose this advantage in the latter half of the 1980s as new weapons systems enter Western arsenals. The revolution of rising consumer expectations among the Soviet population may well limit the flexibility of any future government. And the impact of growing economic problems on Soviet domestic and internal behaviour cannot be dismissed, though it is difficult to foresee whether this could be more or less accommodating to liberal values and Western interests.

For all that, great changes do not seem likely in the 1980s. Andrew Marshall speculates that there might, in the next few years, be a major deliberate contest between East and West, on the scale of the Cuban missile crisis of 1962. Yet it is difficult to envisage that a future Soviet leadership, even if less deterred by memories of the Great Patriotic War than the present one, would be willing to take the enormous risk that such action would constitute. Moreover, there will be other ways for the Soviet leadership to deflect attention from internal difficulties and to gain political stature.

That the Soviet Union has acquired a stake in the international system is a central argument in Robert Legvold's paper. It is, indeed, a plausible one. The Soviet Union, previous preferences notwithstanding, has not succeeded in shaping the international system to her own rules and, therefore, has had to adjust to those determined by Western patterns of power and traditions. But this does not mean that she has a stake in international stability as understood by the West. For the West, stability is an almost universal value, but it is not a value shared by what

Hedley Bull has called the underdogs of the international hierarchy – the USSR and third-world countries. The Soviet Union may come to appreciate the advantage of predictability in international affairs, but she is likely to be selective – in Europe, as argued by Jean Laloy, perhaps in the Middle East, as argued by Galia Golan. This does not, however, indicate a general acceptance of the Western notion of *status quo* – indeed, given the ideological under-pinning of Soviet policy as well as the precariousness of stability in volatile areas of the world – from South Africa to the Persian Gulf – what interest would the Soviet Union have in recognizing a system which is in such disarray?

The Military Component

That military power is the chief instrument of Soviet policy has become a familiar assertion although, from the Soviet viewpoint, military power is but one element in the changing 'correlation of forces'. Yet there is little question that military power has acquired increasing weight in the Soviet definition of what constitutes changes in this correlation: the Soviet Union is regarded as a major power because of her military strength and this must affect both the Soviet Union's perception of what is her due and how other countries see her power in relation to their own efforts to achieve security. Soviet literature is paying increased attention to military power, and there is little expectation of any general decline in the military emphasis this indicates: economic constraints, while inevitable, will scarcely be powerful enough to reverse the current trend; the attitude of the present and future leadership is likely to favour a strong military posture, and the Soviet military will be able to point to sufficient insecurity in the world to justify their demands – not least to the military efforts of other nations which the Soviet build-up has provoked. Moreover, as the paper by David Holloway makes clear, it will not be easy for any Soviet leadership to overcome the inertia of the military-bureaucratic complex which supports this trend.

However, there are indications of a specific change in the emphasis on military power. Andrew Marshall sees the major shift in the continued development of capabilities to project power into distant crisis areas. The Soviet Union will regard China as a growing threat, and

William Hyland suggests that the Soviet leadership might be tempted into military action, not to conquer but to humiliate China. Hyland, in marked contrast to Chinese predictions of where the 'hegemonists' will strike, thinks it possible that the Soviet Union might be willing to contemplate limited military disengagement in Europe, not least so as to be able to shift military efforts towards the East.

Indeed, China, particularly if equipped with modern arms technology from the West, may be the most direct security concern for the Soviet Union in the 1980s, but it will be a very long time before she will pose a serious *military* threat to a Soviet Union increasingly confident in her military might. It is not easy to explain why the Soviet Union is, as Philip Windsor suggests, 'no longer afraid' of her chief military rival, the highly armed and highly developed United States, yet she seems to feel a deep sense of insecurity faced with a militarily and economically backward China.

In the Third World, particularly in Africa, the Soviet Union is likely to be increasingly active, encouraged by her success in Angola and Ethiopia and by the fact that the West continues to be hobbled by its links with white South Africa. These are not merely achievements of opportunity, they reflect a more fundamental Soviet attitude – underdog solidarity with the Third World and a mental disposition in favour of change. It is nevertheless important to ask this question: how great a strategic priority is the Third World for a Soviet Union faced with powerful neighbours beyond her own frontiers and major problems of control within them?

The prevailing consensus that there is no Soviet 'masterplan' but rather Soviet opportunism does not get us much further in this evaluation of priorities. After all, it did not matter whether nineteenth century Britain controlled India as a result of a masterplan or as the result of opportunism. Alexander Dallin quite rightly argues that there is a distinction between appetite and risk-taking. Opportunism as the driving force of Soviet action does not reflect strategic priorities but a readiness to reap advantage if the risk is low. So far, this has been the case for Soviet involvement in Africa – but will it be in the future? In a more hazardous region – the Middle East – Galia Golan argues that Soviet objectives would now be well served by a settlement of the Arab–Israeli conflict rather than by the continuation of the present tension, however many 'opportunities' a more unsettled situation might provide.

What are the strategic priorities for the Soviet Union in the Third World? The most plausible analysis would start from immediate Soviet security concerns. These concerns are very visible along the whole periphery of Soviet territory. The traditional Soviet objective of creating a security *glacis* around her borders will, in future, be reinforced by another, already visible concern: that over ethnic minorities within the Soviet Union and their ties with their relatives across the border. The rise of tribal affinities and Islamic fundamentalism might, in the first instance, offer to the Soviet Union opportunities for exercising influence; but what if the new wave of 'clericalism' and anti-modernization in part of the so-called Third World should spill over into the Soviet multi-nation state? There is likely to be an increasingly close link between the ethnic problems *within* the Soviet Union and the ethnic consciousness *without*. It is as important to ask what the Soviet Union can do to the Third World as it is to ask what the Third World can do for the Soviet Union.

Outside the Soviet periphery – which the Soviet Union will interpret rather generously – it is difficult to find Soviet strategic priorities as opposed to opportunities. If the future of Soviet power is seen to lie most clearly in the Third World this is precisely because it is an area of opportunity rather than strategic priority for the Soviet Union, yet one where perceptions of the over-all power relationship between East and West might be shaped. Yet perhaps, as Philip Windsor warns, it would be too simple to interpret Soviet action in the Third World primarily as probing how far the Soviet Union can go without being reprimanded. The erstwhile revolutionary power, with a growing stake in selective international stability and increasingly risking identification by the Third World with the 'establishment', rather yearns for a clarification of what the United States is up to. The repeated Soviet complaint over American 'zig-zag' policies, and bewilderment over what appear to be unpredictable elements in the Western – and particularly the American – system of government reflect a desire for some reliable pattern of international behaviour against which the Soviet Union can measure her own power and influence.

However, the constraints on Soviet power are unlikely to be felt initially in her policies towards the Third World, and even in her competition with the United States. They will be felt where military power has the most obvious limits and where outside influence can least be blocked – in Eastern Europe. Indeed, it is difficult to avoid the conclusion that it is here that the limitations of Soviet power in the 1980s will be revealed. A combination of economic constraints, a more nationalistic and chauvinistic leadership and a new ideological orthodoxy is a dangerous brew. It holds a serious potential for conflict in that region – Europe – which has symbolized detente and deterrence in the West over the past three decades.

The problems the Soviet Union will face in the 1980s can give little comfort to the West. Moreover, there is relatively little Western policy can do about them – except perhaps to provide a degree of firmness, continuity and consistency of policies so that the risks inherent in their policies and the advantages of co-operation will be more evident to Soviet leaders.

But such consistency will be difficult to achieve almost regardless of who is President in Washington or in Moscow. Security is becoming – for the West as for the East – increasingly diffuse. External protection, security of access to raw materials and domestic priorities will not make the central concern over the East–West military balance disappear. But it will be a part of the security demands of the 1980s which cannot easily be pulled into one coherent policy. With the fragmentation of the international system in the 1980s we could also experience a fragmentation of security purposes and policies. No doubt this fragmentation holds opportunities for the Soviet Union to expand her power, it also will give her fewer incentives to move from the 'zero sum instinct' of the past towards a more confident and responsible involvement in the search for international order. This must, however, remain the long-term Western aim. The Soviet problem is not going to go away; we will have to live with it. We will do well, therefore, to maintain, in the uncertain period of the 1980s, those structures of dialogue between East and West that the past twenty years have fostered, however imperfectly.

4

The Concept of Power and Security in Soviet History

ROBERT LEGVOLD

Beneath the growing concern over the Soviet military threat there rest, unattended, fundamental questions involving the Soviet conception of power, security, order and change. Understandably, grand, difficult, elusive matters like these are not the preoccupation of the practical people who analyse 'the threat' and even less of those who devise a response. But the quality of their analysis and response inevitably depends on our ability to comprehend at this other level. The interpretation of the significance of *Minuteman* vulnerability or of Soviet–Cuban combatants in Ethiopia ultimately requires an honest effort to know what the Soviet leaders think about the place of military power in international politics; how they conceive their national security and what regard they have for ours; and whether they worry in any depth about international stability or the interplay between order and change.

Too long we have contented ourselves with half-formed thoughts and vague impressions of these elemental dimensions of Soviet perspective. Some are impressions transported across the years and converted by now into accepted wisdom, such as the central role attributed to military power in the Soviet approach to foreign policy. According to this assumption, the Soviet leaders, more than most, believe in the utility of military force and even of war, stake their policy on its political exploitation and labour constantly to perfect the fusion of policy and force in a formal strategy. The equally common assumption about the Soviet definition of security stresses the Soviet Union's peculiar insecurity, so great and self-centred that it can be assuaged only at the expense of everyone else's sense of safety. As a result, it matters little whether the Soviet Union is a consciously expansionist state. The practical effect of her obsession with absolute security and her disregard for others' peace of mind amounts to the same. To these loose but enduring impressions we often add a third and ultimate one: beyond her presumed faith in the instrumentality of military power and beyond her menacing insecurity, the Soviet Union has long appeared to many as an adversary with little or no stake in international stability, save within her own camp. In the final analysis, the Soviet Union remains for us an alienated power, disaffected with the world – or at least with our part of it – less dedicated than we are to quieting troubled areas that threaten the peace (indeed, happy to exploit instability where selfish Soviet ends may be served) and lost to the idea of building a more stable global order, particularly, one based on notions of equity and equilibrium.

Others of our impressions owe more to the moment. For example, we dwell on the current growth of Soviet military power not only because of its scale and tempo, but also because it parallels what many perceive to be a new 'global thrust' in Soviet foreign policy. Because we sense a shift in the inspiration of Soviet policy, we tend to dramatize the meaning of shifts in the military balance(s). And because we attach such significance to the changing state of the military balance(s), we tend to regard Soviet behaviour in specific instances (Africa, in particular) as a confirmation of global ambitions. The analysis has a circular quality, however, one fear flowing from the next with no clear starting point, and rarely is its internal logic justified. Little effort, for example, is made to probe the assumed link between the evolution of the central balances and Soviet assertiveness in Africa's instabilities. Even less attention is given

5

to defining the nature of the Soviet Union's 'global thrust' or the way the shifting military balances are to be manipulated to serve it. Yet, to a large degree, these assumptions and fears now dictate the terms within which the discussion of the Soviet challenge proceeds.

At best these are partial truths, draining reality of its complexity and imposing on us associations with no demonstrable basis; truths neither powerful enough to capture the subtlety of the Soviet Union's self-conception nor balanced enough to convey the impact of a changing global environment on the Soviet outlook. If we are to put the Soviet challenge in perspective, we need to release ourselves from these simple assumptions and begin to deal directly with the notions that actually shape the Soviet approach to the primary issues of power, security and order. One starting point is the past, a hill from which to judge the evolution of Soviet perspective.

From Lenin to Kirilenko

No two moments symbolize more perfectly the breadth of a fifty-year span than the time when Maxim Litvinov was waiting in Stockholm in 1918 to learn whether the Allied governments would allow him to come to Paris, so that he and the half dozen other individuals claiming to represent various Russian governments might better follow the fate being decided for his country by Woodrow Wilson, Lloyd George and their colleagues, and the moment when Andrei Gromyko, before the Twenty-fourth Party Congress in 1971, told the delegates: 'Today, there is no question of any significance which can be decided without the Soviet Union or in opposition to her.' One might choose other ways to depict the change: the chaos and fragility of power picked from the rubble, contrasted with a regime long ascendant over the society it commands; a peasant economy, war-devastated, with but the first struts of industrialization in place, contrasted with a large, modern economy, second only to the United States' and many times greater than the original; or, perhaps most strikingly, a rag-tag, anarchic army, with scavenged supplies and a navy in revolt, contrasted with hundreds of ballistic missiles and fifty-eight divisions poised against Western Europe or the 3,500 tanks that annually roll off the assembly line.

But the distance between Litvinov's discomfort and Gromyko's boast communicates better the product of these years. It also touches more directly on the Soviet Union's historic impatience and self-appointed destiny. For even in the early years the imperative of policy was never merely to defend the 'only fatherland of socialism' nor later, when the fatherland was well-defended, was it ever merely the glorification of Soviet power and the expansion of its influence. From the start – or from the point at which the dream of a European revolution began to fade – the Bolsheviks arrogated to their country the role of history's vanguard, a pose requiring a permanent concern for the character of change virtually everywhere.

Because our convictions about the Soviet Union have been so thoroughly shaped by the long interlude of Stalin's rule, and because his rule has always seemed to us so cynical, nationalistic, even anti-revolutionary, we have trouble taking seriously the residual force of earlier ideals. The notion that Leonid Brezhnev and others like him in fact believe that their nation embodies a revolution, has a 'manifest destiny' and stands for change that may not always be self-serving is outside our normal perception and, as a result, rarely figures in our analysis. Reading Gromyko's words, therefore, we reach one of two conclusions: either, as some like to think, he is only confessing to the Soviet Union's long-felt sense of inferiority and claiming the right to a voice on a par with the United States', moderation Soviet leaders find consoling; or, on the contrary, as a great many more conclude, he is in fact trumpeting the momentum of growing Soviet power, telling us that the Soviet Union is ready to throw her weight around and acknowledging in effect a new 'imperial' phase in Soviet foreign policy. Either way, the issue is reduced to a matter of Soviet ambitions, and these in turn to the status of power-seeking for the sake of power. The contest between East and West is kept primitively strategic – it is a contest featuring one side's desire and ability to jeopardize the other side's interests.

In the process we miss the more interesting and significant possibility that Gromyko has in mind less his country's growing power than its original vocation – not in the simple sense of a revolutionary mission, but faith in the course of events and confidence that the Soviet Union has an ever greater role to play in influencing the re-ordering of international politics. This role is not necessarily one of direct intervention or of assault on the strategic positions of the capitalist world, nor is it one predicated on coercion and overt control; it is rather one that transcends the conventional concerns and ambitions of most states. It is this that makes the Soviet Union a special challenge. By ignoring this distinction and clinging to our image of the Soviet Union as a state with conventional concerns and ambitions only more distended, we obscure rather than clarify the problem that the Soviet Union poses for us.

In a sense, Stalin nationalized the Soviet Union's revolutionary personality – that is, he subordinated everyone's revolution to the needs of his nation's own, and thereby persuaded us that the peculiarly ideological impulse of Soviet policy had been largely supplanted by the revival of a commonplace, Russian imperialism. This left us unprepared to observe how much Stalin remained a 'revolutionary' in Henry Kissinger's sense of the word and how little allegiance he felt he owed to the international system of his day. The USSR under Stalin, as under Lenin, was never *of*, only *in*, the prevailing international order. Stalin's strong advocacy of collective security in the 1930s never signified the slightest concession to the 'system' of Woodrow Wilson's hopes, the now crumbling collective security system the Versailles peace-makers thought they substituted for the nineteenth-century balance of power. Collective security was for the Soviet Union an expedient, not a way to give order to international relations. By joining the League of Nations and championing its strength, Stalin's regime meant only to extract from the environment what aid it could in coping with a specific danger; it did not intend to make peace with this environment. Rallying to the principle of collective security, in Stalin's eyes, had no more nor less legitimacy than the decision to strike the bargain he eventually did with Hitler, and both choices involved an equal disdain for the nature and organization of the contemporary world.

His commitment to the post-war order that in theory he helped to design was no greater. On his own terms, he was prepared to tolerate the creation of institutions so important to Hull and to Roosevelt – even to value them for the contribution they might make to great power co-operation – but he took care to build his own security system alongside and, for the rest, assumed that in the long run events would undo whatever structure the Western powers sought to impose on international politics.

This was his legacy to his successors: the continuing faith in the inherent vulnerability of an international system fashioned of, by and for the major capitalist powers. Khrushchev improved on the legacy by convincing himself that the process was already well advanced and that further far-reaching changes were just around the corner. At the heart of his confidence was an exuberant belief in the transfiguration of his own country's power, one involving its military potential but based above all on economic performance. So exhilarated was he by the prospect of growth in the Soviet economy and technology that in the late 1950s he went as far as to forecast the timetable by which the Soviet Union would overtake and then surpass the United States. It was an extraordinary proposition. In little more than a decade the Soviet Union was to become 'first in the world, both in total production and in *per capita* production'.[1] His country was, Khrushchev said, 'moving forward four times as fast' as the United States, and the momentum of such progress, reinforced by the surge of Soviet science and technology, came to epitomize for him the basic shift in power under way between East and West. Coupled with what he took to be an accelerating defection of the newly independent nations from the Western camp, the Soviet leader saw indications of a radically revised international order. For four critical years, between 1958 and 1962, Khrushchev's foreign policy was deeply influenced by this perception.

These years are critical because, more than any others, they mark the origins of the modern Soviet challenge. In 1930 Stalin proclaimed the 'doctrine of capitalist encirclement' and, over the next quarter of a century, let it stand for the Soviet predicament. Khrushchev abolished the phrase, saying that it was meaningless when no one could any longer determine 'who encircles whom'. Thus did he cut his country free of its Stalinist introspection, its narrow preoccupations and its timid assault on a *status quo* repudiated a thousand times over. And, by the same token, thus did he launch the Soviet Union on a new

7

international career, born of a special self-confidence and promising a renewed activism.

The Modern Soviet Challenge

Much of what drives our current concern, in fact, has evolved from this earlier phase of Soviet policy. By slighting this connection, we forsake the insights of the recent past and leave our view of the moment significantly unbalanced, finding new departures where there are none, adventure where there is also restraint, and purposefulness (even a coherent design) where there is greater disorder and opportunism.

We would do better to view present trends from a historical perspective. The transformation of Soviet military power under Brezhnev becomes striking and so too does his readiness to use it in ways previously untried; but at the same time the larger dimension turns out to be more involved and less portentous. Set beside Khrushchev's bold, simple – and credulous – notions of international politics, or his aggressive and often impetuous policies, those of the current leadership appear considerably less sweeping and calculating and considerably more intricate. To a large degree, they emerge as both an extension and a trimming, a refinement and a repudiation of Khrushchev's original impulses.

For it was he, if anyone, who indulged a crude globalism, though even in his case Soviet globalism had neither the imperial nor the pre-eminently military quality often assumed by commentators in the West. He not only believed in the promise of Soviet power and the imminent decay of that of the West, but he acted on his belief, taking the turmoil of decolonization and making of it a theatre in the historic confrontation between capitalism and socialism, challenging the West in Berlin, daring it to prove that its resolve was not already fatefully eroded, and sparring with China over what was, at root, her lack of faith in the spontaneous revolutionary process.

His activism, moreover, fed (as it in turn was fed by) a readiness to celebrate in doctrine the underlying significance of events. In the phrase of the day, capitalism had entered the third stage of its 'deepening general crisis', a ritualized way of saying how important this new historic juncture was, to be ranked with the 1917 Revolution itself and the expansion of this revolution into a 'world socialist system' after World War II, each the occasion of an earlier stage in the 'general crisis'. Only this time it was not the balance of power that was being altered by revolutionary change, but the other way round. At last – to postulate the cause of Khrushchev's exhilaration – the Soviet Union had ceased to be the object of her environment and had begun to shape that environment instead – all of it, not merely parts torn from it and added to the enclave.

Those who drove him from office thought Khrushchev took matters too far. Their demur elucidates the way contemporary Soviet leaders view their country's place in the world, the role of its (military) power and the security requirements. He was, they thought, naive and incautious in his judgment of trends within the Third World and, having finished with him, they swiftly expunged from their policy his simple revolutionary expectancy. Like him, they had learned the futility of trying to intimidate the other side without the substance of power and of the risks inherent in what used to be called 'brinkmanship'. No doubt these lessons, too, they would later begrudge him. They mistrusted his ebullient confidence in his ability to get the better of Western leaders at the Summit and in one-to-one encounters, particularly when, in his last years, he appeared actually ready to do some political trading. But, more than any of these other excesses, it was Khrushchev's confidence in the momentum of the Soviet Union's own development that bothered them. Their doubts, in the end, called into question the whole edifice of his optimism and, in doing so, established the boundaries for another, less fulsome version of the Soviet Union's global vocation.

For nothing had been more central to Khrushchev's 'globalism' than his confidence in the speed with which the Soviet economy would outdistance that of the United States (hallowed in the notion of the 'extensive construction of Communism'). This he merged with a climactic image of change within the Third World (culminating in his theory of 'revolutionary democracy'), and together these two great historic currents, enhanced by the growing internal contradictions of the other camp, were rendered as a fundamental power transition (the third stage of capitalism's 'general crisis'). Khrushchev's successors rejected the premises of each proposition and, after he was gone, they quietly dismantled each of the attending theories. They have never replaced them with new ones – something we ought not to overlook.

Before turning to perceptions of the current leadership and its notion of the Soviet Union's global role, another dimension of the Khrushchev legacy is worth noting, one involving the essence of the Soviet definition of power. For all his intemperance, Khrushchev guarded an essentially economic notion of power. Indeed, the one had to precede and support the other.

Soviet leaders from Lenin onwards have believed that the 'correlation of forces' is the principal dynamic of international politics or, more fundamentally, the dynamic by which international politics will be liquidated. As we are not a part of this tradition, nor are we persuaded of history's determinist pattern, and as we care more about the stability of an international order that, for all its imperfections, remains basically congenial, we think more in terms of a 'balance of power'. There is a profound difference between, on the one hand, an approach featuring the eternal ebb and flow of power and the virtues of equilibrium in international relations and, on the other hand, an approach dedicated to the impermanence of every international order save for the last and the long-running triumph of a single historic force.

By the same token, however, the 'correlation of forces' turns out to be a broader concept than we frequently appreciate. To the Soviet Union it stands for virtually the whole of an era – not merely the growth of Soviet power or the deterioration of the West's, but the vigour of the 'national liberation movement', the *élan* of the peace movement, the fortunes of the Left in Western Europe and even the militancy of capitalist trade unions. It is decidedly not the simple comparison of power, still less of military power, that many in the West assume. Where it is dependent on the strength of the socialist camp, the notion of strength has far more to do with the basic (or comparative) dynamism of these societies than with the size of their armies or the throw-weight of the Soviet intercontinental ballistic missile (ICBM) force.

Khrushchev was the proponent of this essential conception *par excellence*. His euphoric pre-occupation with the material base of power had its natural antecedents in Stalin's own concerns thirty years earlier: 'Those who fall behind get beaten', he said in 1931. 'The history of old Russia is one unbroken record of the beatings she suffered for falling behind, for her backwardness.'[2] Khrushchev was merely on the other side of the pre-occupation. His successors repressed his simple enthusiasms but shared the same understanding of power.

Not that the Soviet concept of power lacks a military dimension; on the contrary, the Soviet leadership has always been keenly sensitive to the role of military power in international politics. One of the first forms of backwardness abjured by Stalin in his famous 1931 speech was 'military backwardness'. When Khrushchev trumpeted the approaching superiority of socialist forces, he also had the Soviet Union's military strength in mind. And a Brezhnev version of the earlier Gromyko quotation goes: 'At the present time no question of any importance in the world can be solved without our participation, without taking into account our economic and military might.'[3] But it is absolutely critical to acknowledge that, in the Soviet mind, military power remains not only a function of other forms of power, economic in particular, but their auxiliary as well – never, as so many analysts in the West surmise, their substitute. So it was Khrushchev's Minister of Defence who last insinuated that the Soviet Union had achieved military superiority when he spoke in January 1962, because it was Khrushchev who thought the claim could justifiably be made precisely on the strength of the underlying shift in the correlation of forces.[4] Having no such illusion, at least none so crude, Brezhnev has denied his Ministers of Defence the same liberty and has himself chosen to emphasize that the Soviet Union 'is not seeking and will not seek military superiority over the other side'.[5]

Security, Power and Contemporary Soviet Policy
Since 1917 the Soviet Union's security concerns have changed radically. The transformation, at one level, is obvious. A regime that has ruled for more than a half century, has endured great trials and has amassed nearly peerless military power clearly worries about the world differently from one with the frailest grip on power, embattled in civil war and isolated among

9

hostile and stronger capitalist adversaries. In the years separating Brest–Litovsk from the Strategic Arms Limitation Talks (SALT) and the first Soviet–German non-aggression accord from the second, the Soviet Union has freed herself from the spectre of any nation successfully threatening her territorial integrity. *En route*, however, she has extended her sway over other nations, creating new insecurities centred on the stability of empire. And in founding this empire, she has stirred a bitter challenge from a great power once ideologically allied and now the more hostile for it. In short, from the security of power, through the security of nation, Soviet concerns have now proceeded to the security of alliance and, ultimately, to the security of the faith.

Each turn has overlaid but not destroyed the previous one, weaving an ever more complex security environment. Thus, the Soviet Union emerges unable to distinguish national security from the security of her authority in Eastern Europe, and this security, in turn, depends essentially on orthodoxy rather than partnership. Similarly, the conflict with China reinforces two Soviet fears at once – the dangers of fragmentation within her own camp and a common front among adversaries. The complexity grows, moreover, because each individual threat has changed over time: China is no longer merely an ideologically disruptive force within the socialist world but a traditional enemy, armed and bent on jeopardizing Soviet policy in every sphere; Eastern Europe is now menaced less by the ill-will of the United States and her allies than by the contaminating effects of detente and interdependence, less by NATO and more by lapses in economic performance; the German threat has been transformed, even in the last ten years; containment has lost much of its force, but American (economic) power increasingly shapes other parts of the Soviet environment – and so on.

Compelling though these factors are, they obscure the full change that has taken place in the character of Soviet security concerns. For at another level the potential hazards to Soviet well-being have not only multiplied and commingled; they have also grown constantly more diffuse. That is, the issue is one not merely of interlocking complexities but also of imperatives existing on different planes and impervious to traditional solutions built from traditional forms of power. Like every other nation, the Soviet Union faces an increasing array of challenges that cannot be met by military power or military alliances. Her ability to integrate her economy into the larger order, beginning with the energy sector, for example, will have as much to do with her security, and perhaps even more to do with that of her allies, than any plausible erosion of the strategic nuclear balance. Her growing stake in selected foreign markets and expanding lines of communication, as well as her fishing, shipping and mining activities, will impose as many demands on the quality of Soviet diplomacy as on her capacity for force projection.

The Soviet leadership by and large knows this, and over the last decade a great deal of Soviet analysis has come to reflect an awareness of the link between interdependence and security. (We have been so preoccupied with our time-honoured notions of what moves the Soviet Union that we have scarcely noticed.) There is an echo of the same sensitivity in Soviet insistence that detente be more than the absence of war, that it involve a conscious restructuring of East–West relations and explicit forms of co-operation. (Again, this is an area of Soviet thought largely ignored by Western analysts.) Indeed, it is this recognition of security's growing subtlety that leads to the crux of the issue.

Profound choices confront the Soviet Union, though not the ones ordinarily suggested by many Western analysts: not the issues of whether or not to press the strategic arms race so that some day soon an overmatched United States can be intimidated at will, or whether or not to intervene wherever local instability offers the prospect of compromising Western strategic positions, but rather the question of how the Soviet Union's increasing stake in the existing international order, even in its stability, is to be squared with her genuine and historic alienation from that order. There is indeed a 'global reach' to contemporary Soviet policy, but its significance derives from the interplay between these two impulses, not from the simple aggrandizement of Soviet power.

At last the Soviet Union has the (military) wherewithal to affect the evolution of the *status quo* almost everywhere, but has also engaged herself at last in almost every dimension of that *status quo*. The purchase of Western technology, the traffic of its merchant marine and the myriad other Soviet involvements – even the effort to displace Western economic influence in third-world nations – amount to an extensive incorporation of the socialist countries into the larger (economic) order. As this sphere of activity swells, the Soviet concept of security does too, but it also creates an unfamiliar security concern, given the mutual dependencies on which it rests – stranger still, since the framework within which it flourishes remains largely the handiwork of the industrialized capitalist powers and is inaccessible to Soviet influence.

In contrast, the regional instabilities of the Third World are more accessible, and for many observers these have long evoked the older and deeper Soviet drive to overthrow an uncongenial international order. It is in this light that Soviet interventions in Africa assume significance. For the first time the Soviet Union has been able and willing to use her military power to decide the outcome of distant crises. Angola and the Horn of Africa pose the question of whether or not the Soviet Union henceforth intends to play a more active role in regional instabilities and sees her growing military power in these circumstances as a useful instrument for laying siege to the *status quo* where it is most vulnerable. (A starker but inapposite version of the same question is whether the Soviet Union means to conquer facilities and destroy Western strategic positions throughout the Third World.) Behind this question lurks the more fundamental apprehension that Soviet assertiveness in Africa stems from a new 'arrogance of power' based on the general shift in the military balance.

This, it seems to me, misstates the challenge of the Soviet Union's growing military capabilities. In the first place, in the Soviet outlook military power has always constituted an important element of foreign policy, but never its central element and never the blunt instrument that some make it out to be. Neither has it ever been the perfectly matched complement of political strategy that others perceive. In fact, for all their praise of Clausewitz, the Soviet political and military élite have done less to integrate defence and foreign policy than their American counterparts. The language of Soviet strategists and leaders has misled us on this score, trapping us into confounding rhetoric with authentic conceptualization. In truth, the Soviet leadership has never worked out (at least not publicly) an integration of military force and foreign policy comparable with the American doctrine of 'flexible response', spelling out the hierarchy of threat and moulding a response across the balances. Nor has it laboured over the place regional instability and low-level violence should occupy in its overall political-military strategy. Until Admiral Gorshkov's modest efforts early in the decade, the gulf between political strategy in areas outside the central theatres and military strategy (designed essentially for these theatres) was very wide.

Second, as a practical matter, the central place assigned to military power in Soviet thinking is said to be a function of the central place military power occupies in Western, particularly American, foreign policy. Thus, when Soviet analysts deal with the political implications of military force, they link these with the way the United States has allegedly used her military power in the post-war period. No independent significance is ascribed to Soviet defence-building. How exclusive the Soviet Union conceives her military power to be in countering the effects introduced into international politics by Western military power is, of course, a matter for debate. Nonetheless, there is a distinction that we often lose sight of between a military effort predicated on the challenges raised by the reality of others' forces and one based on the inherent superiority of military power as an instrument of foreign policy. Whatever we think of the validity of the first, the second simply cannot be demonstrated in contemporary Soviet thought.

All the phrases that we employ to describe the modern Soviet challenge fail us: a new 'imperial' era, a 'global thrust', a new stage of 'acquisitiveness' and the old standby, Soviet 'expansionism', all fall short, saying either nothing or too much. We need, instead, formulas spanning the dual impulses of interdependence and alienation, the constraints of extended involvements and the temptations of increased military power; formulas representing the complexity of Soviet security concerns, their subtlety, their diffuseness and their contradictions. We need ways of capturing the tension between the Soviet stake in acceptance, status and even stability, and the Soviet urge to play an ever larger role in influencing change. To the extent that the Soviet leaders find their growing military power an increasingly handy recourse for influencing change, particularly in unstable areas, we require knowledge of the actual inspiration of Soviet behaviour, not assumptions based on what we fancy it to be. Only if we confront the Soviet leaders with analyses of those of their ambitions that trouble us, analyses *that they find recognizable*, do we have much chance of dealing effectively with the threat. We tell the Soviet Union too often these days that the heart of the problem is the growth of her military might, when the real problem is the aspirations guiding the use of that power – aspirations, to make matters worse, that we insist on distorting or over-simplifying.

Knowledge of the past will at least help to produce a sounder perspective from which to judge the evolving Soviet challenge. Soviet insecurities, and even more Soviet disregard of others' insecurities, for example, continue to bear the scars of Stalin's day. But we underestimate Soviet policy (and the opportunities for our own) when we overlook the degree to which the Soviet Union has outgrown the crudest of these earlier apprehensions, how much she has enlarged the notion of security, and even how far she has come in addressing herself to the concerns of others. Khrushchev's global vocation, too, has left its mark on Soviet policy, although it no longer bears the stamp of his original extravagance. By ignoring the extent to which his successors have moderated

Khrushchev's expectations, have avoided the risks he willingly ran and have tightened up on his commitments, we deny our policy a measured sense of the challenge before us.

For the past offers only partial insights into contemporary Soviet policy. It cannot represent the new choices facing Brezhnev and those to follow, or the degree to which they are already affected. These are the choices facing all of us, but in the Soviet case there is always a further dilemma. For the powerful, as Stanley Hoffmann has argued, the alternatives are the 'politics of world order' and 'politics as usual'; for the Soviet Union there is the further consideration that the 'politics of world order' unfold around institutions and ideas that are often objectionable to her and beyond her power to shape, while 'politics as usual', which the Soviet Union interprets as 'politics to change the world', dominate situations in which she is increasingly powerful but her power is becoming less relevant and more costly in application.[6] The world presents odd choices: between the insecurities of interdependence and the securities (or familiarity) of instability; between the power to compromise and importence to control; and between change sought through restraint, in an effort to induce others' restraint, and a *status quo* frozen through permanent revolution or permanent intervention. We pay a foolish price in pretending that the Soviet Union is not part of this world.

NOTES

[1] Quoted in Wolfgang Leonhard, *The Kremlin Since Stalin* (New York: Praeger, 1962), p. 316.
[2] *Pravda*, 5 February 1931.
[3] 14 March 1970: speech on the occasion of Dvina manoeuvres, as quoted by Hon. Foy D. Kohler, Hearings before Subcommittee on Europe and the Middle East, 95th Congress, First Session, 27 September, 11, 13, 18 and 26 October 1977, p. 33.
[4] For Rodion Malinovsky's ambiguous comment and an interesting discussion of this phase in Soviet foreign policy, see William Zimmerman, *Soviet Perspectives on International Relations* (Princeton: Princeton University Press, 1969), p. 191.
[5] *Pravda*, 3 November 1977. This is a new development, but since late 1977 it and other assurances on the nature of Soviet military ambitions have been repeated a number of times. See, particularly, Brezhnev's speech to the 18th Komsomol Congress, *Pravda*, 26 April 1978, and his interview with *Vorwärts*, reprinted in *New Times*, No. 19 (May 1978), pp. 4–7.
[6] Stanley Hoffmann, *Primacy or World Order* (New York: McGraw-Hill, 1978).

The Soviet Union in the International System of the 1980s

PHILIP WINDSOR

It is, of course, impossible to discuss the role of the Soviet Union in the world of the 1980s. The nature of that world, and the part played in its determination by the power of the USSR, are so totally interdependent that one might just as well attempt to discuss the role of the trade unions in the British economy. Developments in Africa and American reactions, the prospects for the control of the arms race, the chances of a global attempt to deal with imminent energy problems: all these will help to determine, and will all be in part determined by, the domestic politics of the Soviet Union and the interaction of these politics, in the form of agreement, conflict or understanding, with those of the United States and other centres of power. But this initial admission also offers a starting point for a discussion, and the starting point itself carries a further implication. The starting point is obvious. The Soviet Union has become a global power. But the manner in which she has done so also merits a little consideration. Long before she acquired anything like a global reach, the Soviet Union was regarded as a super-power. At first, this title smacked rather of an ascriptive courtesy than of any existing reality; but nature gradually came to imitate art, and the USSR emerged as the true bipolar partner of the United States.

Initially, however, bipolarity was always a phenomenon that reflected the power of the United States. It was because the United States was a true super-power – one that could order the economic system of most of the world, one on whose strength other countries depended for their prosperity or their chances of growth, one whose political influence took myriad forms, from the overt patrolling of frigates to the covert activities of intelligence – that the world could

be deemed to enjoy (or to suffer from) a bipolar system. And it was only because the United States gave overriding consideration to the military power of the USSR, and to the need for preserving a stable alliance against war with that country, that the Soviet Union could really enjoy her status as a bipolar associate. She became a super-power purely by virtue of her strategic strength and her consequent strategic relationship with Washington; and she did so before she acquired any of the dimensions of a global power. The difficulty is that whereas the experience of the United States reflected a global involvement, an assumption of responsibility – albeit unwilling on occasion – for a global order to which her resources as a super-power were later harnessed, *before* she became a super-power, the Soviet Union has acquired the status of a global power having already been acknowledged as a super-power. For the Soviet Union this position is a luxury, reflecting little of the pattern of her economic or political intercourse with the rest of the world and few identifiable or quantifiable interests. The nature of her involvement in global politics and the character of her intentions are enigmas.

Yet the manner in which the Soviet Union emerged as a global power is suggestive and its implications paradoxical. The Soviet Union is weak. Indeed, it might well be argued that her military strength is a function of her weakness in other spheres. Her economic aid to developing countries consists largely of showpiece projects – a steel mill in India or Turkey, or the guaranteed purchase of cash crops like Egyptian cotton, or direct currency subventions to places like Cuba. She is in no sense capable of sustaining a programme of widespread economic growth. She has little to offer in the way of agronomic

13

expertise or advanced technology. Since she can hardly play a forceful part in a world system in which economic and political considerations interact constantly, her political influence is, in fact, restricted, and it is notably absent from such attempts (for what they are worth) to reconstitute relations between the rich and poor of the world as the North–South dialogue. The principal vehicle of her power is military hardware, supplemented by a sometimes transitory military presence. The policies which result are notoriously unstable, and for all her temporary successes, the number of countries from which the Soviet Union has been expelled outside her immediate alliance system is almost equivalent to the number in which she has gained a foothold. The global presence of the Soviet Union is a demonstration of her strength, but also an indicator of her weakness.

What, then, have we seen? The development of an apparently bipolar system, but one whose bipolarity has in fact depended on the power of only one country; and the emergence of its partner as a global power, but one whose very range and involvement has helped to demonstrate its own weakness. In consequence, Soviet involvement in the affairs of the world has not helped to confirm the bipolar system, as it should logically have done were the USSR truly powerful: it has challenged it. This is not, of course, to suggest that the Soviet Union was, or might have been, interested in securing her acceptance by the United States as a *status quo* power, co-responsible for world order and security and enjoying *à titre d'égaux* the imperial benefits of condominium. Often she has shown a degree of political interest in doing so, however, though this has been coupled with an ideological aversion. The military and strategic constraints of her position have prompted her in part to accept the stability of the controlled adversary relationship; but an adversary relationship it has always been. The history and ideological evolution of the USSR since 1917 suggest that she would always seek to challenge the reigning assumptions of the Western capitalist system, in the post-imperial age as much as during the imperial era itself. Nonetheless, if Soviet involvement in the affairs of other regions had taken more deeply-rooted economic or political forms, it is possible to suggest that it would have been easier to reach some degree of accommodation or compromise with Moscow: if the Western countries, and they alone, had not been so visibly and exclusively responsible for the economic development of the Third World, if the Soviet Union had been able to challenge the United States with money as well as with abstract models of economic development, then she would have been less able to exploit grievances in what has so often appeared to be a subversive and irresponsible manner, to turn social and economic discontent into bloody conflict, to challenge that very bipolar order on which her acceptance as a super-power originally depended.

The global emergence of the Soviet Union is thus a double phenomenon. Not only does it indicate Soviet weakness, but it also suggests that such weakness is almost bound to present Soviet activity as subversive to any global understanding and potentially dangerous to the super-power relationship. But not everything, of course, can be laid at the door of Soviet history or attributed to the character of the Soviet system.

The bipolar system has been crumbling for a long time anyway. Political scientists have long taken pleasure in charting its decay. It was a tight system when the Soviet Union was globally at her weakest; it became a looser system as the Soviet Union became stronger. In part, this merely reflects the gradual tidying-up of Europe. As Europe became less and less likely to cause general war between the two super-powers, so other crises in the world fed less directly into European crises. By the time the Four-Power Agreement on Berlin was concluded in 1972, there was very little connection left between the original causes of the Cold War in Europe and the general pattern of conflict elsewhere. But in part, too, the decay of bipolarity has reflected the comparative weakness of the United States – weakness in comparison not merely with the growing strategic strength of her Soviet rival (a strength which in many important areas has still not reached parity with that of the United States) but also with the emergence of other forms and centres of power.

In the end, bipolarity might be said to have depended upon a neat, artificial and perhaps almost fortuitous relationship between the different forms and the single centre of power. When Washington was the centre of almost all political, economic and military influence, bi-polarity was a world order. Since then different centres have begun to compete with Washington in different ways. There would be few today who would still abide by the brave futurology of a few years ago, when Japan was held to be the 'emergent super-state' (since futurology is really the study of the present), but it is obvious that Japan can cause acute discomfort to her Western partners in trading and monetary matters. Yet Japan is still a relatively insignificant military power and is likely to remain so for some time to come. Similarly, the countries of the European Economic Community (EEC) have on occasion appeared to be the centres of economic decision-making; on other occasions some of them have shown an ability to intervene, with a rapid and effective show of military force, in the affairs of Africa, and European optimists could still claim that they exercise very considerable political and economic influence on the Third World generally through the Lomé Convention. However, not only has the success of Europe been intermittent in time and variable in content, but the EEC has always depended for its fundamental security and its very continuance as an entity on the strategic guarantee of the United States. Such a bewildering variety – even sometimes, one might say, succession – of different forms of power has made it very much more difficult for the most powerful state in the world to organize and co-ordinate a global order. The President of the United States is today accused of being weak and indecisive in his foreign policy. In part such accusations reflect a nostalgia, of which some of his critics may decently be convicted, for the elegant simplicities of the Cold War; in part they reflect the yearnings of those for whom Henry Kissinger was the cynosure of Machiavellian management; but in large part they simply reflect the fact that it is very much more difficult today to orchestrate American policy in so many different areas than it has been at any time since 1945.

This change in the American position relative to that of other powers, and in the management of different forms of power, has meant that the international system is no longer really bipolar, except in one sense: clearly, it is still bipolar in the context of strategic management and is likely to remain so for the foreseeable future. But the interaction of the concerns of strategic management and the avoidance of nuclear war will almost certainly take an increasingly confused form over the next few years. If the pattern of world relationships can no longer be ordered into a system of bipolarity through a single centre of power, and if instead it is likely to acquire an increasing number of fissiparous characteristics, then the manner in which the two super-powers maintain their strategic relationship while pursuing their rivalries in other spheres is going to present difficulties for both – conceptual difficulties, difficulties of domestic politics, difficulties in determining the relationship between effective threat and effective conciliation. It is possible that acts of policy, and particularly, perhaps, the process of agreement in SALT, which were once seen as the keystone to a whole structure of detente, will come to be regarded as partial and functional arrangements without any great relevance beyond the borders of their own immediate agenda. But if this possibility (which seems already to be taking shape) should coincide with a period of increased tension or with a pattern of apparently meaningless subversive activity on the part of the Soviet Union, if above all the Soviet Union is still so weak that she continues to strive for influence through the medium of military power, it is further possible that the avoidance of nuclear war will lose all relevance to the control or avoidance of conflicts elsewhere. Detente will be remembered as the last gasp of a bipolar understanding which was born in antagonism and which died in the hubris of mutual esteem. As the super-powers reach the limits of their ability to control the world in order to save it, so other countries will be less ready to sacrifice their interests or stifle their conflicts in order to preserve the super-power relationship.

Trends in the 1980s
It is worth considering, therefore, the potential characteristics of the world of the 1980s, with an eye on the way in which the USSR might fit into this world and an ear for its effects on the super-power relationship. The first characteristic – a decline in the ability of the super-powers to control developments outside the immediate systems of their alliances – has already been implied, at least in the case of the United States, but it applies *a fortiori* to the Soviet Union. This is not to say that they will lack allies or

quasi-allies beyond the confines of NATO or the Warsaw Pact; such creatures already exist. But, as the experience of the United States with Saudi Arabia or that of the USSR with Vietnam will indicate, such alliances are themselves a symptom of declining super-power control, of the need for partners, of a degree of dependence, in fact. Such interdependence might constrain not only the scope for unilateral super-power action, but also the scope for super-power understanding. It could also mean considerable tension in the management of the central alliances themselves: Vietnam might be useful in helping to contain what the Soviet government regards as Chinese ambition in Asia, but it does nothing to prevent the visit of Chairman Hua to Eastern Europe or the consequent need for 'frank' discussions between the leaders of the Soviet and Romanian Parties. The relationship between the United States and Saudi Arabia might help to underpin the world economy and serve the interests of the West European allies and the United States herself, but it cannot prevent rivalries, antagonisms or misunderstandings between the major NATO allies about the future of the Middle East. In fact, relationships within the central alliances can be complicated by the super-powers' need for partners elsewhere; and complications within alliances can also mean complications between them. The super-powers *might* find a way of controlling the military confrontation in Europe, but this does not mean that they can set the pattern for the development of other relations between East and West. In this sense it will probably remain urgently necessary to minimize the risks of war in Europe; but this task will not help either power to reconstitute a working relationship in other spheres.

The second characteristic follows from the first. It is a growing tendency towards regionalization in the world. In part this tendency arises from the failure of the Western economic system to develop any restructuring of the world economic order and to adapt to the consequences of the economic growth which it has itself helped to promote. The emergence of the Newly Industrialized Countries (NICS) has been accompanied by protective measures, and just as Japan is regarded with alarm and apprehension by its Organization of Economic Co-operation and Development (OECD) partners as a kind of super-NIC, so Japan's prosperity is sometimes deemed to be threatened by the more recent NICS of South Korea or Taiwan. Protectionism is a poor alternative to a logical division of labour, in which some NICS might engage in primary production while the older industrialized countries proceed towards a more advanced technology; but given the social structures and employment patterns of most Western countries, protectionism is the most likely choice. Summit meetings and functional agreements can perhaps help to palliate the effects of such policy, but it is most likely that a regionally based series of protective associations will nonetheless arise.

But the origin of increasing regionalization does not lie only in economics. One of the effects of the Nixon Doctrine was to encourage the emergence of strong regional powers. Iran is an obvious, though somewhat anomalous, case in point – anomalous because her ability to obtain significant credits and sophisticated armaments from the United States dates back at least to the time of the Kennedy administration. The case of Brazil is perhaps more clear-cut. But even where the power concerned is a ramshackle country, prone to internal decay and hardly, by any yardstick, internationally strong, it can still be significant as a test case for Western intentions or as a 'key' to the future of regional security. If Iran and Brazil might count as emerging NICS, this is hardly the case with Zaire; but Zaire meets many of the criteria of the Nixon Doctrine. Yet what happened in Zaire? The United States certainly supported French and Belgian action there, but her own role was limited. It was a Chinese Foreign Minister and not an American Secretary of State who went to offer diplomatic and material support against the threat of Soviet influence borne by Cuba out of Angola. The indirectness of American support matched the indirectness of the potential Soviet threat. The case for Zaire confirmed the importance of regional security considerations both to the super-powers and to their allies, but it also confirmed that neither of them felt free to engage in a direct confrontation with the other.

The products of such considerations are somewhat paradoxical: on the one hand, the two super-powers seemed to see themselves as engaged in a world-wide competition for influence, a sort of 'neo-zero-sum' game, in which each is sensitive to the advances of the other as constituting a repulse for itself; on the other hand, this global competition merely emphasizes the fragmentary nature of the world and the increasing regionalization of criteria. In 1977 it was perfectly possible for President Carter to come to an agreement with President Brezhnev on a Joint Statement on the Middle East, even while showing acute anxiety at Soviet penetration in Africa. This is a trend which is likely to continue and, except perhaps where crises are acute, to prompt a political informality and an *ad hoc* style in dealing with problems and conflicts.

Regionalization and the fragmentary diplomacy which follows from it also prompt reflection on the third likely characteristic of the international system in the 1980s. This is simply a proliferation of conflict. Again, such a phenomenon can scarcely be considered without some direct reference to the Soviet Union. It is Soviet action – again reflecting Soviet weakness – which helps to transform indigenous social conflict in developing countries into bloody fighting with international implications. But even if the Soviet factor is subtracted, it is clear that the turmoil of development, of territorial disputes arising from the legacy of imperial boundaries, of the clash between the idea of the nation and the concept of the state, of religious hatred in an age in which economic programmes demand secularization, is going to produce endemic and frequently violent conflict in large areas of the world. Not all violence is inevitable – indeed much could be avoided with a degree of East–West co-operation about North–South questions – but since it is precisely the North–South questions that provide a field for East–West rivalry and help to stimulate violence through competition, it is probable that this will continue to be a characteristic feature of the 1980s. In a sense, one could argue that such violence will matter in terms of human sorrow but need not matter at all in terms of the international system. There have been many massacres in the world since 1945, yet few of them have had much impact on the relations of states. But such sanguine cynicism is probably misplaced. The relative tightness of the international system did help for many years to contain the implications of conflict. Today its relative looseness can help to disseminate those implications. It is not merely the internationalization of terrorism – promoting, as it does, both the

prospects of unilateral exploitation and the need for multilateral co-operation among governments – which is at stake here; it is rather that certain kinds of international force can exacerbate and relate conflicts which would otherwise have been left unnoticed. To take one example, the international character of Islam relates violence in the Philippines to the export of arms, to the price of oil and to rivalries among Arab states. In circumstances such as these the potential certainty exists for an increase in tension at the highest level, even if particular conflicts themselves would appear to be no more than local and without any relevance to the major issues of international relations. Equally, of course, the potential exists for a deliberate exploitation of conflict and of tension – for the re-introduction of the Soviet factor.

Closely related to this third characteristic is a fourth, namely, a heightened watchfulness and jealousy in many parts of the Third World about access to, and the use of, raw materials. Everyone is familiar with the problems of oil and the questions of future energy resources. It can also be convincingly argued that other commodities do not provide a basis for the activities of an international organization such as the Organization of Petroleum Exporting Countries (OPEC). But this does not mean that shortages of important commodities, or allied questions of nationalism, might not be of the highest importance. A shortage of phosphates could have consequences for the future of the world at least as grave as a scarcity of energy fuels – and an enormous proportion of the global stock of phosphates is concentrated in Morocco, Mauritania and Jordan. It is not hard to imagine how problems arising from this distribution could impinge on the future problems of political relations of the Middle East and the Arab world, nor how easily these could affect relations between the major powers. Similar arguments clearly apply to the related questions of seabed resources and the law of the sea.

All the foregoing potential characteristics of the 1980s create the framework for an aggravating factor, which by now bids fair to become a further characteristic in its own right. This is the proliferation of the conventional means of military power. It is possible that the superpowers, and perhaps even their allies, might find means of controlling the future transfer of arms from advanced to developing nations. There are even signs that the super-powers might be about to acknowledge a common interest in doing so. For all that, however, it is now an established truism that small countries can fight big wars – even big civil wars. This will not be easy to reverse in the foreseeable future, if ever. Such wars will become easier to start and harder to stop, and will draw the major powers into a pattern of competition for advantage and collaboration in control which has already been adumbrated in the Middle East war of October 1973. The difficulty here is not that such behaviour is likely to lead to the risk of direct super-power confrontation – that will probably remain the least likely possibility – but that the careful balance between competition and collaboration will enable either or both to pursue advantage or to take revenge in future conflicts for losses experienced in a current one. In turn, such attitudes can discourage any proper curtailment of the transfer of arms (at least as long as arms transfers are held to be a means of influence) and thereby favour a Soviet policy of purchasing dependencies in one of the few areas where it is truly strong.

One must enter a caveat here. In some countries at least, the proliferation of conventional hardware would be accompanied by better options for nuclear weapons. Everything suggests that, as in the recent case of South Africa, such a prospect would provide a powerful impetus for intensified super-power collaboration. Nonetheless, two questions arise. The first is how successful either super-power could be in preventing other states from acquiring a nuclear option or even a limited nuclear armoury. The case of Israel might in many ways be exceptional, but other exceptional cases could follow that example. To the degree that local conflicts could also become nuclear conflicts, super-power behaviour would be critically affected. But, and this raises the second question, the super-powers would, to the degree that they were successful in avoiding nuclear proliferation, also find themselves under great pressure to supply sophisticated conventional armaments to threshold states and to get drawn into their conflicts in the manner sketched above.

All these characteristics suggest that the world of the 1980s will be very different from the world in which the basic code of conduct for super-

power relations was so painfully drawn up. It will be a world of looser arrangements, in which it will be harder to contain the global implications of local conflicts; a world in which the incidence of such conflicts is likely to increase, along with their scope; a world in which the criteria for their management will have become fragmented and in which the successful resolution of one issue will establish no precedent for the next – in short, a world which will become very much harder to control than the rules of global confrontation or global detente might suggest. Perhaps this would have no great significance if the two super-powers and their alliance systems were merely powers in the traditional European sense of the term: divided by rivalry, prepared to engage in limited hostilities over issues of *realpolitik*, but united by a common conception of an international order. But they are not. Both states are informed by a powerful ideology, and both, though in varying degrees and in fundamentally different ways, appeal to this ideology to hold their diverse populations together and to defend the legitimacy of their governments against those who challenge it. Obviously, these ideological concerns also influence their international conduct.

But such symmetry is more a matter of presentation than reality. In their appeal to the Third World the two are very different. In discussing this issue, it might at first be tempting to advance a fashionable contemporary thesis – that ideology is generally on the decline, that as a socially unifying credo it has lost much of its appeal to developing nations and that it is generally supplanted by a more organic form of nationalism. It is indeed frequently suggested that nationalism has reappeared to take revenge on those supra-national ideologies which were once thought to have displaced it, from China to Peru. But to argue in this way is to ignore the different functions which nationalism serves, which range from the noble atavism of Poland to the programmatic deliberation of Tanzania. It also ignores the fact that much of the nation-building in developing countries is deliberately allied to an ideological form of thinking, rooted in anti-colonialism but also perpetually casting about for more positive prospects of social advance. In this sense, non-alignment and nationalism find it very hard to challenge more explicitly 'progressive' forms of ideology, as

Cuba's recent reception among the non-aligned countries has shown. Finally, the assumption that nationalism and ideology are hostile in kind ignores the manner in which a continuing nationalism can embrace alternative but resolute ideologies. Chile is merely an outstanding example. In other words, in much of the developing world nationalism is necessarily ideological; it simply changes its ideology over time.

The nationalism of the post-colonial countries does therefore provide a battleground between East and West which is likely to continue to exist for some time to come, and will probably exacerbate conflicts of interest by focusing attention, in the United States Congress and elsewhere, on developments which might not otherwise seem to matter very much. On this battlefield the Soviet Union will probably enjoy a short-term advantage – partly because the history of imperialism still generates powerful emotions in the Third World, and partly because the idea of socialism is still attractive to many élites, but above all because the ideology of Marxism–Leninism specifically encourages dictatorship. The Soviet Union can support her most ruthless and dictatorial adherents anywhere in the world without any sense of domestic discomfort, whereas the United States can only support her more tyrannical followers at the price of betraying her own political and moral principles. The recent history of President Carter's human rights campaign is a working model of cognitive dissonance. It might be true that in the long term Western ideological beliefs will prove immensely powerful; it is probable, however, that in the 1980s the USSR will benefit from numbering a series of effective dictatorships among her friends.

The Soviet Role
The characteristics of the world of the 1980s which are suggested here provide, therefore, an ambiguous context for a discussion of the Soviet role. The looseness of that world will certainly give the Soviet Union scope to operate; and the weakness alluded to at the beginning of this paper need not be an impediment. While she really has very little to offer, the USSR will still draw apparent strength from tanks, guns and a degree of ideological appeal. How far she will be tempted to exploit this in a manner which runs counter to Western notions of an international order is an open question which has already aroused violent and opposing emotions in the latter years of the 1970s. The difficulty with any attempt to analyse it is that so much of the activity of the Soviet Union has been unrelated to any set of identifiable interests, and many people, even among those who know the Soviet system well, have been driven to conclude that she acts from a motiveless malignancy. But is she merely a Iago? Clearly, the answer will in large part depend on the evolution of Soviet society and on the new leadership that emerges in the next decade. These are broad issues, and two questions only are addressed here: the first concerns the Soviet Union's self-image as a super-power, and the second the constraints that operate on Soviet behaviour.

In one sense, the Soviet claim to super-power status implies an interest in legitimacy. This is not only because the Soviet Union emerged into a world whose bipolarity depended on the great power of the United States, but also because her continuing survival depends on continuing dialogue with Washington. In this sense, it is very hard to underestimate the anxiety to gain acceptance, the need to demonstrate equality, which have been so characteristic of the Soviet leadership and are likely to remain so. But if this need for legitimacy ever implied a common interest in a world order, as perhaps it did briefly during the high summer of detente in the early 1970s, that interest now seems to have died. Legitimacy by now would seem to imply no more than a series of functional arrangements, most notably in the SALT talks, which, while designed for survival, may also be helping merely to keep the world safe for conflict. If, as has been suggested, SALT comes to be seen as a partial and functional arrangement which no longer informs a more generalized detente (and indeed SALT might well depend for any continuous success on its being clearly and positively uncoupled from the more general questions of detente) then the status of the Soviet Union as a super-power will have quite other implications. Some of these can perhaps already be discerned. The recent Japanese Defence White Paper has voiced apprehension at the USSR's attempts to create a position of political and psychological dominance in the Northern Pacific; and this overbearing pattern of behaviour is paralleled, at

19

the other extremity of the Soviet landmass, in her attitudes to Norway and the Barents Sea. In many respects the Soviet Union seems to be developing a peculiar notion of legitimacy: that super-powers are not as other nations, and that they enjoy special dispensations from the norms and rules of international conduct.

This truculence is, however, also accompanied by anxiety. Indeed, one needs not be a very sophisticated psychologist to discern a connection. The USSR has shown repeated apprehension lest her very power bring about a further *rapprochement* between the United States and China or a working co-operation between China and Europe. And the Soviet Union's fear of China has two implications, one for Asia and one for Europe.

In Europe, it has been suggested here, both super-powers may find it harder to control the developments of relations between their respective alliances. But it is only the Soviet Union which is likely to find this very disturbing. It is now ten years since, with the invasion of Czechoslovakia, she abandoned her earlier assumption that part of the price for detente might be to allow a greater degree of autonomy to Eastern Europe. In recent years, and especially since President Brezhnev's visit to Belgrade and Bucharest in 1976, the signs have all pointed the other way. Detente for the Soviet leadership now seems to impose the necessity of maintaining tighter ideological and political control; even in its fragmented form, detente in the future is likely to involve the same measure of control. But it is here that the weaknesses of the USSR become most apparent and most dangerous. The attempt to impose agreed forms of political and economic development on her East European allies depends, in the end, on very little leverage. It is maintained by the threat to use tanks. How far the complexities of social and economic change in Eastern Europe can be contained within a ring of steel and for how long, and how far initial success in suppressing discontent might help to create irresistible pressure for the future are questions which the United States and the NATO countries will have to consider in painful detail during the next decade. An Eastern European crisis could prove to be the major test of Western foreign policy and alliance cohesion that was not quite provided even by the Middle East war of 1973.

In Asia the Soviet Union is less likely to prove a *status quo* power than an increasingly activist one. It is virtually impossible to imagine any lasting reconciliation with China, and Chinese successes in foreign policy have in the recent past only prompted greater Soviet drives for containment. In the fragmented system of the 1980s the Soviet government might still try to contain Chinese influence by a generalized approach to Asia on lines similar to those of its proposal for an Asian security conference. But, given the poor record of such approaches, it is possible that we will see a series of separate involvements leading to separate conflicts or coincidences of interest with different Asian powers or with the United States. In South-east Asia, in South Asia and in the Central Treaty Organization (CENTO) area Soviet diplomacy will be active, will probably contribute to the lability of relations throughout the continent and will be consistent only in its desire to limit Chinese influence. A nexus of concerns, such as that which could develop from the situation in Afghanistan, involving as it does the watchful interests of India, Pakistan, China and Iran, would obviously be of major importance to the Western powers, whatever their other separate interests in different parts of Asia. And Western powers, for those purposes, very clearly include Japan, whose own relations with the USSR will remain delicate, difficult and potentially tense if she becomes increasingly involved in the development of China.

In the rest of the world a truculent and anxious Soviet Union will continue to operate from an unpredictable mixture of motives. Her anxiety to secure resources for her further development will not necessarily make her more co-operative, as her history of the exploitation of the sea has already shown. Her anxiety to assert her global reach, irrespective of whether real interests are at stake or not, will probably continue, and here her underlying weakness will probably still impel her to rely on the military instruments of influence. She will perhaps concern herself intermittently with developments in Africa and the Middle East – without any coherent strategy, without any identifiable long-term aim, but with a degree of opportunism equal to her undifferentiated ambition. In this sense, the fragmentation of the world order already represents a Soviet success, providing greater local opportunities and imposing fewer constraints than did the earlier period of super-power detente.

But if this illegitimate legitimacy, this hag-ridden grandeur, prompt some foreboding, are there nonetheless any constraints on Soviet behaviour? One is obvious: the need to maintain some sort of dialogue with the United States in order to prevent crises from becoming too dangerous. But here the Middle East probably serves as a good example for the future: the Soviet Union has shown interest in controlling crisis but not in preventing it; she is not necessarily opposed to a peace settlement between the Arab states and Israel, but she is opposed to a *pax Americana*. She collaborates with her rival in avoiding war, but if war can be avoided, she pursues her rivalry without inhibition. In this sense, the constraint is itself also a guarantor of antagonistic ambition.

Do economic constraints indicate a different kind of future? Both super-powers have become increasingly dependent on raw materials from areas which lie outside their political control, and the process will continue. In the case of the United States this has led to a close working relationship with certain other countries, notably Saudi Arabia. But there is very little connection in the Soviet case between economic need and political association. It is true that for some years the Soviet Union has had close political relations with Iraq and has also imported Iraqi oil – but this was, in fact, largely for re-export to Japan. On the whole, economic and political business are conducted separately in the Soviet Union, as they have been ever since Stalinist autarchy was dismantled. Indeed, the USSR depends on the United States for two major items on her shopping list: computers and oil-drilling equipment. Yet it is obvious that such dependency has made very little difference to the management of political affairs; it is rather that the onus of deciding whether a particular form of political relationship should be allowed to determine a particular form of economic conduct is left to the other side. In this sense, such events as the cancellation of the Tass computer after the condemnation of Shcharansky may give the United States a little leverage, but it is not likely that such leverage would be either consistent or powerful. In fact, the Soviet system cannot afford to allow its economic interests to determine its political structure:

the primacy of politics is essential to maintaining the role of the party; and even a party increasingly interested in technocratic criteria is still going to be concerned primarily with its own social and political destiny. In these circumstances it would be misleading to suggest that the weakness of the Soviet Union will allow economic constraints to influence her political behaviour. The contrary could even be the case: that, in so far as she feels herself slipping in any form of competition for influence with her principal rival, she might be tempted to use what means she has to redress the balance.

There is, however, a different kind of consideration which might be worth bearing in mind. It is that while the Soviet government might not be open to direct influence from the leading Western powers, it might have to tread more warily in its dealings with others. It will, if it continues to develop economically, depend on imports of energy and commodities to an ever greater extent. Since it does not have much to offer to the developing world, it could find that the temptations to exploit its own power are tempered by its need. An interest in maintaining stability, at least in partial and separate areas of the world, could be related to an anxiety to secure reliable supplies. In this respect, the Soviet Union could, in some areas and over certain issues, come to accept some of the premises of the Western view of international relations – that is, she could come to behave like any other post-colonial power.

This is, perhaps, a depressing projection. But it is probably the best that can be hoped for. A country which has cut itself off so much from its own culture and its own past, a country which is still a moral desert, a country whose ardent ideology has been transformed merely into an offer of pragmatic materialism to the majority of its citizens, will depend more on material inducements than on any other considerations. The behaviour of the Soviet Union will be cross-cut in appearance: prudence and interest will modify ambition. At times her postures will still seem random and threatening to Western observers, but her need to advance, prompted by an acknowledgment of inferiority, will be hampered by constraints.

The dialectics of weakness: this is the framework in which to consider the role of the Soviet Union in the 1980s.

Ideology and Soviet Foreign Policy

LEOPOLD LABEDZ

The relation between ideology and Soviet policies is one of those perennial subjects which has been analysed to the point of exhaustion in the past, but it seems that the question still continues to provoke curiosity. The old duality of ideology versus *Realpolitik*, and hackneyed formulations about the primordial role of ideology as against power motives and national considerations or *vice versa* in Soviet external conduct, still recur regularly in articles and books. New debates on these subjects are occasioned by current developments in East-West relations, by discussions on them among Soviet dissidents (between, say, Solzhenitsyn and Sakharov, or Medvedev and Shafarevich), or simply by the emergence of new generations of analysts.

But if the subject is not exactly unexplored, there is still nothing approaching consensus on it. As Pierre Hassner has remarked, 'the same crude dichotomies between ideology and power have re-emerged intact after a generation in current debates about detente, the significance of Soviet arms policies, Soviet attitudes towards change in Western Europe, and the source of Soviet conduct in Africa'. Although many analysts (Lowenthal and Brzezinski, for example) pointed out twenty years ago that the two factors are interdependent, attitudes to the problem continue to polarize: there are those who see ideology as the ultimate source of Soviet conduct and those who see in it nothing but *post hoc* rationalization of other basic drives. Thirty years ago Kennan saw the problem as one of interaction between Marxist–Leninist ideology and the 'circumstances of power', even though he argued that the former provided 'a highly convenient rationalization' for the 'instinctive desires' of the Soviet leaders. Recently, however, he has come to the conclusion

that 'the rhetoric of revolutionary Marxism' is today just a 'verbal smokescreen' for traditional nationalist foreign policy.

Where, then, do we stand now in relation to this evergreen question? Is the end of ideology in the Soviet Union in sight? If the answer is yes, what are its implications for Soviet foreign policy? If the answer is no, and ideology continues to play a role in Soviet conduct, even if it is changing, how does this change affect the Soviet leaders' concern for the power of their party and their empire? Does it imply in either case that the Soviet challenge to the West would become easier to manage?

Western Simplifications

Before tackling these problems in any detail it is necessary to clear away some of the verbal fog in which the concept of ideology is shrouded. Past debates on the subject may be forgotten, but they did help to avoid the confusion which usually tends to accompany current discussions on the relationship between ideology and Soviet policies.

One of the sources of confusion in controversies about the role of ideology is the absence of a clear distinction between the significance of its particular and its general features.[1] To be concerned with the first aspect is to deal with the modification or abandonment of specific tenets of the Marxist–Leninist gospel, be it the 'dictatorship of the proletariat' or the 'withering away of the state'. Doctrinal change of even the most cherished tenets is compatible with the preservation of ideology. It is only the modification of the general features of ideology that might hint at a basic change in its character or presage its demise. Such general features include the utopian perspective of Marxism, its millennial nature and a belief in the scientific character of its historical 'laws'. As long as these general features of Communist ideology are preserved, any alterations of its particular features can be rationalized.

Dialectics are always at hand to reinforce the dogma 'when the prophecy fails'. Indeed, specific parts of a utopian doctrine *must* change in confrontation with the reality of historical development if ideology is to survive. Otherwise the credibility gap could grow too wide even for true believers. But the ideology survives despite the credibility gap; it does not depend just on the existence of true believers. Those who say that ideology is 'nothing but rationalization' do not ask what role rationalization performs in the maintenance of ideology, or why there is a need for rationalization rather than the abandonment of ideology – in short, how pertinent is the relationship between ideology as rationalization and ideology as a motivating force. Even for an individual, 'motivation' and 'rationalization' can be mutually reinforcing mechanisms; this is even more true of political processes in society, and particularly in Soviet society, where power rests on doctrinal authority. The crux of the matter is that ideology is a necessary part of the system because it provides the principles of its legitimacy and imposes the general framework for the perception of reality. Thus, inevitably, it also conditions Soviet attitudes towards foreign policy.

To grasp the nature of the evolution of Soviet foreign policy it is not enough just to analyse the changing condition of foreign policy. It is also necessary to be aware of doctrinal evolution in the Soviet Union, of the current state of ideology there (which is a related but distinct problem) and of the specific relation between these, power and other factors. To treat the problem as if it were only one question is to over-simplify it to a point at which fallacious conclusions about foreign policy inevitably follow.

Those who dismiss ideology as 'nothing but rationalization' stress the 'pragmatic' character of Soviet policies; but this overlooks the Leninist distinction between short-term considerations (which impose limitations on policies) and long-range ideological goals. In a certain sense, all politics, ideological or not, tend to be concerned first of all with short-term considerations. But there is a difference between policies which appertain to nothing else, and those which take long-term considerations, ideological or other, as their frame of reference. To confuse the two as 'pragmatic' in the same sense is to misunderstand the character of Soviet policies both in the past and in the present.

It is this fallacy, this indiscriminate use of the term 'pragmatism' when describing both Soviet and Western foreign policies, which accounts for most of the erroneous expectations generated in the West by political leaders and commentators on many occasions. Whenever the Soviet Union comes out with what looks like a particularly flagrant violation of her ideological articles of faith, they find in this a confirmation of their pre-conceived ideas about Soviet policy. This was the case with the treaty of Brest-Litovsk, the Stalin–Hitler Pact, Yalta and detente. Throughout this period all too many voices in the West have been ready to disregard the persistence of the ideological factor in Soviet foreign policy. 'Bourgeois' politicians tended to see only the Soviet need for 'pragmatic accommodation' and 'compromise'; revolutionary 'true believers' in the West treated these occasions as instances of ideological betrayal (which only reinforced the short-sighted illusions, or wishful thinking, of their less 'progressive' brethren).

No amount of official avowal would induce most Western politicians to treat Soviet ideological utterances seriously. When confronted with a myriad of Soviet assertions which contradicted American assumptions about detente, the usual Western pattern of reasoning was to explain them away as no more than 'ideological rationalization' or 'ideological rhetoric'. Another stock argument was that they were for home consumption only, though they were also addressed to foreign Communists.

Henry Kissinger provided the grand premise for this type of Western self-deception. He assumed that what he imagined to be the 'rules of the game' in detente were also binding on the Soviet Union. According to him these 'rules' precluded: (a) attempts by either country to achieve a position of predominance either globally or regionally; (b) any attempt to exploit a policy of detente to weaken our alliances; and (c) the exploitation of relaxation of tension . . . as a cover to exacerbate conflicts in international trouble spots.[2]

These 'rules' were based on the Declaration of Basic Principles of Relations between the United States and the Soviet Union, signed in Moscow in May 1972, and on a similar document signed in Washington in June 1973. They solemnly proclaimed that neither of the two powers would try 'to obtain unilateral advantage at the expense of the other'.

The illusions about Soviet 'pragmatism' die hard, as does wishful thinking about the Soviet approach to detente. After Yalta there was disenchantment in the West when it finally dawned that Stalin's use of the word 'democracy' did not quite coincide with Western usage. Now there has been another painful discovery of the obvious – Brezhnev's concept of detente differs from the Western one. But if the *sancta simplicitas* of the earlier period was to some degree dispelled in the West (only to resurface in the 1960s), traces of a new *naiveté* (or of self-induced *faux naiveté*), which has again been challenged by Soviet behaviour, are still lingering. It is still assumed by many that the Soviet leaders accepted (in fact) the Western 'rules of the game' in detente. Zbigniew Brzezinski complained in May 1978 that the Soviet Union has violated her 'code'. This presupposed, of course, that the signing of the pieces of paper by the Soviet Union in Moscow, Washington and Helsinki amounted to her serious acceptance of such a 'code'.

Just as on past occasions, there was no dearth of voices in the West warning against such interpretations of current Soviet policies. They predicted their significance quite precisely on the basis of past experience, but they were not heeded. Many doctrinal and ideological pronouncements were quite explicit about the Soviet attitude to 'peaceful coexistence'. In fact, Soviet words matched Soviet deeds in anti-Western policies and propaganda. They were, of course, incompatible with Soviet diplomatic declarations, but there was nothing new in this: Soviet policies in the past have always displayed such duality when engaged in a diplomatic 'soft-sell' during the periods of 'offensives of smiles'.

Now that the period of 'bourgeois' euphoria over detente is ended it is interesting to recall how Soviet political commentators tried to persuade the Western New Left that the Soviet Union remained faithful to her revolutionary ideology. Here is the American 'independent Marxist' journal, *Science and Society*, describing how Eduard Batalov explained in his book *The Philosophy of Revolt*[3] that the ideological *angst* of Western radicals is groundless:

> The problem of violence, according to Batalov, exposes the New Left's lack of grasp of the correlation of class forces. Certainly in our epoch revolutionary transformations have thus far been carried out only by means of violence. But a premature outbreak of violence incites an overwhelming reaction from the right. Consequently, this question must be handled with extreme tactical skill and must be based on a careful analysis of class alignments and forces . . . Many New Leftists use guerrilla warfare, the revolutionary method *par excellence*, as a pretext for attacking 'Soviet revisionism' and detente – even though no other country has been a more consistent supporter of authentic guerrilla movements. Detente submits capitalism to two pressures, the external one of socialism and the internal one of the working class. Detente favours the liberation of people from imperialism, and helps consolidate socialism.

Ideology in Evolution

One way to approach the problem of whether ideology is 'nothing but rationalization' is to ask whether without it some Soviet policies would be the same. Even if it is only an inhibiting or exacerbating factor, it does play a role in important specific cases. It is difficult, for instance, to imagine that a pragmatic approach would maintain the present structure of Soviet agriculture, a source not only of domestic but also of international weakness for the Soviet leaders. Or, to move to foreign affairs, whatever the historical roots of the Sino–Soviet conflict may be, its character would be different without the ideological dimension which makes it not just a clash between national interests and powers, but a contest which is even more profound because it also affects the legitimacy of the respective ruling parties.

If, then, one is of the opinion that ideology does indeed play a role beyond that of mere rationalization, one still faces questions about its evolution and its present role with regard to both general and specific aspects of Soviet conduct. The fact that we are dealing here with long-range consequences which are difficult to determine is no reason to disregard them altogether.

Ideological evolution during six decades of Soviet history can be summarized as a reluctant retreat from the utopian and universalistic claims of Marxist doctrine – not, however, their abandonment. The content of the doctrine has been undergoing constant modification in line with the dual impulses coming from the intractable reality on the one hand and from the need to legitimate power on the other. There is, of course, nothing historically extraordinary in reluctance to retreat from the universalist pretensions of a doctrine. Even at a time of decline, Byzantium stuck obsessively to its imperial claims on Christian universality. So did Rome, faced with the Reformation. Tribal religions evolve into universalistic ones, as history testifies, but there is usually no reverse evolution in places which claim to be the *fons et origo* of such universal doctrines, and the same applies to the secular ideology of Communism. There is usually only a fragmentation through schism – into Christian churches, Islamic sects or national Communist parties – each faction adapting the universal doctrinal truths to local conditions. This is the one formula on which all Communist parties in this polycentric age agree in theory, but the Soviet Union continues to emphasize the universal validity of her own interpretation of Marxism in the face of those who deny it.

Despite sociological parallels drawn by Crane Brinton, Jules Monnerot and S. F. Kissin, Communism is not a religion: it has no transcendental concern. Certain social and political consequences follow from this. The promise of Utopia is not the same as the promise of Paradise; it is to be realized in this world rather than the next. Therefore the legitimacy of Churches, even where Christianity was a state religion, was a different problem from that faced by Communist parties in power. The latter cannot accept the separation of Party from State. Their legitimacy depends on successful construction of a Communist society with its utopian features and not on attending to the spiritual needs of the faithful.

It is not surprising, therefore, that this part of Marxist doctrine has undergone modification in the Soviet Union under the dual impulses mentioned earlier. Communist Utopia has been postponed ever since Lenin wrote his *State and Revolution*, but it has never been abandoned as unrealizable. From War Communism and the first Party Programme, through Lenin's 'Dictatorship of the Proletariat', Stalin's 'sharpening of contradictions under Socialism', Khrushchev's 'State of All People' and the promise of Full Communism within two decades in the third Party Programme (1961) to Brezhnev's 'Developed Socialism' – all these doctrinal formulas testify to the same problem: power needs legitimacy, legitimacy needs Utopia, Utopia cannot be realized, so it has to be both preserved and constantly postponed. But, needless to say, the state has not withered away and is even no longer expected to do so. The Party has become not only *de facto* but also constitutionally the *alter ego* of the state; classes are officially on the way to extinction, but social and political hierarchies flourish in all their rigidity.

That is not, of course, how *Pravda* sees it. In an editorial article published in 1978 the following passage appears:

Marxist–Leninist ideology of the working class, which triumphed and became firmly established for ever in the motherland of October, is an ideology of genuine humanism and of social justice, of socialist patriotism and internationalism, of freedom, equality and brotherhood of nations. It joins workers, *kolkhozniks*, intelligentsia and toilers of all nationalities of our country; it unites the nations of the socialist commonwealth; it manifests growing influence on the broadest masses of toilers all over the world. Marxism–Leninism has become the ruler of the minds of all advanced humanity. This has been in many respects helped by the active ideological and theoretical work of the Communist and workers' parties and their increasingly strong ideological cooperation. Mentioning this in his speech at the ceremonial meeting in Prague in the spring of this year, the General Secretary of the Central Committee of the CPSU, Chairman of the Presidium of the Supreme Soviet of the USSR, Comrade L. I. Brezhnev said: 'Today Marxist–Leninist ideology occupies an *avant-garde* position in the world's social thought. It is a focus of passions, it attracts various social movements. This is to a very great extent the outcome of the common creative activity of our parties, the result of the influence of the richest practice in building a new world.' The growing influence of real socialism, of Communist ideals in the consciousness of working men, is the most important factor in the ideological struggle between the two social systems at the present stage. As the 25th Congress of the CPSU indicated, the problems of the ideological struggle are coming more and more to the fore in present conditions, and the truth about socialism is a mighty weapon in this struggle. In co-operation with other fraternal parties, the CPSU is doing its best to make the example of victorious socialism radiate more and more brightly, to make the magnetic attraction of Marxist–Leninist ideology grow ever stronger.[4]

Reading *Pravda* regularly teaches one how to perceive its emphases. They reflect, without fail, Soviet leaders' concerns in however inverted or camouflaged a form, and the example above is no exception. There can be little doubt that, after sixty years of doctrinal acrobatics, Soviet ideology is showing strains; its credibility is wearing thin. It is no longer a living faith, but a ritual code and a mental straightjacket. From the point of view of the mechanism of Party power it is necessary, a kind of ballast which cannot be thrown out. Once a source of strength, it is now becoming a source of weakness. Internally, even the attenuated utopian perspective necessitates the continuing flaunting of the reality principle. Externally, Soviet ideology has lost most of its persuasiveness and is more and more frequently forced to confront polycentric ideological challenges within the international Communist movement. What was once a source of unqualified support is now often a burden and an embarrassment. Revolutionary romanticism is dead in the Soviet Union. She has consequently lost almost all power to attract 'idealistic' radicals abroad (she has to use Cuba as a substitute). Her political appeal is increasingly based on crude power.

The rise of the Soviet empire coincides with its downfall as an ideological Mecca of Communism.

Ideology: A Wasting Asset?

All this cannot but have some negative repercussions, not only for the general image of the Soviet Union, but also for her performance in specific areas of international relations. The long-term implications of this are yet to be assessed, but present consequences can be discerned, even though they are contradictory.

Their contradictory character stems from the fact already mentioned: Soviet expansionism finds its justification in Soviet ideology, but this ideology is now becoming less effective for Soviet power projection. This is important because, among other reasons, Soviet geopolitical strategy, which is rooted in Leninism, has always aimed at changing the *status quo* at the margin by employing the expedient of an indirect approach to achieve a shift in the 'correlation of forces' in favour of the Soviet Union. It is a strategy which recommends itself particularly in the nuclear age because the risks have become inordinately high and the need for caution considerable, even when strategic parity has been formally achieved by the USSR. But Soviet Leninist strategy and Soviet Leninist ideology have somehow got out of step. Ideology is now hardly an asset which can tip the scale.

Politically, the Soviet Union has almost achieved a state of splendid isolation. Her so-called 'allies' in Eastern Europe are unreliable satellites. She has always been pre-occupied by the spectre of two-front confrontation. Stalin avoided it by helping to deflect the Japanese imperial drive southwards (during his conversation with Matsuoka he told him: 'We are both Asians'). But after the war the Soviet Union managed to frighten the West sufficiently to provoke the creation of NATO, and it is no exaggeration to say that it was Stalin who was the architect of German rearmament. Thirty years later the flagrant ambiguity of Brezhnev's detente, combined with the Soviet arms drive and expansionism, provoked the very situation the Soviet Union feared most: a two-front strategic confrontation. Brezhnev cannot claim all the credit for the Sino–American *rapprochement* and the Sino–Japanese Treaty, but he has a major share in it. Even if there is no complete symmetry, because neither *entente* is a military alliance and in both China's partners are apt to pursue a less stringent anti-Soviet policy than China herself, it is nevertheless clear that in both cases the Soviet Union is the losing party. She cannot prevent the United States from 'playing the China card' or Japan from supplying technology and economic assistance to her neighbour instead of to herself, as she had once hoped. On the other side the Soviet Union is, of course, hemmed in by the Western alliance. A policy which succeeds in mobilizing as adversaries of the Soviet Union not only the United States and Western Europe but Japan and China as well is not exactly a great political achievement, even though it can be defended in the cause of the 'ideological struggle' on all fronts. And indeed the Soviet Union is now involved in such an 'ideological struggle' with China and the West, not to mention Eurocommunism, Albania and parts of the Third World.

The real questions for the Soviet Union, however, are how impenetrable is the present adversary line and how invulnerable are the emergent countervailing coalitions? In short, can they contain Soviet expansion or not? The Soviet 'ideological struggle' has of course, to be taken in conjunction with geo-political and military factors. This poses three basic questions for the future:

- How will the dynamic of Soviet expansionism be affected by the fact that ideology no longer helps it?
- Soviet expansionism provokes countervailing coalitions, while Soviet ideology is finding few supporters abroad. In view of the gap between traditional Soviet strategy and the debilitation of its ideological appeal, is it not possible that the Soviet leadership might in future adopt a higher-risk strategy to compensate for its internal and external frustrations? This may be tempting in view of the increased Soviet military strength and of what is perceived as failure of the Western political nerve.
- If the Soviet Union tries to break her 'splendid isolation' (as China did when Chou En-lai started 'ping-pong diplomacy' to make up for the self-inflicted wounds of the Cultural Revolution), what political and military strategy can she conceivably adopt?

A Balance Sheet

If one were to borrow the Chestertonian technique and create a sovietological Father Brown, who would look on the political and strategic developments in the world through Soviet eyes, he would be struck by the number of ideological juxtapositions and political dilemmas that face the Soviet Union at present. For one, he would notice that the Soviet Union has now abandoned her previous perspective on the Third World. As *Kommunist* has recently put it:[5]

> There is no sufficient basis . . . for calling the developing countries a 'Third World' which allegedly has a parallel existence with the capitalist and socialist worlds. To determine the common features of developing countries it is necessary to take as a starting point two fundamental observations: the division of the contemporary world into two opposite socio-political systems, and the historical significance of our epoch as a period of transition from capitalism to socialism. This predetermines the objective impossibility of the liberated countries developing in a 'third' direction.
>
> Among developing countries there are already states which are following the capitalist path and states which have chosen the socialist orientation, and simultaneously there can be. and there is going to be, a gradual erosion of their commonality as a result of some developing countries associating with the world socialist system and some others joining the developed capitalist countries.

Among the former group, *Kommunist* lists Angola, Congo (Brazzaville), Ethiopia, Afghanistan, Madagascar, South Yemen, Benin, Tanzania, Algeria and Libya (neither Iraq nor Syria is mentioned). Among the latter group are Egypt, Iran, Kuwait, Saudi Arabia, Somalia, Sudan, Pakistan, Sri Lanka and Bangladesh. It is clear that inclusion in one or other group is determined by Soviet political interests and hopes and not by any Marxist, social or economic criteria. Some of these countries have fully-fledged Communist regimes; others are included in the 'progressive' group simply on account of their pro-Soviet foreign policies. What matters to the Soviet Union is obviously the strategic and geo-political opportunities they may be providing, and in this respect Afghanistan, South Yemen and Ethiopia (after its reconquest of Eritrea) are offering particularly good prospects as the staging ground for pressure on the Persian Gulf riparian states with their access to oil, the jugular vein of Western industrial economies.

If our sovietological Father Brown were to divine Soviet political perceptions, his approach would certainly differ from the usual Western approaches to the problem. He would certainly not imagine that the Soviet Union was committed to the maintenance of the international *status quo;* he would know that she was ideologically against it and striving to change it. Unlike most of his Western colleagues, he would be at least as much concerned with the geopolitical strategy of the Soviet Union as with her military stockpile, which is almost the only focus of Western perceptions (which is not to say that he would be more concerned with Soviet intentions than with Soviet capabilities). He would realize that both intentions and capabilities depend on opportunities and temptations, which are sometimes provided by fortuitous circumstances but are exploited by strategic and tactical foresight.

Finally, Father Brown would trace the historical evolution of foreign policy in the Soviet Union. He would bring to light her perceptions of her position in the world at different stages of her history. He would emphasize the erosion of ideology in Soviet short-term foreign-policy conduct from the beginning. (When Trotsky, on becoming a Commissar for Foreign Affairs, imagined that he would soon be able 'to close the shop', as there would no longer be any need for foreign policy.) He would also bring to light the long-term modifications of the role of ideology in Soviet foreign policy. He would stress in particular that in the early period, under Lenin, it was still playing a direct role, that its significance diminished under Stalin, that it was overshadowed by economic and strategic perspectives under Khrushchev and even more by military power under Brezhnev. But all this time, despite doctrinal erosion, Soviet foreign policy was firmly rooted in the *politique d'abord* principle derived from ideological perception. Despite the erosion of its role, ideology itself has never become entirely irrelevant, though its specific impact has not always been easy to discern and though it has gradually been overshadowed by other factors which have been seen as having a more effective impact abroad than dwindling Soviet ideological influence.

How would Father Brown perceive the strengths and weaknesses of Soviet foreign policy? He would not be able to see them objectively (the West tends to overestimate Soviet political skill; the East tends to overestimate Western political will). Nor would he be able to see the overall historical perspective on Soviet foreign policy properly through Soviet ideological lenses. This can only be done from outside. But he could try to see how the historical balance sheet of Soviet foreign-policy successes and failures looks from inside.

The past foreign-policy record is indubitably a positive one from the Soviet point of view. The Soviet Union has managed to achieve the status of a super-power and has registered many gains in the Third World. She has even managed, despite detente, to avoid the stigma of ideological betrayal, the stigma with which she now brands China for her bedfellowship with the 'imperialists'.

The overall achievement of the Soviet Union has been summarized by a Polish commentator in a recent issue of *Trybuna Ludu* as follows:[6]

In the long run the attitude of the capitalist countries to detente . . . is determined and will be determined in future, by objective circumstances. As far as the United States is concerned there are several. But I will limit myself to the enumeration of only a few of them.
1) The change in the balance of power between the socialist and capitalist systems. During the more than thirty years since World War II there have been substantial shifts in the political, economic and military correlation of forces between East and West [in favour of the former] . . .
2) The inability of the United States to win the strategic race with the Soviet Union. In spite of great arms expenditures in the United States, the doctrine of 'assured' strategic superiority over the USSR has ended in fiasco . . .

3) Changes in the world political configuration. The emergence of about 100 new states after World War II, despite their political differences, has generally weakened the capitalist countries. On basic questions of war and peace many new states have supported the concepts of the socialist countries...

4) The West has not won the Cold War. It has not achieved the goals of its policy, it has not 'contained Communism', nor reversed the progressive social and political changes in the world...

Although this points to real developments, it is far from being the whole picture. The post-war balance sheet of East–West relations is undoubtedly marked by Western strategic backsliding, but the Soviet advance has been accompanied by so many unwanted occurrences which complicate both the power and the ideological perspectives that the prospects of the triumphal Soviet march into the radiant future are somewhat less than certain.

Internally, the erosion of ideological momentum spells long-term trouble for Party legitimacy and position. Soviet economic performance is on the decline. Nationality problems are on the increase. The handling of any one of these problems would intensify the difficulty of resolving at least one of the others, while immobilism renders future action on them even more difficult.

Externally, it is enough to read the fifth page of *Pravda* (which covers foreign affairs) to see that the self-congratulatory exultation on page 1, its editorial page, is bunkum. In just the short period of summer 1978 it was filled with indignant outcries against almost everybody, as well as warnings and threats to the United States and China, Japan and Pakistan, France and Germany, Yugoslavia and Romania, Iran and North Yemen, Egypt and Saudi Arabia.

More than one spectre is haunting the Soviet Union: the spectre of anti-Communism (in the United States), the spectre of Eurocommunism (in Europe) and the spectre of Communism (in China). Ideological polemics in Soviet publications are now more variegated than ever. The Sino-Soviet dispute has reached the high point of absurdity. The Soviet Union accuses China of persecuting dissidents, of violating human rights, of using show trials against political opponents and of staging 'legal farces' against those 'suspected of dissatisfaction'.

But such high-minded sentiments, expressed in the Soviet press shortly after the trials of Orlov, Ginzburg and Shcharansky are not only directed against what *Pravda* (27 August 1978) called 'reprisals from above' in China. Similarly indignant denunciations are also made regularly of the abuse of human rights in Britain and the United States – hardly a case of the pot calling the kettle black. Yet it continues. One article condemns a 'War against Dissidents' in the United States; another compares the strengthening (by 4,000 men) of the much-reduced British Army in 1978 with the Nazi military build-up in the 1930s; a third cavils sarcastically at the misuse of psychiatry in capitalist countries, and so forth. Day after day, country after country and personality after personality, from Chile to Israel, from Santiago Carillo to Zbigniew Brzezinski, become the targets of Soviet obloquy.

These unrelenting castigations make the black list longer and longer. Fukuda is attacked for getting ready to sign the 'anti-hegemony clause' in the Sino-Japanese Treaty and Hua Kuo-feng for visiting Romania, Yugoslavia and Iran. Even Albania has not escaped censure, although her split with China was seen as opening up promising possibilities for the Soviet Union in future. Albania was harshly reprimanded because she 'has still not changed her extremely dogmatic ideology, nor her policy, which even today equates the socialist Soviet Union with the imperialist United States, the Warsaw Pact with NATO, COMECON with the European Common Market'.

But if dogmatic Albania was sternly rebuked, so were the 'revisionist' Eurocommunists. The Spanish Communists like Azcarate are already beyond the pale, but even the more accommodating Italian communists are getting stiff lessons in elementary Leninism. Thus *Kommunist* reminded them of Gramsci's warning that 'not a single revolutionary movement can be dictated to by a national assembly', that the problem of power cannot be decided by 'arithmetic majority', that revolution 'cannot be decided by voting' but must transcend 'the framework of the formal principles of bourgeois democracy'.

As can be seen, 'ideological struggle' in the Soviet Union has become a matter of *défense de tous les azimuths*. And this is as good an indication as any that, contrary to the historical reflections of the *Trybuna Ludu* commentator, not everything is for the best for the Soviet Union in the worst of all possible imperialist worlds. It may even suggest that some waves of the present may never reach the future. Lincoln Steffens thought that he 'had seen the future, and it works' in Soviet Russia, but sixty years later it looks less and less likely that this is the case.

NOTES

[1] The distinction is related to, but differs from, what Martin Seliger calls the 'restricted and inclusive' conceptions of ideology (*The Marxist Conception of Ideology:* Cambridge, 1977). The former refers to specific political belief systems, the latter to all political doctrines.

[2] For one of Henry Kissinger's major speeches on detente, see his statement, *Hearings before the Committee on Foreign Relations, US Relations with Communist Countries,* US Senate, 93rd Congress, 2nd Session, 19 September 1974 (Washington, DC: USGPO, 1975).

[3] Eduard Batalov, *The Philosophy of Revolt* (London: Central Books, 1975).

[4] 'The Strength of Our Ideology', *Pravda*, 24 August 1978, p. 1.

[5] No. 11, 1978.

[6] 14 August 1978.

[7] No. 10, 1977.

The United States in the Soviet Perspective

ALEXANDER DALLIN

The Soviet view of the United States is inherently ambiguous. The United States is the object of both envy and scorn; the enemy to fight, expose and pillory – and the model to emulate, catch up with and overtake. There are multiple sources, reinforcing each other, for this ambiguity. There are traditional Russian views going back a century or more, as well as the 'scratches on their minds' in the Bolshevik leaders' grudging admiration of symbols of industrial efficiency such as Pittsburgh and Detroit, along with their conviction that American capital has been responsible for crises and abuse in the world economy from the Great Depression to the multi-national corporations of our day. There are the Soviet ideological biases which, coupled with overwhelming ignorance regarding the United States, shaped much of Moscow's attitudes in the Stalin days. And, it must be recognized, the reality of American life and behaviour often validates and reinforces such uncertainties: however distorted the Soviet image, both American intervention after the Russian Revolution and Allied partnership against Nazi Germany did indeed occur; there is a basis for the images of both abundance and squalor; there are the Pentagon and populism, optimism and opportunity, as well as racism and the shallowness of a mass culture symbolized by such figures as Mickey Mouse and Elvis Presley.

The difficulty in defining the Soviet perspective on the United States is due, however, not only to the simultaneity of contradictory elements, such as admiration and fear, in their perception of a system and a society they do not, by and large, understand or trust, but also the existence, within the Soviet political élite, of *different* images, perceptions, assumptions and policy preferences regarding the United States – and each set of mental pictures of the adversary gives rise to a set of congruent attitudes.

We must, then, start out by rejecting for the Soviet Union, much as we have done for the West, the model of a unitary, rational actor represented by the 'state' (or the 'party'). Even if the range of Soviet views is less sweeping than its Western counterparts, one could show that the differences among Soviet observers are significant, have often been consistent, have persisted for a long time and fit logically into and inform distinct and fairly coherent world views and political priorities.

Conflicting Images

A careful reading even of public pronouncements and publications will reveal at least two distinctly different clusters of Soviet images and arguments concerning the United States (and some analysts would say more than two). While this is an over-simplification, it would not be grievously unfair to label one a moderate-realistic and the other an intransigent-hostile perspective; the former is likely to be pragmatic, the latter dogmatic.

Curiously, one can trace back both these sets of pictures and the policies that flow from them at least to the end of World War II; and one can show (as, for instance, Franklyn Griffiths has done)[1] that there has been a remarkable degree of consistency in the outlook and analysis which each cluster of images has helped define. If Maxim Litvinov took seriously the need for the wartime Allies to continue working together when the war had ended and believed that they could, others like Molotov and Zhdanov were convinced that the ultimate clash between the two opposite world systems was inevitable. Before long the orthodox Stalinists would condemn those Soviet economists (Eugene Varga being, perhaps, the best known) who had begun to argue that government regulation and a Keynesian policy served to mitigate the strains of private enterprise, and that the expansion of productive capacity and GNP heralded a massive rise in the American standard of living – forecasts which led to their authors being suspected of being soft on capitalism. The dominant perspectives in the years of late Stalinism (as Frederick C. Barghoorn, among others, documented at the time)[2] more and more resembled a caricature, and Soviet accounts of American policy and American life were candidly described as 'weapons' in the cosmic contest.

All the more important, then, was the fundamental reversal that came in the post-Stalin years. International relations and foreign-area studies came into their own, with changing views of nuclear war and deterrence, an end to self-isolation and the gradual emergence of a new corps of Soviet analysts and consultants who, with all their shortcomings, were increasingly knowledgeable and influential – trends which William Zimmerman and others have carefully traced and examined.[3] Needless to say, it took time to shake off some of the habits of predictable dogmatism, self-serving distortion and phoney optimism, and to stop reporting what it was assumed the boss wanted to hear.

Meanwhile Nikita Khrushchev found it convenient to fall back on Lenin's old formula that there were 'two tendencies' at work in Western (and now particularly American) society. Over the past generation Moscow has often invoked the notion of two conflicting attitudes (towards the USSR as well as other issue areas) competing for support in the United States. In as much as the outcome of this internal American tug-of-war is not predetermined, the United States is not doomed to clash with the Soviet Union; and it follows that one cannot speak of the 'autonomy of the superstructure', that 'subjective factors' (including personalities) do matter and can make a difference – in short, that politics are not merely a by-product of the ownership of the means of production.

In the early 1960s Khrushchev argued that in each camp there were both 'men of reason' (or realists) and 'madmen'; that in the nuclear age it was imperative for the former on both sides to get together so as to freeze out the madmen, who took a future showdown for granted, and thus to forestall nuclear catastrophe on a world scale. Here was an example of a symmetrical or mirror image, in which each actor perceives the adversary camp in substantially the same terms as his own. (Khrushchev's description of his conversation with President Eisenhower about the 'greedy and self-seeking' nature of the men who run the armed forces, both in the United States and in the USSR, has often been cited as a telling example of the same approach.)[4]

There are very distinct limits, however, beyond which such images of symmetry or convergence cannot publicly progress. Ideologically it has remained impermissible to erode the organic, qualitative difference between the Soviet system and Western capitalism. Many aspects of American politics and culture have remained genuinely baffling to Soviet observers, and some sophisticated insights by Soviet commentators must remain concealed behind rhetoric.

Soviet commentators gradually came around to acknowledging that the American bourgeoisie, the business community and the power élite are by no means monolithic either. Curiously, a more pluralist image of the United States appears to have been proffered more readily by those who are themselves prepared to see a more diverse USSR as well. To illustrate differences among Soviet perspectives, one might refer to Khrushchev's arguments with Molotov, Mao or Malinovsky. Since the Stalinists and Maoists have been better known. it may be useful to refer to the repeated instances in which Khrushchev spoke of the necessity of coexisting with the United States, while Marshal Malinovsky, as head of the armed forces, would insist (without challenging Khrushchev) that the imperialist beast could not change its spots, that it was (and was bound to remain) the enemy of socialism and national liberation movements. A comparison of statements made some ten years later by Leonid Brezhnev on the one hand and Marshal Grechko on the other shows each using very similar formulations, the one laying stress on the necessity (and benefits) of getting along with the other side and the other the impossibility of doing so.

It is important to note that neither of these major Soviet orientations has asserted, either in the 1960s or now, that the United States is a 'paper tiger' or that the Soviet Union or the Soviet bloc is stronger than the United States or NATO. Neither has taken riots and protests in the United States as indicators of a looming collapse; nor has either exaggerated the crises engendered by American economic setbacks, inflation or unemployment (while making propaganda capital of strikes and dislocations, the more serious media have spoken of the economic problems as cyclical and transient). Soviet observers have often condemned the New Left for under-estimating the 'objective' problems of an effective revolutionary movement in the United States. At all times Moscow has given the United States high marks in science, technology and, of late, the 'science of management'. And, whatever their differences over other issues, virtually all Soviet policy-makers and experts seem agreed in discounting at least for the foreseeable future all prospects of either an economic collapse or a successful proletarian revolution in the United States.

Assumptions about Detente, 1969-75
The current phase in the Soviet assessment of the United States goes back to 1969, when the basic decisions were taken in Moscow regarding Soviet aims for super-power relations in an age characterized by (1) strategic parity, (2) the Sino-Soviet conflict and (3) increasing Soviet awareness of slowing economic growth and technological innovation. By then the Institute for the Study of the USA and Canada had begun to function in Moscow under Georgii Arbatov's direction and to offer expert advice to the Kremlin (on the whole, from the moderate end of the political spectrum). Fundamental decisions were made in favour of arms-limitation talks and, more broadly, of multiplying various forms of (carefully controlled and highly selective) trans-actions with the outside world. An escape from economic and technological autarky and self-reliance to greater interdependence was vastly preferable to a risky, destabilizing and uncertain reorganization of the Soviet economic and administrative systems.

With some over-simplification, it may be said that this stage involved an overall Soviet assumption that 'realism' in American policy (the result of objective trends, including the shifting international balance, as well as trans-

ient events such as the Vietnam war) made the United States a possible partner in a variety of common enterprises; that the American economy would continue to function and pro-duce, and that peace would be maintained (or else the whole calculus made no sense, either in terms of Soviet gains from grain purchases, technology transfers, and joint development projects, or in its anti-Chinese implications); and that both sides stood to gain from a better Soviet–American relationship. Such a capsule formulation credits the dominant orientation in Moscow with a rather benign view – even some wishful thinking – with regard to the United States. The deeply ingrained approach symbolized by the formula *Kto Kovo* (who-whom) had not disappeared, but it does seem that even at that time Soviet fear of the United States was considerably greater than the Soviet Union's commitment to, or even optimism about, 'doing her in'. While there was un-doubtedly a strong temptation to exploit the new situation for unilateral gains, the Soviet Union never seemed to have the confidence to take such a step, nor the willingness to run risks. There may have been some officials who saw the new course as a façade for mischief-making, but if so, there is no way of document-ing their existence or their views.

While such a perspective became dominant from about 1969, it reached its peak with the Nixon and Kissinger visits to Moscow in 1972-3. Though its basic assumptions and arguments have persisted, as we shall see, a change has set in since 1976, and both the *amerikanisty* and the policy-makers are concerned about the resurgence of 'rightist' tendencies in the United States and the deterioration of Soviet–American relations. As yet, this has not led to an abandon-ment of the assumptions underlying the Soviet detente calculus – partly because it is so completely identified with the Brezhnev leader-ship that its abandonment would imply an attack on the incumbents, but also because the signals Moscow receives from the United States are ambiguous and unclear and the Kremlin is unwilling to conclude that things cannot yet get back on track.

Once again, it would be a serious misreading of the evidence to assume that the question of whether one can do business with the United States, literally and figuratively, has been settled in Moscow. It remains an open question, and here there is indeed some symmetry between the two super-powers. Carl Sandburg is believed to have remarked once that every time an argument breaks out in Chicago over whether there is such a place as hell, there is a debate in hell over whether there is such a place as Chicago.

By contrast with the Khrushchev years, élite conflicts and differences in the Soviet Union have certainly received far less publicity in recent years. Yet there has been periodic confirmation of the continued existence of the basic cleavages. And one major cluster which currently brings together divergent assessments and preferences linking domestic and foreign policy issues in Moscow might be identified under the headings: (1) assessment of the United States; (2) SALT II; (3) detente – the Soviet calculus. Those Soviet observers who have tended to see the United States in less ideological, and more moderate terms have also been more inclined to be optimistic about the prospects of detente (at least until 1977) – both as to its expected benefits and as to the likelihood of its enduring.

This is not the place to exhibit the evidence in support of this general argument. It ranges from Soviet materials – an occasional remark by Brezhnev or an oblique attack by Gromyko on certain comrades who see 'any agreement with the capitalist states . . . almost [as] a plot',[5] – to *samizdat* documents (such as the summary of a speech by Moscow *gorkom* secretary Vladimir Yagodkin, assailing both 'dogmatic negativism' and 'opportunist illusions' regarding detente)[6] and several American doctoral dissertations carefully analysing diverse perceptions found in Soviet sources. The testimony of recent Soviet emigrés (such as Dimitri Simes, Alexander Yanov and Boris Rabbot), who had an opportunity to hear what was being said in Soviet élite circles, is also relevant. Whatever questions one may raise about their particular assertions, there is little reason to doubt that 'the internal debates over detente in Moscow reflected uncertain perceptions of American intentions among the Soviet leaders . . .'[7]

Given the nature of Soviet élite politics, it is often impossible to reconstruct the alignment of particular actors or groups on a given cluster of issues. It remains uncertain just how importantly perceptions of the United States figured in the removal of Shelest, Shelepin or Podgorny (probably more in the first two, least in the latter case). Sophisticated and informed efforts have been made by Vernon Aspaturian and Astrid von Borcke, for example, to see how particular occupational and bureaucratic groups in the USSR perceive their self-interest *vis-à-vis* an improvement in Soviet–American relations (and thus their perspective on the United States).[8]

It is clear that a number of 'hardliners' in Moscow (in the Party, in the police apparatus and in the armed forces) opposed both the new and more benign image of the United States and what they saw as the implied opening of the USSR to 'subversive' influences from, and contacts with, outside. (Michel Tatu has suggested that, in addition to the ideologically orthodox Party functionaries, the policy is 'opposed by a mass of lower cadres who are prisoners of the dogmas and the primitive views of the world imposed upon them . . . How can they avoid being more "hawkish" than their leaders?')[9] Some perceived this change in attitude as a threat to their own roles and careers; others (as Marshall Shulman has suggested) saw the abandonment of autarky as opening the way to a fatal Soviet dependence on the adversary power, felt threatened by new prospects of American 'bridge-building' to Eastern Europe (let alone Soviet nationalities), opposed sharing Soviet natural resources with foreign countries and described the effects of anticipated economic transactions as objectively postponing the twilight of capitalism.[10] To a degree, Brezhnev was able to take the wind out of their sails by insisting on a policy of repression calculated to minimize the political costs of the new course at home, but this dealt with only one dimension of the problem. It is also likely, though harder to show from compilations of Soviet sources (such as those analysed by Stephen Gibert),[11] that some Soviet 'hardliners' have more recently complained about the excessive price of detente – in effect, that interdependence deprives the Soviet Union of freedom of action and that she is not getting enough in return to warrant the degree of self-restraint which Washington demands of Moscow.

At the other end of the spectrum the 'experts' have sought to counter these muffled attacks on the Brezhnev policy and the underlying perspective on the United States; in particular, these are the staffs of the United States and World

Economy and International Politics institutes, who have access to influential people in the Kremlin. In all likelihood their views have often been endorsed by senior Foreign Ministry personnel.

The level of competence in studies produced by these and other research bodies and the conclusions contained therein are, by and large, good indices of the substantial advances made over Soviet analyses of the United States a generation ago. Monographs on particular institutions and processes – the Federal Reserve system, for example, or the National Security Council – are serious academic studies, despite their obligatory rhetoric, occasional lapses and predictable distortions. Those who have studied the Soviet output conclude that Soviet analysts are far more comfortable in dealing with the Executive branch (in particular, the State and Defense Departments and the White House) than with Congress and public opinion. Bureaucracy, decision-making and factional politics are categories they understand and can deal with. On the other hand, there was surprise at such developments as the passage of the Jackson Amendment. More generally, Moscow failed to understand what Watergate was all about. It tends to see the human rights issue as a strictly manipulated special-interest gimmick. Soviet observers have typically misjudged the role of media in the United States, unwittingly seeing newspapers and television as the equivalents of Soviet media in their role as mouthpieces. As Morton Schwartz remarks:

> They do not seem able to understand, for example, the principle of limited government, the rule of law, the separation of powers and majority rule. They have difficulty even conceptualizing the value we place on individual liberty, freedom of speech and the press, the concern we have regarding the morality of our public leaders . . . Obviously, Soviet comprehension of the American political process is severely hampered by their truncated political preconceptions.[12]

Still, the dominant school in Moscow correctly saw a shift in American outlook on world affairs and on the affairs of the Soviet Union in particular, and it liked what it saw. And yet doubts and fears remained, even in the years of greatest euphoria, when Arbatov, for example, argued that the United States tends to embark on foreign-policy adventurism to take the heat off the Administration at home—as it ostensibly did in Cambodia in 1970 and in the Middle East (in the middle of the Watergate crisis) in 1973. The USA Institute has reminded its readers that the United States has typically been committed to changing *internal* aspects of the Soviet system (a perception that was bound to be revived in 1977–8 and make the human rights issue an even more sensitive nerve than it already was). From time to time Soviet commentators would speak of the efforts of 'reactionaries' to reverse the general course of American foreign policy, of the attempts of 'militarists' and 'Fascists' to gain greater influence on policy and public opinion. And yet Moscow appears to have been unprepared for what it has perceived, with some bewilderment, as a serious deterioration in Soviet–American relations – unprepared because such a deterioration was not predicted and because the 'objective' conditions which gave rise to the detente policy (the incumbents in Moscow convinced themselves) have not essentially changed.

The New Uncertainties

When the Soviet dignitaries were served baked alaska at a banquet at the American Embassy in Moscow during Nixon's visit, Brezhnev was observed shaking his head as he remarked to Kosygin, 'Hot ice-cream: crazy Americans!' Indeed, 'hot ice-cream' may be a good way to characterize the dominant Soviet perspective on the United States. While the diehards have an easy time mumbling the Russian equivalent of 'I told you so', most of the others are baffled or disappointed as they observe contradictory elements in American behaviour. As one Soviet visitor remarked privately, 'If I had not experienced the Khrushchev years, I wouldn't have believed that a great power could behave so *ne-ser'iozno* (unseriously).'

Soviet doubts began multiplying during the Ford Administration. The abandonment of the term detente was first written off as pre-electoral childishness. The platform adopted at the 1976 Republican National Convention was a bit more bothersome in so far as it amounted to a repudiation of the Kissinger line. There was evident concern over the new strategic policy which reportedly allowed for limited nuclear strikes. And there was disappointment that the SALT II agreement was not completed – and the United States was blamed for dragging her feet. Moscow seemed to be even more surprised by the galvanization of 'hysterical' and 'primitive' anti-Soviet forces, such as the Committee on the Present Danger and the 'Team B' national intelligence estimate of Soviet intentions and capabilities. While Arbatov warned that there would be a price to pay for the 'dishes broken' during the presidential campaign, in the end the Soviet experts somewhat hesitantly banked on the incoming Carter Administration as the best bet – an estimate which was reasonable enough in the circumstances, but which has apparently cost the same advisers the loss of some influence within the Soviet élite since their misjudgment became manifest. (It is ironic that, time and again, developments in the West have aborted Soviet 'revisionist' reconsideration. Thus the looming Soviet discussion of the nature of capitalism – and its crises – and the role of the state was arrested by evidence of failures after the 1973 energy crisis and its effects in the West. Similarly the argument that the United States welcomed detente for economic reasons seems to have been rejected.)

In substance, Moscow observers saw the United States as:

– 'hypocritically' accusing the Soviet Union of seeking military superiority, while she herself was dragging her feet on arms limitation, developing new weapons and strengthening NATO as well as Japan, and was also prepared to sanction the transfer of advanced military technology to China by her allies;

– launching a 'hysterical' human rights campaign, which amounted to intolerable interference with the domestic jurisdiction of a sovereign state (particularly galling, moreover, as it has been applied selectively against the Soviet Union but not others, be it China, Romania or Iran, whom the United States chose to overlook for political reasons);

– erecting 'artificial barriers' to commercial intercourse and other forms of economic and technological co-operation;

– playing the 'China card';

– over-reacting to events in Africa, which Moscow does not see as a violation of prior Soviet-American understandings (the Soviet leadership seems agreed that the USSR never promised – indeed, could never have promised – to freeze the international *status quo* or not to give aid to national liberation movements);

– stepping up a variety of covert operations in and against the Soviet Union and her allies.

Even if some of these and related points, when raised in the Soviet press, are clearly inflated for propaganda purposes, there is reason to think that the substance of the above 'charges' has been taken seriously by many thoughtful and influential observers in Moscow. This is true even if some of them are privately embarrassed by Soviet handling of dissidents and other forms of repression.

In particular, Soviet authorities evidently do not believe that the USSR has moved ahead of the United States in military power. Operating from a position in which a sense of inferiority is deeply ingrained, they do not claim to have gained the upper hand (being, no doubt, more keenly aware of Soviet shortcomings than outsiders are likely to be), and they have thus deprived themselves incidentally of any political advantage they might have gained from such an assertion. Surely, if the more complex 'correlation of forces' which Soviet analysts refer to is taken to include economic capabilities as well as levels of scientific and technological development, Moscow cannot seriously believe that the United States thinks the Soviet Union has pulled ahead. But even in strictly military terms (whatever the reality of the situation, which goes beyond the bounds of this paper), Soviet commentators point out that the build-up of the Soviet navy, armour and combat aircraft, and recent Soviet missile programmes, have all been natural products and parts of the Soviet acquisition of global parity and super-power status. Why, they ask, should the United States retain control of the seas as well as superiority in strategic weapons? According to the Soviet perspective, Washington has continued to resist the logical implications of parity, refusing to acknowledge that the USSR is equally entitled to a presence far away from her shores, to a global navy and to a voice in all international disputes – in short, that she is entitled to act much as the United States has been acting all along.

Irritation among Soviet political leaders has been heightened by what they perceive to be an

American challenge to the Brezhnev policy and, to a degree, to Brezhnev himself. From Moscow's vantage point, it has become far more difficult to make a compelling case for the continuation of detente policy in the terms in which it was originally 'sold' within the Soviet élite. The neglect of the Vladivostok formula during the first Vance mission to Moscow in 1977 betrayed an ignorance of Soviet bureaucratic politics. The espousal by President Carter of the human rights issue, from his letter to Andrei Sakharov to his defence of Anatoli Shcharansky, has amounted to a challenge which the Politburo has evidently concluded it cannot afford to ignore. It has been prepared to pay a price in Soviet–American relations for the sake of proving to the United States that her efforts are bound to be counter-productive. Finally, the tightening-up of American policy on scientific exchanges and technology transfers has threatened to deprive the USSR of one of the few remaining tangible benefits to be gained from her new policy towards the United States.

Many Soviet observers have had genuine difficulty in seeing how Soviet actions in Africa have violated understandings with Washington. They do not see the Soviet Union as 'getting away with something'. They judged correctly that the risks of American involvement over Angola or Ethiopia were negligible, but Soviet policy-makers evidently erred seriously in dismissing the effects of Soviet behaviour (in Africa, over 'human rights', in relation to weapons procurement or naval deployment) on American public attitudes towards, and suspicions of, the Soviet Union.

In turn, the key analysts in Moscow appear to have been alarmed by the 'China card' played in the Brzezinski orchestration of 1978. After insisting for some twenty years that the Soviet Union was no longer the victim of hostile encirclement, Soviet comments have begun to reflect new fears, especially after the signing of the Sino–Japanese friendship treaty, with the Sino–Japanese–American 'coalition' in the Far East and NATO in the West looming as a two-front threat. The new *rapprochement* between the United States and China has permitted Soviet analysts to return to a 'two-camp' view of the global alignment – from the cognitive dissonance generated by the Sino–Soviet rift back to orthodox primitivism.

In the end, Moscow has been inclined to explain the 'counter-offensive' against detente as part of the general onslaught from the political 'right' within the United States, backed by a coalition of professionals (bureaucrats, journalists, academics) threatened by it, by special interests (above all, the 'Zionist' lobby), by the military-industrial complex and by 'primitive anti-Communists'. Soviet comments reflect surprise that business has not exerted a stronger influence in favour of better Soviet–American relations as Moscow had assumed capitalist self-interest would demand. As for American labour, Moscow has in effect decided that it no longer counts in the equation.

Soviet observers have thus found themselves confused. For one thing, it has not been clear whether they should attribute the Carter policies to incompetence, confusion or mischief. Soviet journalists have remarked that it is hard to believe that every four years all American policy has to stall before and after an election, and that every time a new team takes over, people without memory start from scratch, acting out their pet fantasies! And yet the dominant voices in Moscow have continued to affirm that a new SALT agreement could be reached (though they probably underestimate the difficulties it will face in the US Senate). The conclusion of such an agreement might indeed have the effect of 'reassuring' some of the Soviet doubters. But the questions are bound to go deeper than that. If (except for the diehards) they have had difficulty in making sense of the American scene, their confusion is due not only to Soviet misconceptions but also to the contradictory signals received from Washington and the inherent ambiguity of the situation. Meanwhile, the 'objective' pressures and constraints that propelled Moscow towards its present course – demographic, economic and scientific trends, as well as the power constellation, including the arms race and the Sino–Soviet dispute – remain as valid and as vivid in Soviet eyes today as they were ten years ago.

In the latter part of 1978 Soviet foreign policy-makers seemed to reaffirm the basic direction of their policies towards the United States. If progress with the new SALT agreements and some symbolic gestures on the part of the United States (such as visits of Cabinet-level officials and the silencing of the shrillest anti-Soviet voices in the Administration) provided reassurance, Soviet concern over China once again heightened a perceived need to forestall closer Sino–American ties. For their part, Soviet authorities seemed to recognize more clearly than before the importance of trying to manage American opinion (for example, by permitting continued emigration in substantial numbers), and the relatively forthcoming Soviet response to the private effort by Senator Edward Kennedy to secure exit visas for a number of specified individuals was apparently meant to indicate to Washington that it was possible to exact an occasional concession, provided this was done unofficially and without the glare of publicity. Moscow seemed to take seriously the message communicated by American businessmen and officials that a repeal of trade restrictions and other new steps could be seriously considered only if the United States Senate ratified SALT II, and that this was only likely if Soviet behaviour in the meanwhile did not again alarm, upset or antagonize American public opinion. While admitting with unusual candour that there were, in fact, differences within the Soviet establishment over relations with the United States in general and over SALT in particular,[13] the dominant policy-makers in Moscow seemed prepared to live with the irritations associated with American behaviour which they had come to expect – if only because they could think of no preferable alternative.

It is ironic to find that neither super-power has been exactly skilful in pursuing its own interests (as it sees them) *vis-à-vis* the other, and that the Soviet Union, now more powerful than at any time in her history, should find herself on the brink of greater dependence than ever on American technological and economic assistance, at the very time when the American economy is suffering from serious disorders, American society is experiencing a crisis of morale and confidence and American politics lack both leadership and clear purpose. For better or for worse, most Soviet observers did not expect to perceive the United States in such terms.

A View of the Future

It is impossible to predict the dominant Soviet perspective on the United States in the years ahead with any confidence because it will depend on at least two major variables and their interaction: first, who is in charge in Moscow (and, correspondingly, what the nature of Soviet priorities and policies will be) and, second, what American policy will be – including, in particular, American signals to the policy-makers in Moscow. While one may want to exclude some ludicrous extremes from the range of the possible, the gamut of possible scenarios for the 1980s is too great for comfort or any degree of certitude. Moscow acknowledges that the situation is open-ended and that there is room for will and choice.

Some years ago Herbert Dinerstein suggested that distortions in Soviet–American relations have been due, to a significant degree, to each side's failure to comprehend the complexity of the other's decision-making.[14] While there may be a danger in over-stressing cleavages and conflicts in the Soviet élite, I would consider this a lesser caricature than the customary proclivity to 'black-box' Soviet foreign-policy outputs.

In this light it may be wrong to ask, as is often done, whether the United States can influence Soviet outlook (and hence behaviour). It can be argued that whether she wants to or not, and whether she knows it or not, the United States inevitably contributes, through what she says and what she does (and by what she fails to say or do), to the dialogue which is being carried on among members of the Soviet élite. The mutual perceptions of the super-powers are shaped, in large measure, by each other's behaviour (along with domestic pressures and constraints). The United States is thus an unwitting participant in internal Soviet arguments and reassessments, and this is likely to be the case particularly at times of genuine debate and uncertainty in Moscow – times which are once again upon us.

Though neither side likes to hear it said, one may also speak of tacit alliances between adversaries. The 'moderates' in Moscow and Washington share an interest in promoting agreements they deem mutually beneficial, such as those covering a comprehensive test ban or the exploration of outer space. The military-industrial establishment on each side cites the research and procurement of the other to justify its own demands for budgets and allocations. Indeed, it has been suggested that in a number of branches – for instance, the navy and foreign trade – Soviet and American counter-parts are in effect functional bureaucratic allies and act as 'external pacers' for each other.[15]

Even the hawks on each side unwittingly co-operate: they need each other to validate each other's expectations. The commitment of each to worst-case analysis requires the assistance of the other to provide support (at least in their own minds) for self-fulfilling prophecies of doom. The ringing of tocsins in the United States when Moscow genuinely finds them unjustified – which is not the case with Soviet objections to American construction of B-1 bombers, cruise missiles or *Tridents*, which are transparently tactical and manipulative – is bound to strengthen the hand of those Soviet diehards who deny the possibility of meaningful and useful accords with the United States, who see no evidence of American goodwill and who confidently expect an eventual military showdown.

The record of recent years would seem to show that the Soviet Union, or at least her most sophisticated experts, have learned a great deal when it comes to understanding and analysing the United States. It also suggests that there is still much more learning to be done. It is true that at times the messages the Soviet Union has received from the United States have been less than clear: thus, for example, Moscow has not perceived an explicit American 'price list' of rewards and penalties for Soviet behaviour. The next generation of Soviet leaders will have to learn that, as a matter of self-interest, the USSR has more to gain from getting along with the United States than from confronting her. If the United States wishes this lesson to be learned, she can (and must) make a vital contribution to the process. Whether she is capable of making this contribution is an altogether different question.

NOTES

[1] Franklyn Griffiths, 'Image, Politics and Learning in Soviet Behavior towards the United States' (doctoral dissertation, Columbia University, 1972). See also, Robert W. Hansen, 'Soviet Images of American Foreign Policy, 1960–1972' (doctoral dissertation, Princeton University, 1975).

[2] Frederick C. Barghoorn, *The Soviet Image of the United States* (New York: Harcourt, Brace, 1950).

[3] William Zimmerman, *Soviet Perspectives on International Relations* (Princeton, N.J.: Princeton University Press, 1969).

[4] For his own version, see *Khrushchev Remembers* (Boston: Little, Brown, 1971), pp. 519–20.

[5] *Pravda*, 4 April 1971.

[6] *Samizdat* Register, Document AS 1461. See also, V. Yagodkin, 'Nekotorye voprosy ideologicheskoi raboty ....', *Kommunist* (Moscow), No. 3, 1974.

[7] Boris Rabbot, 'Detente: The Struggle Within the Kremlin', *Washington Post*, 10 July 1977; Dimitri Simes, *Detente and Conflict: Soviet Foreign Policy 1972–1977* (Washington Papers, No. 44 [1977]); Alexander Yanov, *Detente After Brezhnev* (Berkeley: Institute of International Studies, 1977).

[8] Vernon Aspaturian, 'Internal Politics and Foreign Policy', in his *Process and Power in Soviet Foreign Policy* (Boston: Little, Brown, 1971); and Astrid von Borcke, 'Der Kreml und die Entspannungspolitik', in *Elemente des Wandels in der östlichen Welt* (Jahrbuch für Ost-West-Fragen, 1976), pp. 252–70.

[9] Michel Tatu, 'Decision Making in the USSR', in Richard Pipes (ed.), *Soviet Strategy in Europe* (New York: Crane, Russak, 1976), pp. 62–3.

[10] Marshall D. Shulman, 'Trends in Soviet Foreign Policy', in Michael MccGwire, Ken Booth and John McDonnell (eds), *Soviet Naval Policy* (New York: Praeger, 1975). See also, Wolfgang Leonhard, 'The Domestic Politics of the New Soviet Foreign Policy', *Foreign Affairs*, October 1973.

[11] Stephen P. Gibert, *Soviet Images of America* (New York: Crane, Russak, 1977).

[12] Morton Schwartz, 'Soviet Perceptions of the United States' (forthcoming, Berkeley: University of California Press).

[13] Craig Whitney, 'Moscow Aide Concedes Differences', *New York Times*, 7 November 1978, based on an interview with Valentin Falin, First Deputy Chief of the International Information Department of the CPSU Central Committee.

[14] Herbert S. Dinerstein, *Fifty Years of Soviet Foreign Policy* (Baltimore: The Johns Hopkins Press, 1968), p. 7.

[15] Colin Gray, 'The Urge to Compete', *World Politics*, January 1974; Edward L. Warner, 'The Bureaucratic Politics of Weapons Procurement', in MccGwire *et al.*, *op. cit.*; George Hudson, 'Soviet Naval Doctrine and Soviet Politics, 1953–1975', *World Politics*, October 1976; David Holloway, 'Foreign and Defence Policy', in Archie Brown and Michael Kaser (eds), *The Soviet Union Since the Fall of Khrushchev* (New York: Macmillan, 1975).

Western Europe in the Soviet Perspective

JEAN LALOY

The expression 'Western Europe' does not belong in the Soviet political vocabulary. The term, rarely used, was accepted only after the creation of the European Economic Community, which in its turn was considered to have been established only after the great crisis of 1958–62, and then usually in an economic sense. In official texts (speeches, reports to the Party Congress, etc.) Western Europe is referred to only in terms of its member states: Britain, the Federal Republic of Germany, France, etc.

On the other hand, Soviet leaders speak of 'Europe' in connection with their proposals for security or co-operation agreements, or the Geneva UN Economic Commission or simply in designating the continent to which they (at least partly) belong. It is noteworthy that, since 1978, the Council for Economic Co-operation (COMECON) has been active over four continents and has thus assumed a universal role.

In the Russian tradition the term 'Europe' had a special meaning, as indicated by the many works dealing with Russia and Europe. This underlined the fact that Russia had her own past and that she considered herself to be separate. Slavophiles and Westernists alike emphasized this difference, the former arguing that Russia should maintain her own tradition in the course of her development, the latter that Russia should assume in Europe a role befitting her importance. Both schools dreamed of a unique role for Russia. At the beginning of the twentieth century these feelings became less evident, but they reappeared with Bolshevik messianism and still survive today.

Since 1945 there has been the added problem of relations with the United States – both American–Soviet relations and relations between the United States and Western Europe. There is no well-established tradition in this field. Ideas vary, ranging from attempts to expel the United States' presence from Europe to efforts which aim to create a special relationship between the United States and the Soviet Union. This extension of the West to the other side of the Atlantic cannot be completely ignored when examining the evolution of Western Europe as Soviet leaders see it.

The Problem over Time

Four periods can be distinguished – two under Stalin and at least two others under his successors.

At the end of World War II there were traces in Stalin's thinking of a pan-European, or rather pan-Continental policy. But this was difficult to reconcile with his policy towards Eastern Europe. From 1947–8 Stalin tried to prevent the creation of a political system in Western Europe, his instrument being Germany, as his instrument for influencing Germany was Berlin. He failed in this, as he failed to eliminate Yugoslavian dissidence. In trying to break the links then forming between the United States and Western Europe, he only managed to contribute to their strength.

After the 20th Party Congress (1956) the horizon broadened considerably. Phrases like 'peaceful coexistence', 'peaceful transition to (a diversified) socialism', 'peace zones' and plans for 'European and Asiatic security' reflect this. The existence of an economic Western Europe was recognized and a new effort made to prevent it becoming a political unit (as in the second Berlin crisis). The special relationship between the United States and the USSR became fundamental.

During the present period, beginning in 1969, the USSR has developed a European policy which bears some resemblance to the one adopted in 1945 and which faces the same dilemma. Yet conditions have changed radically in the meantime. Different prospects for Soviet policies have opened up as a result, but they are contingent on a number of conditions, many of which remain unfulfilled today.

Liberated Europe (1945–7)
Did Stalin have a European policy? The record is mixed:

- In October 1939 Stalin said to Paasekivi: 'Whoever wins this war will inevitably attack the USSR'.[1] This was possibly an argument for negotiation, but it does not indicate any particular affinity with any of the Western or Central European states.
- In December 1941 Stalin proposed a *quid pro quo* to Anthony Eden: bases in Eastern Europe for the USSR in exchange for bases in the West for Britain (Dunkirk) and for the United States (Dakar). This offer, confirmed during the Anglo–Soviet negotiations in the spring of 1942, was reiterated in Tehran in November 1943 in a modified form (in Dakar and Bizerta).
- During the war several Soviet statements refer to the USSR as having saved 'Europe' – on 9 May 1945, for example. At the same time, projects for a 'Western Bloc' are severely criticized.

More concretely, between 1941 and 1945 Stalin stayed in close touch with Europe, acting successively on Poland, Czechoslovakia, the Balkans, Germany and France, without neglecting the Mediterranean states in the south – Turkey, Greece, Italy – and the Baltic states in the north – Finland and Sweden.

As to Poland, even in July 1941 Stalin did not abandon the Ribbentrop-Molotov line (which in 1941 had become the Curzon line after a few modifications) that the British Government had agreed to as early as the autumn of 1940 (in a letter from its ambassador in Moscow). Stalin refused to discuss any of the compromises drafted after Tehran by Mikolajczyk between February and October 1944. In 1944–5 he imposed upon Poland a government which agreed to this tough line.

In respect of Czechoslovakia, Stalin signed an alliance treaty in December 1943, which the British Government had tried to prevent and which killed, more effectively than any formal declaration could have done, any prospect of a Polish-Czech federation. He assured Benes that the liberal regime would be maintained in Czechoslovakia. This was a rather mild policy, though it was not without its irritations.

Stalin could convince himself in Tehran that his predominance in the Balkans would be accepted. In October 1944 Churchill confirmed that Romania and Bulgaria would remain in the Soviet sphere of influence. From the summer of 1944 Stalin controlled the battlefield in the East and started to show an interest in the Turkish Straits (Yalta 1945).

During the war Germany was a matter of great interest to Stalin. From February 1942 he pointed out that Germany would survive even after Hitler. He did not rule out dismemberment of that nation, which would enable the extension of Poland to the Oder (and of the USSR to Koenigsberg); but, once this was settled, he had no intention of obliterating Germany from the map. In 1943–4, he began to bring the German Communists and the Wehrmacht closer together in the *Freies Deutschland* Movement. In 1943 he obtained an unsolicited undertaking from the Allies that all of Germany would be occupied and, above all, that all German political authority would be suppressed after the capitulation. In 1944 he exhorted General de Gaulle to relinquish his claims to the left bank of the Rhine. In December 1944 Stalin signed an alliance treaty with France modelled on the Soviet–Czech Treaty, with its serious constraints on the weaker of the two signatories (Article 4 obliged one of the two parties to enter the war if 'the other one is *dragged* into hostilities against Germany').

No precise proposals were put forward by Stalin during the war which revealed his longer-term intentions towards Europe. The best indication of his plans is contained in a memorandum written by Charles E. Bohlen on his return from Tehran:

Although is not possible to call it precise, the picture one has of Soviet intentions is sufficiently clear to give an idea of what is planned for Continental Europe after the war. Germany is to be broken up and kept broken up. The States of Eastern, South-eastern and Central Europe will not be permitted to group themselves into any federations or association. France is to be stripped of her colonies and strategic bases beyond her borders and will not be permitted to maintain any appreciable military establishment. Poland and Italy will remain approximately their present territorial size, but it is doubtful if either will be permitted to maintain any appreciable armed force. The result would be that the Soviet Union would be the only important military and political force on the continent of Europe. The rest of Europe would be reduced to military and political impotence.[2]

The network of pacts signed by the USSR between 1943 and 1945 with Czechoslovakia, France, Poland and Yugoslavia (the Anglo-Soviet Treaty of May 1942 is of a different nature) foreshadows a continental security system that would be dominated by the Soviet Union. Between 1945 and 1947 Warsaw and Prague attempted to conclude alliances with France to complete this system. There is, therefore, reason to believe that Stalin did have a European policy or at least some notion of such a policy in the back of his mind and that this left little room for the autonomy of the non-Soviet participants.

The Crises of 1947–52
There are only three ways in which such a system could have evolved: if the USSR had physically dominated Germany as far as the Rhine following the armistice; if the Western leaders had turned a blind eye to Soviet ambitions; or if relatively liberal regimes had been established in Eastern Europe. The first two contingencies did not arise. The third was blocked by a problem that was neatly summarized by a remark Stalin made to Philip E. Mosely in Potsdam: 'Any freely elected government would be anti-Soviet, and that we cannot permit'.[3] The only exception was Finland, and the course she followed can be explained by specific factors.[4]

Thus Stalin's European policy, designed to be as progressive and cautious as it was persistent and disguised, broke down and gave way to an Eastern Europe based on the prototypes of Ulbricht's Eastern Zone, or the Poland of

Bierut, and a Western Europe in which liberal trends began to emerge from 1946 onwards (for example, the Fulton speech, the rejection of the first draft of the French Constitution in May 1946, etc.).

Between 1945 and 1947 one can detect two trends in Soviet attitudes towards the outside world, especially towards Europe and the United States. Many within the USSR hoped for a period of rest and a relaxation of the constraints imposed by discipline and terror. The theories of Vargas supported this trend, arguing that the capitalist world after the war would be able to discipline itself and avoid a break-up.[5] The other view, especially prevalent in the Party, was hostile to any detente, either within or outside the country, and favoured a military policy. Zhdanov is believed to have been its main proponent (although whether he really held that position or was forced to adopt it when put in charge of the repression of the intellectuals in the summer of 1946 remains uncertain).[6] It is the second view which carried the day, primarily because of the apparent risks that internal relaxation within the Soviet system might bring. External factors played no more than a secondary role in 1946.

At the same time, there were also differences of view within the United States between those who remained partisans of Roosevelt's policies and those who advocated a position of firmness towards the Soviet Union. General Marshall made the historic choice when, on his return from Moscow, he said of Europe: 'The patient is dying while the doctors argue'. He decided to restore Western Europe, including Western Germany as far as the demarcation line, without waiting any longer for Stalin's consent.

Stalin, influenced no doubt by memories of the Four-Power Pact (1933) and of Munich, probably regarded this as the dawning of a new European coalition against the Soviet Union. He responded strongly: the Marshall plan was rejected; Czechoslovakia was forbidden to join it (June-July 1947); a campaign of strikes was launched against the Marshall plan (autumn 1947); and the Cominform was set up (September 1947). There followed the Prague coup (March 1948), the blockade of Berlin (June 1948-May 1949), the Yugoslav crisis (June 1948) and purges in the East (from Mostov, 1948, to Slansky, 1952). Thus the hard line was confirmed, with the USSR in the predominant position in the Eastern camp. The policy included a cautious but nonetheless determined use of force to prevent the establishment of the Federal Republic of Germany and a massive campaign against American influence in Europe, against any coming together of Western Europe and against the atomic bomb. The explanation for this new policy was provided by Zhdanov in his speech at the inaugural meeting of the Cominform: 'The question of Germany . . . is the main problem of international policies and one which will sow discord between the United States, England and France'.

In the spring of 1949, despite the earlier signing of the Atlantic Treaty, Stalin lifted the blockade of Berlin. The German Democratic Republic was born a few months after the Federal Republic of Germany. Stalin sent a message to Wilhelm Pieck which stated that as long as the USSR and Germany were friends, 'there can no longer be war in Europe'. A detente of sorts emerged in Europe. The Coal and Steel Community was launched in May 1950, disproving the predictions of Zhdanov (who had died in August 1948). This first period of detente was interrupted by the Korean War (the causes of which remain difficult to ascertain) and by the plans for West German rearmament that represented Western reaction to it. But it reappeared in 1951–2, with the negotiations of Panmunjom, the Economists' Conference in Moscow (April 1952) and the exchange of notes on Germany up to September 1952.

Could the first great European crisis have been avoided? Perhaps a better American understanding of the problems facing a Soviet Union victorious but ruined could have softened some of the blows. But would that have been sufficient to make Stalin think any more kindly towards Western Europe? We have an answer from his own entourage. In a private conversation with an American journalist in Moscow on 18 June 1946 Maxime Litvinov was pessimistic: 'Hottelet asked him [Litvinov] if Soviet suspicions . . . would be mitigated if the West were suddenly to give in and grant all Russian demands. . . He said it would lead to the West being faced, after a period of time, with the next series of demands'.[7] One month earlier Litvinov had remarked privately that, in his opinion, 'the best that can be hoped for is a prolonged armed truce'.[8] The

conclusion that can be drawn from this second period is that, confronted with an obstacle, Stalin's choice was a 'prolonged armed truce'.

'Peaceful Coexistence' (1953–64)

In the years between 1953 and 1955 three trends appeared in the policies of Stalin's successors: a hard-line approach; a trend towards revisionism; and attempts to reconcile the two. Led by Molotov and Kaganovitch, the hard-liners proposed to maintain Stalin's old policies abroad but in a less severe manner.

Revisionism, on the other hand, had no known leaders: it became visible primarily through the criticism levelled against it. There were, for example, claims that from 1952 some 'capitulators' wished to 'appease' capitalism or, in 1955, that there were philosophers 'denying the objective existence of general laws on the development of societies' and economists looking for an 'intermediate degree between capitalism and socialism'.[9]

The middle way was that of Malenkov, later that of Khrushchev. It maintained in theory the fundamental principles of Leninism, but accepted in practice that there might be periods of slower progress, even detours along the way. This is the meaning of 'peaceful coexistence' as defined by the 20th Party Congress in 1956: war is not inevitable, nor is revolution, but the victory of Soviet socialism *is* inevitable.

As regards Soviet policies towards Western Europe, this new approach was demonstrated by the following episodes:

- During the Big Four Conference in Berlin (January 1954) the Soviet Union proposed a pan-European Agreement for collective security, aimed at replacing the European Defence Community (EDC) – and probably the Atlantic Treaty – and neutralizing the two German states.[10]
- After the defeat of the EDC in the French Parliament (August 1954), Soviet leaders showed a surprising degree of passivity, no doubt as a result of disagreement over what should be the best strategy to be adopted against the Paris Agreements (winter 1954–5).
- The German problem and the question of European security remained deadlocked at the Summit Conference (July 1955). Diplomatic relations were established between the

USSR and West Germany. The Western powers renounced their earlier conviction that any agreement on European security should embody some disposition about a future settlement of the German problem.

The 20th Party Congress considerably broadened the horizons of Soviet policy, which has, since then, included the Third World. The idea of a 'peace zone', which would group around the USSR the more or less progressive countries of the Third World (and, to begin with, those of the Middle East), had a clear anti-European slant, as the 1956 Suez Crisis demonstrated.[11]

The signing of the Treaty of Rome in 1957 provoked vigorous opposition from the Soviet Union.[12] 'The Seventeen Theses', published by The Institute of World Economics and International Relations (IMEMO) in July 1957,[13] sharply criticized the project but also testified to a certain amount of uneasiness, which was to become even more marked in 1959 and to lead, three years later, to *Pravda's* 'Thirty-Two Theses' (25 August 1962). These were still as severe in their criticism but the European Community's success, which was so out of keeping with Lenin's predictions, was causing considerable embarrassment. It is only during the present phase of Soviet policy that a more positive view has been advanced.

In that earlier period the Berlin crisis, launched one year after the first *Sputnik*, can be seen as an all-out Soviet effort to paralyse Western European enterprise and as part of the dialectical relationship between detente and peaceful co-existence. Perhaps it was also designed, if successful, to restore Soviet prestige in the eyes of China as well as in those of Communist Parties elsewhere, which were beginning to move away from Soviet control. In any case, Soviet policy of this period, in contrast to that of 1948, was not just a reaction to a Western initiative. The failure of this initiative, in conjunction with failure over Cuba in 1962, engendered a new phase in Soviet strategy. The manifestation of this was the treaty of August 1963, banning nuclear tests, which revealed the existence of a special Soviet–American relationship not directly linked with European issues. But Khrushchev did not survive to benefit from this new phase. He was replaced by a group of men who announced their intention of pursuing a more considered policy, one founded on a 'scientific' basis.

European Security (1964–78)

At first, relations with the United States, complicated by the Vietnam war, were conducted through negotiations in a United Nations framework, especially those concerning the Non-Proliferation Treaty of 1968, the Outer Space Agreement of 1967 and the Ocean Bed Agreements. With regard to Western Europe, two policies emerged. One advocated the improvement of relations with France in particular (especially after 1964) and the pursuit of bilateral relations in general. The other, nurtured by the fight against the Multilateral Nuclear Force (MNF), led to the reactivation, after 1966, of plans for a European Security Pact and the Bucharest Appeal. These two trends were characterized by hostility towards the United States and the Federal Republic of Germany. Soviet military intervention in Czechoslovakia in 1968 brought the first part of this phase to an end.

The election of President Nixon (4 November 1968) and the formation of the Brandt government in the Federal Republic of Germany opened up new perspectives. Chancellor Brandt's policy towards the East led to treaties with the USSR (1970), Poland (1970) and the German Democratic Republic (1972), as well as to the Four-Power Agreement on Berlin (4 September 1971). The improvement of relations with the United States cleared the way for the Conference on European Security, which involved the United States and Canada as full participants. In the Soviet literature this period is referred to as one of 'decisive change' (*perelom*) in Europe, the culmination of more than twenty years of Soviet effort to obtain 'the confirmation of the territorial status resulting from the Second World War'. At the same time as the Helsinki negotiations on security and co-operation got under way, those concerning mutual and balanced force reductions in Europe were initiated in Vienna in 1973.

From 1972 onwards the attitude towards the European Economic Community (EEC) changed. The idea of integration was no longer criticized by the Soviet Union; it was even used to define the programme of economic co-ordination in the East. As early as 1965 a Czech economist envisaged 'theoretical common models' which

44

might be applied to both the socialist and the capitalist form of economic integration. He was severely criticized.[14] From 1974 onwards contacts were being established between COMECON and the EEC. Was this the dawning of a new era, in which the two halves of Europe would recognize each other as different but compatible? This was perhaps a long-term prospect, but its revisionist nature made it unacceptable to the leadership of the Soviet Union.

Several new elements emerged in the second half of the 1970s which tended to undermine the stability which the treaties signed between 1970 and 1975 were supposed to provide for the USSR. First, the 'capitalist' world no longer fitted the traditional patterns of Soviet ideology. A new technological revolution was taking place. The notion of the 'working class' no longer reflected the new realities. New ideological currents were developing on the political Left. Second, the development of economic relations between East and West had had unforeseen consequences. The economic crisis in the West which began in 1973 had also had a deleterious effect on the economies of Eastern Europe. The idea that common interests might transcend ideology began to emerge. Third, there seemed to be no remedy for the crisis within the Communist movement. Throughout the world the Soviet myth had collapsed. Moreover, the Communist Parties, beginning with the Chinese, all contested to a certain degree the Soviet claim to hegemony. This led not only to Western 'Eurocommunism', but also, in Eastern Europe, to centrifugal trends in public opinion which national leaders had to take into account. Finally, in the USSR itself, the Helsinki principles encouraged political dissent which demanded the right to express itself openly.

Faced with these problems, the Soviet leaders displayed considerable uneasiness. In the USSR they opted for repression, but in Eastern Europe they were forced to tolerate a situation which was far from satisfactory to them. In relations with Western Communist Parties they tried to solve problems over doctrine at the Berlin Conference in July 1976, but without success. 'Eurocommunism' was neither sanctioned nor condemned and it continued to manifest itself. The tactical problems were even more delicate: how were the Soviet leaders to direct, from Moscow, the tactics of the Chilean Party between 1970 and 1973, for example, or those of the Portuguese Party in 1975? As for the latter, there seem to have been some differences of opinion among the Moscow leadership during the summer of 1975. Although Moscow cannot be blamed entirely for Cunhal's failure, failure stemming from the very basis of the system is serious.

These and many other phenomena probably explain the greater trust the present leaders have placed in organized force and armed strength. First, the Soviet Union has redressed, in her own favour, the two global military imbalances (nuclear and naval) which until now have enabled the United States to compensate for regional European imbalances. Second, she relies increasingly on military forces for overseas influence (Cuba, Ethiopia and even Vietnam) rather than on political movements, be they Communits or Progressive. Third, she enjoys a military superiority in Europe which she continues to protect and reinforce.

Thirty-three years after World War II, therefore, we see the contours of a policy towards Europe that contains both constant and changing elements. In view of Soviet activities in the Middle East and, since 1975, in southern and eastern Africa, one can almost envisage a scenario in which the USSR would accept the existence of a separately organized and non-Communist Western Europe, dependent on the Third World (which the USSR hopes to influence) for her energy and raw materials and on the United States (with which the USSR hopes to establish links) for her defence. It is unlikely that such a scenario will become reality, but the possibility nevertheless deserves mention because it would not leave much choice to the European countries themselves; they would have only to consent to a situation which would not warrant any vigorous reaction on their part. Many other possible scenarios might produce 'irreversible military detente' – a state which Leonid Brezhnev has declared to be indispensable for European security.

Today Western Europe is still far from genuine peace. It remains vulnerable to crises which can either erupt spontaneously (in Eastern Europe, for example) or result from a more or less deliberate policy (for instance, the case of Berlin). We should never forget that, as demonstrated by the experience of the past thirty years, for the Soviet Union Germany is the main problem and the main instrument of leverage. On the other hand, it cannot be denied that important changes are taking place in the East and in the West. These are linked, in one way or another, not with the 'end of ideologies' but rather with the weakening, not to say the withering, of Marxist ideology – not only its Leninist but also its socialist variety. It remains to be seen whether this phenomenon may not in itself generate future crises. That is why, to conclude, we must examine whether past crises have been due to misunderstandings or whether, on the contrary, they can be explained by clear-cut and more or less constant factors.

Past and Future

If Stalin made a mistake in the first and second phases of his European policy (1945–53), it was to assume that the three Western Allies could never agree on their attitudes towards Germany. He counted on a long period of indecision in the West and was surprised by General Marshall's initiative (probably more than by the Truman Doctrine of March 1947). This error resulted partly from ideology (the 'contradictions of capitalism', etc.) and partly from the experience of the inter-war years, 1919–39. When Stalin realized his mistake in the winter of 1948–9 he retreated. He re-launched the attack in the winter of 1950–1 (Korea and German rearmament), retreated again in 1952 (exchange of notes) and died dissatisfied. His second mistake was over the relations between the United States and Europe. He made a major effort to bring about in Europe a climate hostile to the United States ('US Go Home'), only to achieve the opposite. However, his measurement of the balance of forces was accurate and he retreated without too much difficulty. This taught the West European countries a lesson: it was possible, with American backing, to stay firm without provoking a war. Stalin was no Hitler.

In the third phase the years 1953–5 are of particular interest. Malenkov had it within his reach to torpedo the Paris Agreements (and therefore, eventually, to push West Germany out of the Western System). He did not seize his opportunity. The Soviet leaders recognized the opportunity when it came but were paralysed by their own internal divisions. Or did they unconsciously prefer the system which took

shape in 1955? To this major question the second Berlin crisis provides the answer. Those four years of effort to impose on the United States and her allies a symbolic retreat in Berlin (with considerable political consequences) indicate that, in this third period, the Soviet Union indeed aimed at establishing a greater fluidity in Western Europe and at separating Europe from the United States. Other factors also intervened, such as the necessity of restoring the prestige of the Soviet Communist Party in the eyes of the Chinese and all other Communist Parties.

In the fourth period, that of 'scientific' foreign policy, two specific changes occurred: first, there appeared a tendency to accept as a fact the coming together of Western Europe; and second, there was a move towards creating direct and special relations with the United States based on 'realism' ('Let's get together and not be bothered about our allies!'). These changes have resulted in considerable gains for the Soviet Union in Europe, but they have also produced new problems, both in the USSR and in Eastern European countries, and with these problems have come new risks. Thus, what to do about Eastern Europe seems to be one of the central issues facing the leaders of the Soviet Union: to what extent can the real world be allowed to penetrate their systems (their systems of ideas and their systems of force)? Or should they, rather, continue to reinforce the total impermeability of these systems to foreign influences? In the first case, the Soviet Union runs the risk of causing major centrifugal forces to emerge, with unpredictable consequences. In the second, she will have to maintain and expand all those instruments of military power which isolate her from the outside but which at the same time allow her to operate beyond her borders. Such are the limits within which the team that will succeed Mr Brezhnev must operate. Their choice will probably reflect an unsatisfactory compromise between the two alternatives.

Western Europe can only influence this choice if it is strong enough to resist future pressure, if it is able to define its own long-term political objectives in a way which the USSR will have to take into account, and it it succeeds in encouraging the Soviet Union to move beyond mere coexistence towards the idea of a true peace (notwithstanding the fact that, for the time being, such a concept remains alien to the Soviet regime).

Such a policy, which presupposes a sense of solidarity between the United States and Europe, could include:

- the definition of long-term objectives such as peace and reconciliation instead of struggle and coexistence, with the various consequences that arise from this;
- continuation of the efforts for a real transformation which began in Europe in 1950 and which has already had an effect on the thoughts and experiences of many Eastern leaders (co-operation instead of rivalry, agreements with instead of exploitation of the southern countries, progressive solutions to internal social tensions instead of the alternative of revolution or dictatorship, etc.);
- all other measures which tend to replace the 'rivalry in decadence, which Pierre Hassner has referred to with a 'rivalry in renovation'.

This would add to the inevitable pragmatism of Western policies a general conceptual thrust which would, by drawing on the experiences gained since the end of World War II, affect not only the West but the East also.

NOTES

[1] Cf. Max Jakobson, *Finnlands Neutralitätspolitik zwischen Ost und West* (Dusseldorf, 1969), p. 30.

[2] *Foreign Relations of the United States: The Conferences at Cairo and Tehran* (Washington: USGPO, 1961), p. 845.

[3] Philip E. Mosely, *The Kremlin in World Politics* (New York: Vintage Books, 1960), p. 214.

[4] Cf. Jakobson, *op. cit.*, pp. 46–89.

[5] G. von Lrauch, *Geschichte der Sovjet Union* (Stuttgart: Alfred Kröner Verlag, 1969), p. 465.

[6] Zhdanov's speech in *Conference of Representatives of Certain Communist Parties* (Moscow, 1948), pp. 13–48.

[7] *Foreign Relations of the United States*, 1946, Vol. VI (Washington, 1946), p. 764.

[8] *Ibid.*, p. 763, fn. 11.

[9] Cf. article by Tchesnokov, *Kommunist*, January 1953; editorial, *Voprosy Filosofii*, November 1955; article by Glouchkov, *Voprosy Ekonomiki*, 9, 1955.

[10] Cf. V. P. Nikhamin (ed.) *Contemporary International Relations and Foreign Policy of the Soviet Union* (Moscow, 1978: in Russian), p. 98: 'The Soviet proposals at the Berlin Conference would have led to the neutralization of the two German states . . .'

[11] A. Sakharov, *Mon pays et le monde* (Paris, 1975): 'The long-term objective', (declares in 1955 a functionary of the USSR Council of Ministers before a group of Soviet scientists) 'is to use Arab nationalism in order to cause difficulties for the oil supplies of the Europeans and thus render them more malleable' (pp. 7–9).

[12] Cf. A. P. Binns, 'From USE to EEC: The Soviet Analysis of European Integration under Capitalism', *Soviet Studies*, 30 (2), April 1978, pp. 237–61.

[13] Cf. *Kommunist*, September 1957, pp. 88–102.

[14] Cf. Binns, *op. cit.*, p. 256.

Soviet Power and Policies in the Third World: the case of Africa

WILLIAM E. GRIFFITH

There are three prerequisites to an understanding of Soviet policy in Africa.[1] First, because it is a part of Soviet global competition with the United States and with China, one must understand Soviet global strategy. Second, one must appreciate that Soviet African policy is primarily responsive to Soviet opportunities and capabilities and is not the result of a 'master plan' for Africa or the world. Furthermore, while Moscow has seen its African opportunities increasing, and has been the more attracted to them because of its losses in the Middle East, Soviet priorities, like American ones, remain centred on Europe, the Middle East and Asia. Third, one must be aware of the immense complexity of African politics.

Since the 1959 Sino–Soviet break the Soviet Union has been competing with the United States and China, working to prevent an alliance between them and trying to lower the risk of nuclear war – and of such an alliance – through arms-control negotiations with the United States, while simultaneously attempting to maximize Soviet power and influence as other young, dynamic empires have always done. The more problems Moscow has had (notably with China) and the more opportunities it has seen (notably recently in Africa), the more it has used its rising military power to compensate for the former and to exploit the latter.

Unlike the West, the Soviet Union regards power and influence as Party (organizational and ideological) as well as State concerns. Khrushchev abandoned Stalin's passive third-world posture for a forward strategy there. Brezhnev has concentrated on more selective third-world targets and has recently used greater Soviet military capabilities to score dramatic gains, notably in Africa (Angola and Ethiopia).

In the early 1960s, after early Soviet challenges to American power failed, notably in the ex-Belgian Congo and during the Cuban missile crisis, Moscow concentrated on achieving strategic nuclear parity with the United States, a seven-ocean navy, a long-range air- and sea-lift capability and, most recently, a non-Soviet ground-intervention capability, first demonstrated by the Cubans in Angola in 1975. In the 1970s the Soviet Union also profited from the Vietnam–Watergate syndrome, which led to popular American opposition to military involvement (especially covert involvement) in developing areas, the weakened power of the Presidency and a more powerful but institutionally fragmented Congress. Thus by 1974, the year of the most recent 'great turn' in Africa, the position had changed: the Soviet Union had much greater military capabilities; she faced an uncertain and indecisive United States; she had drawn the lessons of her African failures in the 1960s; and she saw new opportunities in Africa, which she thereupon proceeded to exploit.

It is often forgotten that in 1945–6 Molotov demanded not only a Soviet mandate over ex-Italian Libya but also Soviet control over the ex-Italian Eritrean port of Massawa (which it now seems likely to achieve).[2] These ambitions having been pre-empted by the West, Moscow became active in Africa when the British and French colonies there became independent in the late 1950s and the Belgian Congo in 1960. In the latter, Soviet support for Lumumba in 1960 and for Gbenye and Soumaliot in 1964 was unsuccessful because of an inadequate Soviet air- and sea-lift capability, the opposition of American and of UN will and capabilities and Congolese near-chaos. Moreover, except for Sékou Touré, all the radical, pro-Soviet African dictators –

48

Nkrumah, Keita, Ben Bella and Nasser – gave way to military leaders who turned away from radicalism and broke their close ties with Moscow. In the 1960s Moscow also competed with Peking in Africa, triumphing in the late 1960s, when the Cultural Revolution largely paralysed Chinese African efforts.

Despite her African setbacks, the Soviet Union remained convinced that Africa would go radical because of the fragility of its moderate governments and the struggle of the black 'national liberation movements' (NLMS) against white minority rule in southern Africa which, Moscow knew, could never hope to succeed without Soviet arms and training. In the early 1960s she initiated programmes of military aid, training and financial support on their behalf. She concentrated on the two which were white- or mulatto-influenced, Marxist–Leninist in ideology and pro-Soviet in foreign policy: the Movimento Popular para a Libertação de Angola (MPLA) in Angola and the (South African) African National Congress (ANC), within which the South African Communist Party (SACP) had considerable influence. Moscow also supported Nkomo's Zimbabwe African People's Union (ZAPU) in Rhodesia and Nujoma's South-West Africa People's Organization (SWAPO) in Namibia, neither of which was Marxist at that time. The primarily tribal tensions within the NLMS, which were intensified by Sino–Soviet rivalry, led during the 1960s to divisions in most of them. China supported the groups which split away: the Pan-African Congress (PAC) in South Africa, the Zimbabwe African National Union (ZANU) in Rhodesia and the South-West Africa National Union (SWANU) in Namibia. (The Front for the Liberation of Mozambique (FRELIMO) in Mozambique and the Party for the Independence of Guinea-Bissau (PAIGC) in Guinea-Bissau, which did not split, continued to receive arms from both Moscow and Peking.)

1974: The Great Turn
In 1974 three events greatly increased Soviet opportunities in sub-Saharan Africa: the collapse of the Portuguese African empire, the overthrow of Emperor Haile Selassie in Ethiopia, and the establishment of radical, often Marxist–Leninist, regimes in Somalia, Benin (formerly Dahomey) and Madagascar. Furthermore, notably in Zaire, traditionalism, élitism, tribal rivalries and,

above all, corruption produced instability and tribal rebellions, as later in Shaba (formerly Katanga) province, in 1977 and 1978. By 1974 the Soviet Union also had the air- and sea-lift capability and available Cuban troops to take advantage of these new opportunities.

She had also learned some lessons from her previous African failures. She now generally supported not rebels but Organization of African Unity (OAU)-recognized governments and NLMS, and (except initially for Somalia) she defended existing boundaries, however artificial, against irredentist challenges. (Moscow had tried not to appear to support the Shaba revolts.) Second, given the demonstrable unreliability of its previous radical but non-Marxist–Leninist civilian and military allies, Moscow preferred now to support Marxist–Leninist parties (the MPLA in Angola, for example, and FRELIMO in Mozambique). Yet even so, the Soviet Union (and Cuba) often had to support ethnic, racial and religious minority groups (for instance, Christians in Ethiopia and mulattos in the MPLA) or NLMS – a strategy effective only as long as these allies depended on her for victory or continued their struggles against white minority rule.

The Soviet Union now had Cuban troops as allies, though these troops in Africa were and are not, *pace* Senator Moynihan, the Gurkhas of the USSR. Fidel Castro has long had his own policy in Africa, especially before 1968, when his relations with Moscow were not good. Cuba is too small for him. He failed to revolutionize Latin America. His policies are not the result of Soviet plans but they now run parallel with them. Cuban troops in Africa have become essential to Moscow's gains in Angola and Ethiopia and to Neto's and Mengistu's survival in power. Moscow has also employed East German specialists in police, intelligence and communications-media work in Angola, Ethiopia and Mozambique.

Angola
From the early 1960s a three-way struggle against the Portuguese began in Angola, involving Holden Roberto's Frente Nacional de Libertação de Angola (FNLA) (black, Bakongo-based, Zaire-, American- and later Chinese-supported, with a 25 per cent tribal support among the population), Agostino Neto's MPLA (led largely by mulatto, *assimilado*, urban intellectuals,

Soviet-supported and also with 25 per cent tribal base) and, later, Jonas Savimbi's Uniao Nacional para a Independencia Total de Angola (UNITA) (black, Ovimbundu-based, Chinese- and later South African-supported with a 40 per cent tribal base). After Caetano collapsed in Lisbon in 1974, the increasingly radical Portuguese armed forces movement (MFA) supported the MPLA, as did the Soviet Union, which brought in massive arms support and thousands of Cuban troops. The USSR may well have started this movement in opposition to China rather than the United States, but her successful pro-MPLA policy defeated Western, Chinese and South African interests. (China withdrew rapidly once she realized the extent of Soviet and Cuban intervention.) Without any foreign intervention the FNLA and UNITA would have defeated the MPLA, because together they had a much larger popular base. American public and congressional opposition forced President Ford and Secretary Kissinger to abandon support of the FNLA, whereupon UNITA and South African armed forces, which were only some 60 kilometres from Luanda, retreated and the Soviet Union and her Cuban allies brought Neto and the MPLA to power. Thus, for the first time in Africa, Soviet and not Western military support was decisive. (Savimbi has continued to fight in southern Angola.)[3]

Mozambique
FRELIMO took power in Mozambique unopposed. Until it did, Chinese influence had been more important than that of the Soviet Union, but FRELIMO had remained independent, controlled neither by Moscow nor Peking. The Chinese withdrawal from Angola, the intensification of Mozambique-based ZANU guerrilla warfare in Rhodesia and Machel's consequent fear of Rhodesian military reprisals made him rely on Soviet arms supplies. (Even so, Mugabe's ZANU in Mozambique continued to get its arms largely from China and – recently – indirectly from the Soviet Union as well.) Machel and FRELIMO remained Marxist–Leninist and anti-Western, but they were fiercely independent and refused to take sides in the Sino–Soviet dispute.[4]

The Horn
By the early 1970s Moscow had gained a strong position in Somalia and had acquired naval facilities in Berbera; Somalia's leader, Siad Barre, had set up a Marxist–Leninist party while continuing to endorse Islam. Somalia's pro-Soviet alignment occurred because Somali irredentism, as fierce and unsuccessful as that of the Irish, demanded that the Somali-inhabited Ogaden be 'recovered' from Ethiopia, where American influence was predominant. Somalia therefore needed Soviet arms. Haile Selassie was overthrown in 1974 by a military junta (the *Dergue*), which Lt-Col. Mengistu Haile Mariam rapidly purged and radicalized. He also broke off relations with the United States and moved towards the Soviet Union. Confronted by the threatened disintegration of the Ethiopian empire, historically dominated by the Christian Amhara minority, Mengistu had to repel the Somali invasion of the Ogaden and crush the Eritrean rebellion. He therefore turned for military assistance to Moscow and Havana. He also formed an alliance with one of the seven Ethiopian Marxist–Leninist groups, the *Meison* (a formerly Paris-based, leftist Leninist movement), to crush the other main Leninist group, the student-based Ethiopian People's Revolutionary Party (EPRP), in a bloody wave of terror – only to turn on the *Meison* in August 1977 and drive its members into prison, hiding or emigration.

The Soviet Union staged an air- and sea-lift operation in Ethiopia greater than the one it had initiated in Angola, over-flying Turkey, Iraq and Pakistan and using Aden as a staging base. Soviet command and arms, with the aid of some 20,000 Cuban troops, defeated Somalia early in 1978. Since then, with Soviet and Cuban logistical support but no direct combat involvement (lest the Eritrean rebels' Arab and third-world support be antagonized), Mengistu has driven the rebel Eritrean Liberation Front (ELF) and Eritrean People's Liberation Front (EPLF) out of the cities and back to rural guerrilla fighting. Soviet support of (ex-) Christian, Marxist–Leninist Ethiopia against the largely Muslim Eritrean rebels turned the Arab world, including radical Syria and Iraq, against Moscow on this issue. (Indeed, in terms of global Soviet and Western strategy, the Horn is primarily a Middle Eastern rather than an African crisis area.)[5]

Thus Moscow and Havana won two major victories in Africa – in Angola and in Ethiopia.

The Soviet Union also achieved another victory: an intensified global image of American indecision and hesitation, though she also suffered some losses, in Africa and elsewhere. The rapid and massive intrusion of Soviet and Cuban military power into Africa alarmed not only the conservative African states but also such centrist ones as Nigeria, which by mid-1978 was putting pressure on Neto and Mengistu to cut back on the Soviet and Cuban military presence. The second invasion of Shaba from Angola (May 1978), while in large part tribal (Lunda) in character, could hardly have occurred without Soviet and Cuban knowledge, and East Germany may well have been involved in training the rebels. (Had the rebels won, Shaba, Kinshasa and most of Zaire would probably be in the hands of pro-Soviet radical elements.) The invasion triggered a French paratroop response, followed by a largely Moroccan pan-African force and increased French, other West European and American concern about Soviet operations in Africa. The United States, at the request of France, sent transport planes to fly in French and Moroccan troops and materiel – the first instance of direct American military involvement in Africa since the 1960 UN Congo operation and the first time American resources had been used in support of extra-European French military operations since the first Indochinese War. Franco–American relations improved, to Moscow's disadvantage. A Western–Japanese–Saudi economic consortium was formed to overcome Zaire's near-bankruptcy, and Mobutu was thus at least temporarily propped up. Although the Algerian-backed Sahara Liberation Movement (POLISARIO) and Front de Liberation Nationale du Tchad (FROLINAT) rebellions, against French-supported Mauretania and Chad respectively, were Libyan- and Algerian-armed, the arms were Soviet in origin, a fact which strengthened Paris's view that Moscow was trying to subvert French influence in Africa.[6]

Two other problems arose from Soviet African successes. In spring 1978, hardly without Soviet knowledge and consent, the Cuban troops smuggled back into their embassy in Addis Ababa a major *Meison* leader, Negede Gobezie, who had been abroad when Mengistu turned on the *Meison* in August 1977. (Thereafter Negede had criticized Mengistu for being not radical enough at home and too pro-Soviet abroad, but he later became pro-Soviet and pro-Cuban, presumably after Mengistu turned on him.) Mengistu then ordered out the Cuban and South Yemeni ambassadors and Negede left with them. It thus seems likely that the Soviet Union has reservations about Mengistu's military rule and would like to set up a Marxist–Leninist party under at least partial civilian leadership, which Mengistu promised to do in December 1978. There were also press reports that the Soviet Union was intriguing with three prominent *Dergue* members – Legesse, Gesesse and Tamrat – against Mengistu. Mengistu himself was careful not to break off all relations with Washington and agreed to the appointment of a new American ambassador.[7]

It seemed at first that Neto could not survive in Angola without continued massive Soviet and Cuban help against the continuing UNITA rebellion in southern Angola, the less serious FNLA operations in the north and the dissent within his own leadership. In 1977 a rebellion against Neto and the largely mulatto civilian MPLA leadership, led by Vito Alves and other black military leaders, was crushed only by the intervention of Cuban troops. After the second Shaba invasion in May 1978 the Carter Administration, having failed in an attempt to sound out Congress over covert aid to Savimbi, reversed its course and sent an emissary to Luanda. Angolan–American relations improved somewhat and the United States reportedly got some Angolan help in the Namibian negotiations.[8] At the Khartoum OAU summit Neto and Mobutu agreed to re-establish diplomatic relations, cease support of guerrilla activity against each other's territory and to reopen the Benguela railway for shipment of Zaire's minerals to the Angolan port of Lobito. Neto has since visited Kinshasha.

This kaleidoscopic series of events shows on what shifting sands African alignments are built. While Neto is a professed Marxist–Leninist and is closely linked with the Soviet Union and with Cuba, he is also an African nationalist. It is even more true in Africa than elsewhere that all Communism in power becomes national Communism. Neto can hope for more economic progress, African support and Western economic aid if he at least appears to have, and if possible actually does have, a more remote association with Moscow and Havana. Moreover, an end to

51

South African military presence in Namibia is likely to decrease Savimbi's threat.

Yet because Neto and Mengistu are still threatened, they will hardly want to dispense entirely with the Soviet and Cuban military presence in the near future. It seems unlikely, therefore, that the Soviet Union and Cuba will soon leave Angola or Ethiopia. Nor can Moscow assume that Washington will remain indecisive in Africa indefinitely; there are already signs in the United States which indicate that this is no longer the case. On balance, however, Soviet and Cuban military and political presence in Angola and Ethiopia remains predominant, and the Soviet Union is therefore stronger in Africa than she was in 1974. She may well become stronger still.

Southern Africa: The Soviet Prospects

It is in southern Africa, and particularly in South Africa, that Soviet prospects in Africa seem the brightest during the next decade. This is not because South Africa will soon come under black majority rule, led by a Marxist–Leninist Party (even if she did, the government would then be subject to the same conflicting pressures which now beset the MPLA in Angola and Soviet influence would also come into question); it is because she will not. Soviet influence on the protracted black guerrilla struggle against white rule in South Africa will increase as the guerrillas need more arms, will fail to get them from the West, or enough of them from China, and will therefore have to get them primarily from the Soviet Union.

At an early stage the USSR became the principal supplier of arms and money to SWAPO in Namibia and ZAPU in Rhodesia. When ZANU initially broke away from ZAPU it turned to China for arms and money. As the guerrilla war in Rhodesia intensified, the Zimbabwe African National Liberation Army (ZANLA), the ZANU guerrilla wing based in Mozambique, drawn largely from the Karanga sub-tribe of the Shona and headed by Mugabe, Tongagora and Nhongo, broke with the ZANU 'civilian' leadership, which came to terms with Smith (the 'internal solution'). Mugabe continued to rely on China for arms and training until his recent visit to Cuba diversified his arms supply. SWAPO profited from the Soviet and Cuban camps in Angola and ZAPU from a continuing supply of Soviet arms and some Cuban training in Zambia.

Marxism–Leninism is stronger in ZANU than in SWAPO, but it is primarily of the Chinese, not the Soviet variety. (ZAPU draws on some Marxist rhetoric but hardly much more.) Nor are the ZANU and SWAPO leadership undisputed: the ZANU military leaders, Tongagora and Nhongo, wield much influence and SWAPO's Nujomo is potentially menaced by Toivo. Finally, the Rhodesian and Namibian liberation movements are under strong Christian influence.

The Nkomo- and Mugabe-led Patriotic Front guerrilla activity is on the rise in Rhodesia and the 'internal solution' is therefore in increasing difficulty.[9] In Namibia a Western proposal for peaceful, UN-monitored transition, initially accepted by SWAPO and South Africa, was endangered by rising SWAPO guerrilla activity and by doubts over whether South Africa would tolerate a SWAPO-dominated Namibian government,[10] but South Africa then rejected a somewhat more extensive UN plan (involving UN troop and police presence). The Western powers compromised with Pretoria to persuade the South African government to accept an election in Namibia without a UN presence, and South Africa agreed to accept a UN-sponsored election thereafter. The December 1978 election, in which only the multi-racial South African-supported Democratic Turnhalle Alliance (DTA) and the right-wing Aktur fielded candidates, resulted in a DTA victory. SWAPO refused to run. Whether, and when, a UN-sponsored election will occur remains unclear. In the meantime, Nujomo's position in, and Moscow's influence over, SWAPO have become more entrenched as SWAPO guerrilla activity has continued.

South Africa

The black struggle for majority rule in South Africa will be protracted. The terrain is not hospitable to guerrilla warfare. The formidable South African security forces and their informer networks among the black population are major obstacles to effective black urban guerrilla warfare and industrial sabotage, the most effective violence-orientated strategies for the black majority. Despite the gradual dismantling of petty apartheid, increased political participation for coloureds and Indians and the beginning of contacts between the moderate (*verligte*) Afrikaners and moderate black leaders, the lack of realism and obstinacy of most Afrikaners and the bitterness and despair of most blacks make peaceful transition to black majority rule unlikely. Although some of the English-speaking whites might eventually accept it (and more would emigrate to avoid it), most Afrikaans-speaking whites will long resist black majority rule with the utmost vigour and ruthlessness, and most black activists will hardly accept anything less. For the Afrikaners, nation, language, history, religion and culture are at stake. In their own minds at least, they have nowhere to go. They do not think of themselves as colonialists but, rather, as the victors in their own national liberation war against British Colonial rule; most black activists, on the other hand, feel they have the same right to black majority rule as do the blacks to the north.

Thus a protracted black–white guerrilla struggle in South Africa seems likely. True, after Rhodesia and Namibia move to black majority rule, the black African states may well want to break from hostilities. Yet the South African NLMs are already trying to carry on some sporadic guerrilla activity in South Africa, and urban dissidence there has become endemic since the Soweto black demonstrations in 1976. Nor can the black African states hold out indefinitely against offering their support for the black struggle in South Africa.

The Soviet Union will support it as well, She has the capability, the opportunity and the motive to do so. True, her present capability would be seriously stretched to do in or near South Africa what she and Cuba have done in Angola and Ethiopia, but after what they did there, one would be foolhardy to think it necessarily and indefinitely inadequate. Moscow's opportunities are obvious and multiple. First, without Soviet arms and perhaps Cuban troops, black guerrillas inside and outside South Africa can hardly hope to overcome Afrikaner power and determination in the foreseeable future. Second, South Africa, even more than Namibia and Rhodesia, has strategic minerals which Western Europe needs even more than the United States and for which the former would be more pressed to find substitutes. (Yet a pro-Soviet government would presumably sell the minerals in the West, just as Angola now does

her oil.) Third, South Africa controls the Cape route along which is transported much of the oil destined for Western Europe and, increasingly for the United States. True, Soviet military interruption of oil transport around the Cape would mean general war and is therefore unlikely; however, Moscow may consider that the fact that such a possibility could arise (in the event of a black-ruled South Africa) might prompt some West European governments – although hardly the United States – to be less openly anti-Soviet, that is, somewhat 'finlandized'. Yet this prospect is rather unlikely to be realized, for shipping will become less, not more, dependent on calling or refuelling at South African ports.

In contrast, Western support of South Africa, or even the absence of opposition to her, would turn the black African states and NLMs more towards the Soviet Union than would otherwise be the case. By supporting the black struggle against South Africa, the Soviet Union would once again demonstrate her superiority over China. And finally, during the coming struggle for South Africa and in the present one over Rhodesia and Namibia, pressures will be increasingly applied to the neighbouring black states by the guerrillas who have their bases there and by whites conducting retaliatory raids such as those Rhodesia is now perpetrating against Zambia and Mozambique. These pressures may lead to radicalism in these black states and, perhaps, to rising Soviet influence there.

Moreover, the Soviet Union has other assets in South Africa. The major external South African black NLM, the ANC, has long been armed and financed by Moscow. Some of its leaders are (black) members of the SACP, which has very considerable influence within the ANC. The SACP has a long and faithfully pro-Moscow history. Officially multi-racial, its *de facto* leadership is white and largely of East European Jewish origin. Thus Moscow has some trained black and white SACP cadres at its disposal. (Yet Soviet multi-racialism will continue to be a handicap in the black South African NLMs: the PAC split from the ANC on this issue and turned to China, who has been trying to play the black nationalist card.)[11]

The United States is hardly likely to play a decisive role in the coming struggle for South

53

Africa. For while American liberals and blacks will advocate help for the blacks, American conservatives, prompted by anti-Soviet, anti-terrorist and sometimes racist motives, will counsel assistance for the whites. The two will probably cancel each other out. Britain, with her massive South African investments and rising anti-black domestic racism, will probably do little and the rest of Western Europe even less. China will compete with the Soviet Union. Finally, the more aid the Soviet Union gives the South African NLMS, and the more essential and effective it is, the more her prestige and influence will increase in the more radical and anti-South African black African states.

Thus the Soviet Union and Cuba are likely to be the primary external forces acting on South Africa, and short-range Soviet prospects there seem good. Soviet influence will probably rise and that of the West decline. And although Soviet operations in southern Africa will contribute to some further worsening of the Soviet Union's relations with the Western countries, Soviet activity there may well be stimulated by this very development.

In the end will the blacks, with Soviet aid, eventually wear down the Afrikaners? And if so, will Soviet power in southern Africa decline thereafter? History will tell.

One final caveat. For the West and Japan, Africa is much less important than the Middle East, to say nothing of Europe and Asia. The Soviet Union is not doing very well in any of these areas; China is opposing her more vigorously than ever; and the Sino–Japanese treaty and Sino–American normalization may well be historic turning points, compared with which the subject of this essay, no matter how fascinating (or, probably, how tragic), is of secondary importance.

NOTES

[1] This paper is based primarily on travels in the Soviet Union, Africa and the Middle East, May–August 1978, for which I am grateful to the *Reader's Digest*, of which I am a roving editor, and to its Editor-in-Chief, Edward T. Thompson. For recent general background, on which I have drawn extensively, see the articles by Colin Legum on the African background, David Albright on Soviet policy in Africa and George T. Yu on Chinese policy in Africa in *Problems of Communism*, Jan./Feb. 1978; my 'The Soviet–U.S. Confrontation in Southern Africa', (MIT Center for International Studies, *mimeo.*, Nov. 1976); and Robert Legvold, 'The Soviet Union's Strategic Stake in Africa', in Jennifer Seymour Whitaker, (ed.), *Africa and the United States: Vital Interests* (New York: New York University Press for the Council on Foreign Relations, 1978), pp. 153–86. For Africa in general at present, see Colin Legum (ed.), *The Africa Contemporary Record* (New York: Africana 1977); and for the history of Soviet policy in Africa, see Wolfgang Berner, 'Afrikapolitik', in Dietrich Geyer (ed.), *Sowjetunion: Aussenpolitik 1955–1973* (Cologne: Bohlau, 1976), pp. 713–843. I am also much indebted to conversations with Colin Legum, Robert Legvold and Robert Rotberg, and to suggestions for revision by Christoph Bertram.

[2] Berner, 'Afrikapolitik', *op. cit.*, p. 713.

[3] The authoritative treatment of the Angolan civil war is John Marcum, *The Angolan Rebellion*, 2 vols. (Cambridge, Mass.: The MIT Press, 1969 and 1978). See also the debate between Gerald J. Bender and Chester A. Crocker, *Foreign Policy*, Summer 1978 and Nathaniel Davis, 'The Angolan Decision of 1975: A Personal Memoir', *Foreign Affairs*, July 1978.

[4] The above is based principally on conversations held in Maputo in August 1978. For Machel's recent authoritative declaration of 'Communist neutrality', see his 'Relatorio do Comité Politico Permanente do Comité Central', IV. Frelimo CC Plenum, in *Tempo* (Maputo), 310, 13 Aug. 1978, pp. 30–43: '. . . nunca agiremos para consolidar ou agravar divisoes na familia revolucionaria, agiremos sempre em favor de unidade'. See also Robert D'A. Henderson, 'Principles and Practice in Mozambique's Foreign Policy', *The World Today*, July 1978.

[5] The above is primarily based on conversations in Moscow, Tehran, Damascus, Cairo, Khartoum, Mogadiscio and Nairobi, June–August 1978. See also the analyses by J.-C. Guillebaud and J.-C. Pomonti in *Le Monde*, especially Guillebaud's articles of 27–28 Feb. 1977 and 20 Feb. 1978. For the Soviet airlift to Ethiopia, see *Newsweek*, 23 Jan. 1978; for the Soviet-Somali break, F. Stephen Larrabee in *Radio Liberty Research*, 5 July 1977 and 2 Jan. 1978; for background, Volker Matthies, *Der Grenzkonflikt Somalias mit Athiopien und Kenya* (Hamburg, 1977), and his 'Unterentwicklung, Nationalismus und Sozialismus in Somalia', *Afrika Spectrum*, 1977, pp. 49–75, and 'Somalia – ein sowjetischer "Satillitenstaat" im Horn von Afrika?', *Verfassung und Recht in Ubersee*, 9 (4), 1976, pp. 437–56; for Barre's Islamic posture, *Halgan* (Mogadishu), Eng. ed., Oct. 1977; for general background, Peter Schwab, 'Cold War on the Horn of Africa', *African Affairs*, 77 (3–6), Jan. 1978, pp. 6–20, and Jorge I. Dominguez, 'Cuban Foreign Policy', *Foreign Affairs*, Fall 1978.

[6] For the above, see primarily the running coverage in *Le Monde*. For the DDR's role, see Colin Legum, 'It's Germans, Not Cubans', *The New Republic*, 24 June 1978. For Zaire, see Crawford Young, 'Zaire: The Unending Crisis', *Foreign Affairs*, Fall 1978. I have benefited from conversations in Paris in May and September 1978 and in Kinshasha in August 1978.

[7] For Negede Gobezie's criticism of the Soviet Union, see the interview with him by Guillebaud in *Le Monde*, 17 Sept, 1977; for the rest, the *Economist*, 3 June 1978, p. 68.

[8] The *New York Times*, 23 June 1978.

[9] For ZANU Marxism-Leninism, see the Political Commissariat lecture series in *Zimbabwe News* (Maputo), Jan./Feb. and March/April 1978. For Chinese influence, see the excerpts from Mao Tse-tung's works in the latter number.

[10] Conversations in Moscow, Lusaka, Maputo, Pretoria, Windhoek and Salisbury, June and August 1978. The best running coverage of Rhodesia and Namibia is in the *Economist*.

[11] I have benefited from conversations in Moscow, Johannesburg, Pretoria and Cape Town in June and August 1978. For *verligte* views, see the writings by Willem de Klerk, editor of *Die Transvaler*, especially his 'South Africa's Domestic Politics: Key Questions and Options', *Politikon*, Dec. 1977, pp. 178–89. For the *verkrampte* view, see A. P. Treurnicht, *Credo van 'n Afrikaner* (Cape Town: Tafelberg, 1975). (Dr Treurnicht was recently elected head of the Nationalist Party in the Transvaal.) The best running coverage of South Africa is in the *Economist*.

Soviet Power and Policies in the Third World: The Middle East

GALIA GOLAN

The Middle East[1] has traditionally been of interest to Russian leaders, be they Soviet or not, because of its proximity to the southern borders of the Soviet Union and her need for access to the Mediterranean from the Black Sea. In the nuclear era, however, more complex strategic considerations have come to dominate Soviet interests in this region. The military-strategic factor became increasingly important in the 1960s, as the Soviet Union sought to expand her naval power and reach. This came about primarily as the result of a gradual shift in Soviet strategic policy, in which conventional forces, particularly the naval arm, were to provide the Soviet Union with greater flexibility, thus opening up global options, whether for purposes of intervention, defence or confrontation. It was also to meet the challenge of the American nuclear ballistic-missile submarines that the USSR shifted to forward deployment of her fleet and put massive resources into the development of anti-submarine warfare techniques, despite all the difficulties involved in the latter. Thus it was the general expansion of the Soviet fleet in pursuit of global flexibility in military-strategic competition principally with the United States and her allies, combined with the more specific response to the deployment of *Polaris* submarines in the Mediterranean, that brought about the formation of the Soviet Mediterranean Squadron and, with it, an upgrading of the Middle East in Soviet strategic considerations.[2]

As a result of these military-strategic developments, the traditional Soviet interest in securing passage through the Dardenelles was intensified and a major Soviet effort both to improve relations with Turkey and to encourage her in a less co-operative attitude towards NATO was again attempted.[3] In addition, the expansion of the Soviet fleet brought with it other undertakings, for, inasmuch as the Soviet Union had not developed aircraft carriers (the decision to do so was apparently taken in the 1960s, the first of such carriers entering service only in the 1970s), she sought not only shore facilities for her fleet but air bases as well for the aircraft necessary for the protection and functioning of the fleet.[4] Egypt was the focal point of this venture, mainly because of the relative suitability of her ports and airfields but also because of her geo-political position and the relative stability of her regime. With the loss of Soviet facilities in Egypt, Moscow sought a strategic alternative in Syria and, later, in Libya.

Given the broader scope of Soviet strategic interests, however, Soviet efforts in the Middle East have not been limited to the needs of the Mediterranean Squadron and of what are known as the Arab confrontation states (in the Arab-Israeli conflict). The same interests at play in this area apply further south as well. Indeed, with the deployment of American *Poseidon* and, shortly, *Trident* missiles, the Indian Ocean – and its peripheral states – has assumed an increasingly important role in Soviet thinking.[5] Locations further west in the Mediterranean have become potential targets for Soviet military interests since the USSR succeeded in improving her own means of supporting her fleet and producing larger numbers of modern long-range aircraft. The uncertainty of the Soviet military presence in the area of the confrontation states might be compensated for by facilities in states to the west, such as Libya and Algeria. Moreover, differences of opinion in the Soviet Union, specifically within the military, may have provoked controversy over the relative strategic importance of such facilities in light of the risks and costs of Soviet military involvement in the area. In any case, during the 1970s Soviet strategic interest in the confrontation states, while still operative, has diminished somewhat. In contrast, interest in the Indian Ocean area, as the coming confrontation point between Soviet and American strategic forces (and a stepping-off point for crisis intervention in Asia), appears to have grown.

Soviet political interests in the Middle East have been geared to the achievement and maintenance of strategic objectives. In addition to penetration efforts designed to gain influence over, and even control of, the local security, military and political forces, the Soviet Union has also sought friendship treaties to provide a formal framework for relations and a degree of stability. It might be argued that Communist regimes would be the best insurance for the maintenance of Soviet facilities in the area; indeed, those in the Kremlin who are more ideologically oriented may well be arguing for such an objective, even at the expense of strategic interests. However, the realities of the situation in the Middle East, as well as elsewhere in the Third World, have generally led the Soviet Union to downgrade this ideological objective, occasionally sacrificing it altogether when it threatens to impede progress in the realm of strategic interests. Nonetheless, Moscow continues to nurture this option in anticipation of the right opportunity – that is, a moment when the risk of outside (specifically American) intervention is minimal.[6] Such an opportunity would appear to have occurred most recently in Aden.

Economic Interests

If Soviet interest in the Middle East is primarily strategic and political considerations are sobordinate to strategic ones, and if ideological concerns are less compelling and longer-term, the extent of future Soviet economic involvement with the Middle East is open to some speculation. The Soviet Union herself is one of the world's major oil producers, and a cardinal rule of Soviet trade policy has been strictly to avoid dependence upon outside resources. Together these two factors may account for the fact that the USSR imports very little Middle Eastern oil and, certain Western estimates notwithstanding, apparently has no plans to do so to any significant degree. Rather, for all the expense and

difficulty involved, Soviet energy plans are to develop Soviet sources, with or without outside technological assistance.[7] Moscow has urged its East European allies to import Middle Eastern oil so as to reduce the Soviet obligation to meet their energy needs – and possible to release more Soviet oil for sale on the world market.[8] But the Soviet Union still meets over 85 per cent of these needs, and any indirect benefit derived from the Middle East supplies only marginally reduces this burden, although the burden itself has been lightened somewhat by Soviet demands for dollar payments from Eastern Europe.

Economic interest could be associated indirectly with Soviet control over the flow of Middle Eastern oil to Japan and the West. Certainly the USSR has sought to limit Western influence in the oil-producing states as well as to improve her own relations with these countries. Yet Soviet prospects are greatly limited by the complexities of Persian Gulf as well as inner Arab relationships, to say nothing of the traditional animosity of the major oil producers, Iran and Saudi Arabia. Moreover, given the importance the United States attaches to the unimpeded flow of Middle Eastern oil to world markets and the Soviet Union's own involvement in these markets it is not certain that Moscow is particularly anxious to tamper with the flow of these supplies or risk East–West confrontation over the oil lanes.

Although no figures are available, fairly recent arms sales for hard-currency cash payments may also serve to explain Soviet economic interest in the region.[9] Yet tough Soviet demands in connection with certain arms deals (for example, the proposal to Jordan in 1976),[10] as well as Moscow's own proposals – albeit infrequent and vague – for the limitation of the Middle East arms race, suggest that the USSR does not consider arms sales to the region to be of major importance. On the other hand, whereas economic relations with the confrontation states once constituted something of a burden for the Soviet Union, today Moscow is beginning to demand and receive a return on its investment there, at least in the form of a more favourable balance of trade. At the same time, Soviet trade with (as well as economic and military assistance to) the Persian Gulf states has increased, reflecting perhaps not only a shift in interest from the confrontation area southwards to the Gulf, but also a rise in importance of the economic factor in Soviet Middle East concerns as Moscow seeks to profit from the affluence of the Gulf States.[11]

Soviet Inroads into the Arab East[12]

Many factors contributed to Moscow's successful penetration of the Middle East in the 1950s and 1960s. These include the general collapse of imperialist rule in the area, the retreat of Britain, the limited American interest and the rise of the third-world neutralist philosophy. At the same time, the Soviet Union had not been traditionally regarded as an imperialist power by the peoples of the region, nor did she make exaggerated ideological or even political demands, while her economic model did offer certain attractions to the area's centralist regimes. Moreover, unlike that of the West, Soviet economic assistance was extremely generous, offered with almost no regard for cost–benefit considerations or practicality.

One of the most important contributing factors was, of course, the Arab–Israeli conflict. Beginning with the Soviet-backed Czechoslovak arms deal with Egypt in 1955, and Soviet political support in response to the Suez crisis, which persisted through the Six-day War and which was followed by Soviet resupplies and direct military assistance in the War of Attrition, an Arab dependency upon Soviet military and political support appeared to have been created. There was a direct correlation between the accommodation of Soviet strategic interests, in the form of naval and air facilities, and Soviet willingness to equip, train and otherwise assist the Arab States. Tension in the area, at least Arab–Israeli tension, appeared to serve Soviet penetration efforts, highlighting as it did not only the need of the Arab states for Soviet assistance but also the polarization of the super-powers' position and the United States' commitment to the 'enemy' side, Israel. The positive contribution of the conflict to Soviet interest was so great that it is arguable that Moscow actively sought its continuation, possibly even its aggravation (in the Six-day War, for example), so as to ensure continued Soviet presence in the area.[13]

The above factors did not, however, remain constant. As Soviet military and political penetration of the Middle East increased and as the Soviet Union attempted to influence events through leaders sympathetic or beholden to her, the Arab states gradually began to see her as another imperialist power. This image was sharpened by the Soviet bid for bases, the behaviour of Soviet advisers and personnel in the host country and a tendency on the part of the Soviet Union to treat the Arab leaders in an imperial manner, often disregarding their requests or even humiliating them. Even the 'progressive' regimes balked at these infringements of their independence. In the case of Egypt, these developments led to the expulsion of Soviet advisers and the abrogation of the mutual friendship treaty; with Syria, they provoked a refusal to enter such a treaty, and policies were followed which were contrary to Moscow's preferences with regard to both the local Communist Party and the Lebanese civil war; in the case of Iraq, they prompted a refusal to grant the Soviet Union extra-territorial rights for naval facilities or political concessions.[14] This Arab independence increased significantly, even to the point of defying Soviet attempts at arms blackmail, with the rising importance of the petrodollar and the consequent rise in the influence of the oil-rich states, particularly Saudi Arabia.

A factor which has further complicated Soviet efforts to make inroads into the area is the kaleidoscope of relationships within the region itself. Such problems as the Syrian–Iraqi dispute, shifting Egyptian–Libyan–Sudanese relationships and the Lebanese war confronted Moscow with serious policy dilemmas. Particularly detrimental to Soviet interests in the region has been the rising influence of Saudi Arabia, whose anti-Soviet position carries with it the potential for influencing not only Egypt, for example, but even the loyalties of Syria and the Palestine Liberation Organization (PLO). Neither the periodic cohesion of the more radical states such as Libya and Iraq, nor their relationships with elements of the PLO, will necessarily help to solve this problem, for the radicals' position regarding the Arab–Israeli conflict and other issues does not entirely suit Moscow's own policies.

Indeed, disagreement between the Soviet Union and her Arab clients on various issues of substance has operated against the achievement of Moscow's aims. It was not only the Soviet Union's imperial attitude towards Egypt which led Sadat to expel Soviet military advisers in

1972; it was also – and mainly – Moscow's growing detente with the United States and, in particular, its opposition to another Arab military offensive against Israel. There have also been serious differences between the Soviet Union, the more radical Arab states and the PLO over the issue of a 'political' as opposed to a 'military' solution to the Arab–Israeli conflict, specifically the matter of the Geneva peace conference and Security Council Resolution 242, which both imply recognition of Israel and provide assurances covering her security.[15]

Limits to Influence

What really imposes restrictions on Soviet moves and policies in the region, however, is the super-power relationship. Here, as elsewhere, the estimated American response, specifically the risk of direct Soviet–American confrontation, is the ultimate consideration in Soviet Middle East calculations.[16] From this point of view, Soviet risk-taking was pronounced in the late 1960s, when Soviet involvement was at its height, but even at this time Moscow sought to restrain the Arab states, both by controlling the types of armaments supplied and by persuasion, so as to avoid an all-out Arab–Israeli war and the concomitant danger of Soviet–American confrontation.[17] Soviet caution persisted even when Moscow decided to renew arms supplies to Egypt early in 1973 in view of Sadat's determination to act with or without the Soviet Union. It was this caution which prompted the Soviet Union once again to risk disfavour with the Arabs by pressing them to agree to a cease-fire almost immediately after the opening of hostilities in October 1973, Soviet arms supplies notwithstanding, and by continuing to apply pressure until a Soviet–American cease-fire was more or less imposed.[18] Given the continued volatility of the Arab–Israeli conflict even after the war, and growing American involvement in the region, the super-power relationship continues to act as a constraint.

Thus the situation that once facilitated Soviet entry into the area has tended, over time, to become dangerous, even counter-productive for Moscow. If the Arab–Israeli conflict could have been strictly controlled, it might have retained its value for Soviet purposes, but in the event it has lost much of its usefulness. The Soviet Union herself has been partly responsible for this, for reluctance to fulfil the role of 'war-maker' has greatly reduced her relevance to the Arab states. And, if she is unwilling to provide the war option, she is virtually unable to provide anything else. She cannot play a role as potentially effective as the American one in bringing about a settlement, for she has no leverage over Israel. Nor can she compete significantly with the United States in the peaceful area of economic assistance.

A Balance Sheet

A stock-taking of the Soviet position in the Middle East after twenty-five years of activity reveals a sharply ascending and then a descending curve which tends in the direction of relative failure. On the success side of the ledger there is the Soviet treaty with Iraq; the legalization of the Syrian Communist Party and its inclusion in a front with the ruling Ba'ath Party; the Marxist orientation of South Yemen; improved relations with Libya, Kuwait, Jordan and, within limits, pre-Khomeini Iran, as well as significantly improved relations with Turkey; and Soviet identification with the PLO as it has gained in world recognition. More significant, the Soviet Union has gained at least informal recognition as a political power in the Middle East, even if that achievement is of potential rather than actual importance. This last accomplishment is connected with Moscow's successful strategic achievements, specifically its military presence in the Mediterranean. While opinions vary about the relative strength (and speed and versatility) of this squadron compared with the American Sixth Fleet, its deployment in times of crisis can serve as a check on American freedom of action. To a lesser degree, the same might be said for the Soviet fleet in the Red Sea–Indian Ocean area, though the Soviet naval presence there is still quite limited.[19]

On the negative side of the ledger, Soviet relations with Egypt, the former cornerstone of Moscow's Middle East policy, have been entirely eroded. Syria has guarded her independence jealously, even defying Moscow over such issues as the Lebanese war, while she periodically represses or restricts the local Communists. Iraq has proved problematic, and Libya is a highly erratic political partner. Moreover, Soviet support for Ethiopian action against Eritrea has raised problems for Soviet relations with the radical Arab states. And, in almost all cases, the rising influence of Saudi Arabia – with her potential for underwriting a westward shift by the Arab states – has placed Soviet achievements very much in question. This applies also to Soviet relations with the PLO, which is by no means totally dependent upon, or even responsive to, the USSR. Even in the realm of strategic interests, Soviet policy has met with certain failures: the port and air facilities lost in Egypt and Somalia have not been fully compensated for by moves elsewhere; and neither Libya nor Syria has been as co-operative as Egypt, nor has Iraq (or, to date, Ethiopia) been as forthcoming as Somalia once was. Only in South Yemen (formerly Aden) does there appear to have been whole-hearted co-operation.

On the whole, the price the Soviet Union has had to pay for political and strategic benefits has significantly increased. Given the demands *and* the risks involved in a Soviet Middle Eastern presence, together with the slight shift at least of future priorities towards the Indian Ocean, the Soviet Union has shown that she is reluctant to make the necessary concessions – and to pay the necessary price – in order to regain fully her former position in the region.[20] Soviet unwillingness to compromise with Egypt without the latter's full renunciation of the United States, the threat to the link between Syria and Moscow during the Lebanese crisis, and exaggerated Soviet demands regarding a Jordanian air-defence system, all point to this conclusion. The Soviet Union would appear to have opted for what might be termed a minimal rather than a maximal policy, which would entail two inter-related objectives: the maintenance of Soviet presence at not too great a cost; and the prevention of a total American take-over of the area.

Soviet Interest in a Middle East Settlement

Such Soviet objectives could be served by a settlement of the Arab–Israeli conflict, as long as the Soviet Union herself were a party to the settlement. Soviet thinking along these lines was apparent even in the pre-1973 two-power and four-power attempt at a settlement;[21] it probably clarified following the 1973 war, as the negative aspects of the conflict became more acute. A settlement would eliminate the risks associated with the conflict while (possibly) reversing some of the negative trends that affect Soviet presence in the region. Soviet participation in a settlement, particularly in its guarantees, would provide international, formal recognition of the Soviet Middle Eastern presence. (Such formalities, their apparent superfluity notwithstanding, have traditionally been of importance to the Soviet Union, as shown by her persistent efforts to organize a European security conference to formalize East Europe's post-World War II borders.) Such recognition would provide greater stability for the Soviet presence than the present, uncertain reliance on the good will of host Arab regimes. Thus surveillance flights in the region (including coverage of the Mediterranean area), port facilities and the use of air bases would be granted for the purposes of peace-keeping rather than as a result of a separate agreement with one leader or another. Navigational rights, as the Soviet Union herself has suggested, might well be included. That such a presence might also entail limitations would not necessarily interfere with Soviet interests; the presence of the USSR, at least at sea, lags behind that of the United States, so that restrictions that also affected the latter would not be unwelcome. Similarly, the Soviet Union herself has proposed limitations on the arms race following a settlement, presumably because of the United States' growing role in this sphere as well as the danger of nuclearization of the region.

Soviet participation in a settlement would not, however, be an easy matter and Moscow's quest for a role in the negotiating process has involved it in a number of contradictions. The very interest expressed by the Soviet Union in a negotiated settlement has provoked the ire of the 'rejectionist' Arab states from the outset, while identification with the 'rejectionists' often involves the Soviet Union in the adoption of positions contrary to her own interests on such issues as the Geneva Conference and the existence of the state of Israel. But even in discussions with the more moderate elements Moscow has had to consider the accommodation of requests close to the maximum demands of the Arab states so as to offer them something beyond the more limited agreements that the United States has proposed. Increasing support for the more radical Arab demands became necessary not only to distinguish Moscow from Washington but also to prove to the United States (and to Israel) the absolute necessity of bringing the Soviet

Union into the settlement process as the controller of the war option, or as the only power capable of bringing Syria and the PLO to the negotiating table. (In time this could also become a tactic to isolate, and apply pressure to, a pro-American country such as Egypt.) In addition, increased Soviet influence amongst the radical elements is designed to strengthen Moscow's position in case Geneva or similar multilateral negotiations should be resumed.

Particularly after Camp David and the Egyptian–Israeli peace treaty, this tactic has become more important as Moscow's options in the area have become more limited. Indeed, with growing American inroads into the area, what was once a tactical Soviet interest in the radical Arab elements may now have become the cornerstone of Soviet policy in the region. Not only has Moscow no alternative clients, but a strengthened relationship with Syria and Iraq, for example, serves Soviet interests in the Persian Gulf as well. Yet Moscow's own reservations about the stability of the radical leaders, the permanence of the 'rejectionist' alliance and the cost – and risks – of responding to the demands upon Moscow made by this grouping suggest that the Soviet Union has not abandoned her overall position. She continues to advocate a settlement, through the Geneva mechanism, which recognizes Israel within secure borders (specified as those of pre-war 1967) as well as a Palestinian state. The maintenance of the Soviet position despite, and even in argument with, the USSR's more radical clients (such as the PLO) strongly suggests that Moscow is indeed committed to this position as the most realistic and feasible. The Soviet Union must convince Israel and the United States that she is a reasonable partner for negotiations and therefore has a positive rather than a negative or obstructionist contribution to make in the event of the resumption of the Geneva conference. Part of this tactic is a carrot and stick approach to Israel; the Soviet Union declares her willingness to provide guarantees for, and recognition of, Israel's 1949-67 borders when her participation in negotiations seems likely and adopts a borderline position (apparent, for example, in press references to the 1947 partition plan) when she seems excluded from the picture.[22] Nevertheless, the basic Soviet position on a settlement, multi-faceted as it is, remains relatively constant.[23]

Future Developments

Despite the fact that Soviet policies in the Middle East (particularly in the context of the Arab–Israeli conflict) have become reactive rather than creative, dependent upon clients and events rather than dominant and directive, and tend on balance towards failure rather than significant achievement, there is little reason to believe that Soviet interest in the Middle East, if the area is defined as including the Persian Gulf and the northern Indian Ocean, will decline in the near future. Future Soviet policies for the Middle East and the position of the Soviet Union in the region will probably be subject to most of the constraints operative until now and will be dictated by many of the same interests. In any case, the East–West balance of power and relationship between the two superpowers will constitute the major determinants, although shifts or re-orientations within and amongst the local regimes will continue to play a very significant role.

NOTES

[1] The Middle East region may be loosely defined as the countries immediately bordering the Soviet Union, i.e., Turkey and Iran; the Arab countries, including the confrontation states of the Arab–Israeli conflict; Israel; the Persian Gulf states, which again cover Iran and Iraq but also Saudi Arabia, Kuwait, Qatar, and the Emirates; and the Yemens. One might also include Libya, the Sudan and even Somalia as peripheral states of the region, the last two because of their relationship with the Red Sea (on which Ethiopia also borders).

[2] For a discussion of the development of the Soviet fleet and the influence of *Polaris*, see Michael MccGwire, 'The Background to Soviet Naval Developments', *The World Today*, March 1971, pp. 93–103; Michael MccGwire, 'The Evolution of Soviet Naval Policy: 1960-1974', in MccGwire, (ed.), *Soviet Naval Policy: Objectives and Constraints* (New York: Praeger, 1975); John Erickson, *Soviet Military Power* (London: United Services Institute, 1971), pp. 53–60; Geoffrey Jukes, *The Indian Ocean in Soviet Naval Policy*, Adelphi Paper No. 87 (London, 1972); Richard Ackley, 'Sea-Based Strategic Forces: Mid-term Security for an Era of Nuclear Proliferation', (Halifax (Dalhousie Seminar), 1974), pp. 10, 18. For Soviet references, see A. K. Kislov, 'The United States in the Med iterranean: New Realities,' *SShA: Ekonomika, Politika, Ideologia*, April 1972, pp. 32–3; Admiral Gorshkov, 'Navies in War and Peace', *Morskoi sbornik*, No. 3, 1972, p. 20, or in *Pravda*, 28 July 1974, and *Krasnaya zvezda*, 22 March 1974.

[3] The Soviet Union had made a similar effort after Stalin's death but met with little response. Developments in Turkey itself may account for the relative success achieved in the 1960s (see below).

[4] See J. C. Hurewitz, *The Persian Gulf* (New York: Foreign Policy Association, 1974), pp. 44–7; Arthur Davidson Baker III, 'Soviet Major Combatants', *US Naval Institute Proceedings*, Vol. 100, No. 4, 1974, pp. 47–8; Norman Polnar, 'The Soviet Aircraft Carrier', *US Naval Institute Proceedings*, Vol. 100, No. 3, 1974, pp. 145–61. See Commander Thomas A. Brooks, 'Soviet Carrier Strategy', *US Naval Institute Proceedings*, Vol. 100, No. 4, 1974, p. 103; Bradford Dismukes, 'Roles and Missions of Soviet Naval General Purpose Forces in Wartime: Pro SSBN Operations?' (Arlington, Virginia: Center for Naval Analyses, 1974).

[5] There is some controversy among Western observers over the authenticity of Soviet concern regarding the American strategic threat from the Indian Ocean because of the difficulties involved in submarine detection and the variety of possibilities open to the United States for launching positions against the USSR.

[6] John Cooley, 'The Shifting Sands of Arab Communism', *Problems of Communism*, Vol. 24, No. 2, 1975, p. 33; Robert Freedman, 'The Soviet Union and the Communist Parties of the Arab World', unpublished paper (Milwaukee, Wisconsin, 1974), pp. 28–9. For Arab Communist disagreement with the Soviet Union over this, see Kerim Mroue, 'The Arab National Liberation Movement', *World Marxist Review*, Vol. 16, No. 2, 1973, p. 70; Victor Tyagunenko, 'Trends, Motive Forces of the National Liberation Revolution', *Marxist Review*, Vol. 16, No. 6, 1973, p. 124; A. S. Becker and A. D. Horelick, *Soviet Policy in the Middle East* (Santa Monica, Calif.: Rand, 1970), pp. 30–5.

[7] Dina Spechler and Martin Spechler, 'The Soviet Union and the Oil Weapon', in Yaacov Ro'i (ed.), *The limits of Power: The Soviet Union in the Middle East* (London: Croom Helm, forthcoming); A. S. Becker, 'Oil and the Persian Gulf in Soviet Policy, in the 1970s', in M. Confino and S, Shamir (eds.), *The USSR and the Middle East* (Jerusalem: Israel Universities Press, 1973), pp. 174–85; Franklyn D. Holzman, 'Soviet Trade and Aid Policies', in J. C. Hurewitz (ed.), *Soviet–American Rivalry in the Middle East* (New York: Academy of Political Science, 1969), pp. 104–20; Robert Hunter, *The Soviet Dilemma in the Middle East*, Adelphi Papers Nos. 59, 60 (London, 1969).

[8] Becker, *op. cit.*, p. 181. See also Marshall Goldman, *Detente and Dollars: Doing Business With the Soviets* (New York: Basic Books, 1975).

[9] The Soviet Union reportedly began to demand, and receive, such payments in 1973. The financing even of some Syrian acquisitions has been provided primarily by Saudi Arabia but also by Algeria and Abu Dhabi. *New York Times*, 20, 22 October 1973, 4 February 1974; INA (Iraqi News Agency), 26 April 1974; DPA (Deutsche Presse Agentur), 13 April 1974; (Sadat interview); *Le Monde*, 21 December 1973, 31 March–1 April 1974, 18 April 1974; MENA (Middle East News Agency), 22 September and 8 October 1974 (Sadat interviews).

[10] Moscow demanded not only cash payment but also the stationing of Soviet military personnel in Jordan. MENA, 20 June 1977 (Jordanian military spokesman).

[11] Gur Ofer, 'The Economic Burden of Soviet Involvement. in the Middle East', *Soviet Studies*, January 1973, pp. 329–47, and 'Economic Aspects of Soviet Involvement in the Middle East', in Ro'i (ed.), *op. cit.*

[12] The relative success in the 1960s of the Soviet effort to improve relations with Turkey was attributable, at least in part, not only to the changes which took place in Turkey after 1963 but also to developments connected with the Cyprus problem – i.e., Turkey's dissatisfaction with the position of the United States. For factors affecting Soviet–Turkish relations, see A. H. Ulam and R. H. Dekmejian, 'Changing Patterns in Turkish Foreign Policy', *Orbis*, Fall 1967, pp. 772–85.

[13] The Soviet Union did play a role in precipitating the Six-day War by providing reports of Israeli force concentrations on the Israeli–Syrian border. For various analyses of Soviet motivations see, Yaacov Ro'i, *From Encroachment to Involvement: A Documentary Study of Soviet Policy in the Middle East*, 1945–1973 (New York: John Wiley and Sons, 1974), pp. 436–8; Nadav Safran, *From War to War* (New York: Pegasus, 1969), pp. 269–70, 285, 294–5; Arnold Horelick, 'Soviet Policy in the Middle East From 1953–1968', in P. Hammond and S. Alexander, *Political Dynamics in the Middle East* (New York: American Elsevier, 1972), pp. 581–92. The Arab states claim, however, that the Soviet Union also sought to prevent them from actually going to war; Moscow probably neither expected nor welcomed the results of the war, inasmuch as Soviet prestige in the Arab world was negatively affected and the risk of superpower confrontation increased.

[14] For a fuller discussion of such issues, see Galia Golan, *Yom Kippur and After: The Soviet Union and the Middle East Crisis*, (Cambridge: Cambridge University Press, 1977), and 'Syria and the Soviet Union Since the Yom Kippur War', *Orbis*, Vol. 21, No. 4, Winter 1976, pp. 777–802.

[15] See Golan, *ibid.*, and Galia Golan, *The Soviet Union and the PLO*, Adelphi Paper No. 131 (London, 1977).

[16] Although Soviet leaders and literature often speak of applying the principles of detente to the Middle East, mainly as a means of limiting the risks of super-power competition there and, following the October 1973 war, as a means at least of sharing in the developments involving the area, there is little evidence of any Soviet (or American) linkage of the detente issue with that of the Middle East. See Galia Golan, 'The Arab–Israeli Conflict in Soviet–US Relations: Is Detente Relevant?', in Ro'i, ed., *op. cit.* The contentions of Sadat, Gaddafi and others notwithstanding, Soviet behaviour (particularly during the October 1973 war, but also before and after it) strongly suggested that the Kremlin was willing to run certain risks with respect to detente which, it calculated, could be handled and, in time, overcome.

[17] See Jon Glassman, *Arms for the Arabs: The Soviet Union and War in the Middle East* (Baltimore: Johns Hopkins University Press, 1975) and Golan, *Yom Kippur and After*, *op. cit.*

[18] The cease-fire was even explicitly based on Security Council Resolution 242 and called for negotiations – conditions which, until then at least, had been unacceptable to such parties as Syria, Iraq and the PLO. The massive Soviet material assistance to the Arab war effort represented compensatory action designed (unsuccessfully, as it turned out) not only to preserve Moscow's prestige in the region but also to prevent an Arab defeat on a scale which might precipitate a call for Soviet military intervention. For an analysis of Soviet objectives during the war and Arab criticism, see Golan, *Yom Kippur and After, op. cit.*

[19] This limitation is probably due simply to the limited number of Soviet ships available at present and the rate of ship building. At present the Soviet naval presence in the Indian Ocean is drawn from the Far Eastern Fleet. The military value of the Suez Canal, therefore, is not as great as was once thought. See Jukes, *op. cit.*, and D. O. Verall, 'The Soviet Navy in the Indian Ocean' (Halifax (Dalhousie Seminar), 1974), pp. 53–4.

[20] An exception to this is Turkey, the importance of which has not receded.

[21] See Lawrence Whetten, *The Canal War* (Cambridge, Mass.: MIT University Press, 1974), pp. 67–115, 340–61; chapters by P. M. Dadant and Ciro Zoppo in Willard A. Beling, *The Middle East: Quest for an American Policy* (New York: State University of New York Press, 1973), pp. 169–236; Martin Indyk, 'Israel and Egypt in the October 1973 War: The Effects of Political and Military Dependence on Small Powers in Conflict', unpublished paper (Canberra, 1974), pp. 13–14.

[22] For a more detailed analysis of this aspect of Moscow's position, see Golan, *The Soviet Union and the PLO, op. cit.*

[23] For Palestinian accounts of this tactic, see Zuhair Mohsen interviews in *Akhbar al-Yom*, 23 April 1977, and *al-Asubua al-Arabi*, 9 May 1977.

Sources of Soviet Power:
The Military Potential in the 1980s

ANDREW MARSHALL

This paper presents a view of probable major trends in the Soviet military effort in the 1980s. The most plausible developments are described and major alternatives considered. However, shifts in the internal or external context may perturb current and likely trends, and a few such possibilities are also briefly discussed.

Major Trends

Economic and Political Aspects

Current estimates of the size of the Soviet military effort (in terms of the dollar expenditures that would be required to reproduce it in the United States) put it at approximately 40 per cent more than the current American military effort. Estimated rouble expenditures for defence show a remarkably steady 4–5 per cent real growth rate each year for the past decade or more, and some observers estimate figures up to 2 per cent higher. There is no reason to expect that the Soviet effort will fail to grow into the 1980s at essentially the current rates.

Of perhaps more interest for a discussion of future military trends is the burden imposed on the Soviet economy by a defence effort that is estimated officially at 11–13 per cent of GNP. For a number of reasons, many believe that this estimate is too low. Even if it is not, however, the defence burden will almost certainly increase gradually during the 1980s as the rate of growth in the Soviet economy slows.

The significance of underestimating the percentage of GNP going into the military sector and the 4–5 per cent growth rate in defence spending is magnified by this projected continuing decline in the growth rate of the Soviet economy. The underlying causes for the projected decline are related to a slowing in the growth of major factor inputs, such as labour and capital, and

the continued difficulties that the Soviet Union appears to have in improving productivity. Further, declining birth rates during the 1960s will mean a marked drop in new entrants to the labour force, unless there are changes in military conscription, deferment or retention practices. There may also be some special problems in the energy area.

The combined effect of all these factors, if the projections of a slowing in GNP growth rate are accurate and the estimates of defence burden and of defence-spending growth are too low, is to suggest the Soviet military could be taking up about 20 per cent of GNP towards the end of the 1980s. This might be a major problem for the Soviet Union, as well as for the West.

The Soviet Union could respond by reducing her military effort, but it seems more likely that she will want to keep her growth rate more or less where it is now. Since the early and middle 1960s she has gained in power in relation to other nations through steady military investment. This advance has become clear to the United States, to the West generally, to China and, more recently, to Japan, and it may lead to increases in the defence efforts of these countries. The Soviet Union, therefore, just when she might wish to consider slowing down the rate of growth of her military effort, could be faced with the consequences of this general reaction to her past build-up.

The post-Brezhnev succession process will probably start soon, if it has not already begun. In the past, succession in the top leadership has taken time – the transition from an initial period of collective leadership to the eventual domination by a single ruler has taken something like four to five years. During these transitional periods, the military have played an important role in the success of the leadership that has emerged. This factor argues for continued growth in defence expenditures, at least through the mid-1980s; later a new leadership might try to restrain military spending. On the other hand, there may be more effective competition for resources from other sectors after the succession issue is resolved. Also, Brezhnev has been unusually close to the military; the new leadership may be more inclined to separate itself a little once it has established itself and to try to exercise more control over military expenditures.

The situation that is emerging is very complex, and our ability to analyse the economic problems associated with it is limited. We know little about the internal politics of the budget and planning process. In addition, there is a growing secondary economy in the Soviet Union which the central government cannot easily control. The convergence of these many separate trends, and the interaction and cumulative nature of their effects, make it hard to predict with precision what will happen.

Technology
Another major trend in Soviet military developments will be the continued emphasis on science and technology. The Soviet Union has a long-term goal: technological superiority, particularly in the military area. She has a military research and development programme that is very strong and continues to grow rapidly. However, weapon designs have been constrained by a set of policies and circumstances that has stressed the deployment of what is proven and has limited the use of more advanced (but more risky) technology. The Soviet conscript force is drawn from a less skilled population than in the West, which imposes some limitations on the sophistication of the weapons it could both operate and support. Also, there has been an emphasis on producing large numbers of weapons and, consequently, a desire to keep down unit costs. This has been achieved by using standard materials that are more easily fabricated and weapons designed for production using general-purpose machinery. Weapons have also been designed to require limited maintenance in the field by relatively unskilled personnel; large-scale maintenance demands that the equipment be shipped to factories where a permanent work force of skilled personnel can

be concentrated. A different weapons-design philosophy is also detectable and the approach of the Soviet Union to accomplishing particular missions may be different. An example is the tendency to control fighter aircraft from the ground rather than to put all the sensors and avionics needed to allow the pilot to operate independently in the aircraft itself.

In terms of laboratory facilities, the Soviet Union is probably about equivalent to the West overall, but limitations on manpower quality, manufacturing skills and capabilities, and policies demanding low costs per unit, have constrained the use of high technology in deployed weapons. Nevertheless, the last decade or so has seen major technological improvements in Soviet weapons. This trend is likely to continue into the 1980s as large – and still increasing – R&D investments come to fruition. Soviet military R&D may become more revolutionary as high-risk but potentially rewarding programmes are undertaken; the West may be obliged to catch up in areas in which the Soviet Union has been the first to deploy new technology.

The extent to which the Soviet Union will be able to make the shift to wider deployment of high technology in her weapons is an open question. It is true that manpower quality will improve generally, but there will be the off-setting problem of the changing ethnic composition of the 18-year-old cohort. There are also questions about how she will manage weapon-system maintenance in the future. Will more sophisticated designs force her to change her practices, to resort to more diagnosis and repair and to have more highly skilled people doing maintenance at lower echelons? Will increased use of high technology fit into the current way in which she has organized maintenance and other support functions? The Soviet Union will probably have to select a few areas and make major organizational changes to exploit fully the technologies that she is capable of developing.

Power-Projection Missions
In the main, the missions of Soviet forces will probably remain much as they are. The only major shift is likely to be the continued development of capabilities to project power into distant crisis areas. The Soviet Union appears to

have decided to extend her reach in the middle or late 1960s, having concentrated up till then on power projection into peripheral areas. Since that time the formulation of the statements of military missions has changed somewhat to include the protection of Soviet interests and international socialism world-wide, in addition to the defence of the USSR. There have been visible developments, especially in strategic airlift, airborne forces and naval-related forces since the early 1970s; more subtle changes – such as the appearance of training manuals emphasizing the USSR's international role – have also occurred. At the moment the Soviet Union's capabilities for distant combat remain embryonic, but there is likely to be continued growth in her capabilities to get out into the Third World countries and other crisis areas in the world.

Strategic Forces
The Soviet Union is likely to continue the development of her strategic-force posture, subject to whatever limitations are agreed on in SALT, along current lines. Soviet doctrine and strategic thinking regarding strategic nuclear forces are quite different from those of the United States; strategic nuclear warfare is seen as less distinct from other forms of warfare. Although she is labouring under no illusions about the destructiveness of thermo-nuclear weapons, the objective of her strategic-force programmes is to develop a capability to fight, survive and, if possible, win a nuclear war. For the Soviet Union, a credible war-fighting capability is the best possible deterrent. While strategic arms-limitation agreements may have a marginal effect upon programmes, there has been no sign of the kind of agreement that would oblige her to alter her basic strategic doctrine or that would prevent significant strategic force improvements.

These improvements will include an emphasis on counter-force capabilities and on capabilities to attack an enemy's command and control assets. There will be a continued strengthening of Soviet capabilities to function during and after a nuclear war, including a broad programme for the survival of the political and administrative leadership, the industrial work force and the military infrastructure. Another aspect of the broad Soviet view of the strategic balance is that the USSR looks at all the forces that would be involved in a strategic nuclear war (it is significant that the Strategic Rocket Forces and Long Range Aviation include not only weapons with intercontinental range but also forces for peripheral attack). Except for SALT purposes, it is doubtful that the Soviet Union singles out intercontinental forces for separate assessment.

With this in mind, we can make some informed guesses about the areas where Soviet efforts will concentrate in the 1980s. Most of them will be programmes which appear 'defensive' in one sense or another. Capabilities to attack American missiles, and especially American command and control, have already been mentioned. Anti-submarine warfare (ASW) is likely to be another area of emphasis; the Soviet Union will be interested both in protecting her own SSBN and in attacking and destroying opposing SSBN. She will also concentrate on air defence, for she has already made a major effort in this field and the deployment of American cruise missiles can only serve to strengthen this effort. In much the same spirit, she will probably continue her civil defence programme.

A major issue likely to arise in the 1980s when the Soviet Union considers her forces is the increased vulnerability of her silo-based systems, although the rate at which this problem comes upon her will depend on US actions. She has an especially strong commitment – bureaucratic and otherwise – to maintaining the Strategic Rocket Forces as the main element of her strategic forces. It seems unlikely that she will shift a significant number of her forces to sea or increase the size of her long-range air force; therefore, she will seek solutions to the silo vulnerability problem. This might eventually involve either mobile ICBM or a variety of measures to increase the protection of the silo-based systems. It may well be that she will want to develop some form of site defence using ABM systems.

The strategic forces are a natural area for the fullest application of the desire of the Soviet Union to use high technology in weaponry. She will want to continue with the development of a high-quality MIRVed SLBM during the 1980s. There may also be areas where a use will be found for more exotic technology – as in the deployment of high-energy lasers or space-based weapons of one sort or another.

The Soviet level of effort in this area, measured in dollar cost, has been about two and a half times that of the United States. While strategic arms limitation agreements and a somewhat increased American effort may reduce this margin, it seems likely to remain a major area of Soviet military effort. This is especially so given the broad range of programmes on which the Soviet Union is likely to continue work. The more technically-related parts of this effort – that is, the development of new weapon systems – represent rather specialized resources which the Soviet Union would find the hardest to divert to non-defence uses.

Forces for the European Theatre
We can expect a steady, long-term Soviet modernization effort directed against Europe. While a number of new weapons have entered Soviet forces in the European area, there are still several years to run before current modernization of key weapons, such as the newer tanks, the new self-propelled artillery, the BMP infantry combat vehicle, etc., is completed. The Soviet Union has been modernizing fairly rapidly, and it might be some time before the next wave of new systems begins to come into the force, especially ground-force equipment. Tactical aircraft are likely to be a focus for continued modernization. With some of the newer, longer-range aircraft it would be reasonable to expect continued development of avionics and a fuller exploitation of the capabilities of aircraft through changes in training and tactical doctrine (a major constraint may be the way in which maintenance functions have been organized and staffed in the past).

There is likely to be a very strong effort in the area of command and control. The Soviet Union will be trying to make use of computers to enhance her tactical capabilities in theatre warfare, with its emphasis on speed of decision and execution. She will also continue to focus attention on the protection of her command and control networks which, as she uses more computers and increases the flow of information, may become more vulnerable, requiring greater redundancy or other off-setting measures.

There is likely to be a widening gap between the capabilities of Soviet and other Warsaw Pact forces. Eastern Europeans have lagged behind the recent modernization effort of the USSR and,

with their current and prospective economic problems in the 1980s, they are not likely to be able to support a major programme of modernization for increasingly sophisticated forces. This will introduce or exacerbate a number of already emerging logistic – even perhaps tactical – problems arising from the differences between the weapons and capabilities of the units of the Soviet forces and those of Warsaw Pact units. Romania's recent statements add point to this projection.

The Soviet Union's commitment to the ability to conduct nuclear operations in Europe will continue into the 1980s. This commitment has been evident in the continuing preparation of conventional forces to operate in a nuclear environment, the protection of key facilities and installations and the modernization of Soviet nuclear weapons and delivery systems. Conventional forces of the Pact are generally much better equipped than those of NATO to detect radiological and chemical contamination, better protected against its effects, and better able to decontaminate personnel and equipment. Many operational headquarters for Pact forces are hardened with protective shelters and buried antennae to reduce the effects of nuclear attack. Soviet force modernization includes the introduction of new, dual-capable aircraft and the deployment of the SS-20 missile, which represent improvements in the ability to conduct nuclear strikes.

These current trends are very likely to continue in the future and to become more evident as we learn more about the full spectrum of Soviet preparations for nuclear operations. In the past we have often focused our attention too narrowly on the number of Soviet nuclear weapons, rather than on how all the elements of the Soviet military structure would operate during nuclear conflict. The Soviet Union generally follows a different approach, making no distinction between 'theatre' and 'strategic' nuclear weapons and integrating conventional and nuclear forces more explicitly both in analysis and in doctrine.

There will be important naval developments related to the NATO European area. The seas peripheral to the Soviet Union will remain of great importance to her. She will continue to modernize ships and land-based aircraft to control the northern Norwegian, Black and Baltic

Seas. She will probably be alert to, and will respond to, the naval development of all NATO members.

Soviet naval forces are constrained by geography, especially in the Eastern Mediterranean. How can the USSR support, re-provision and re-arm her forces there? To deal with this problem, we can expect her to try to establish Mediterranean facilities and basing rights. The neutralization of Turkey would offer far-reaching advantages to the Soviet Union, because much of her offensive naval power is contained in her land-based naval bomber force. More generally, she can be expected to expand her amphibious and air-assault capacities to secure straits and to support her flanks in operations in the North, on the Central Front and in the Black Sea and Mediterranean.

In time, she will try to extend her naval defence line further to the South, beyond the Norwegian Sea. Further, she can be expected to apply greater pressure on Norway, and perhaps Iceland, to limit the stationing of opposing aircraft or other military capabilities in these countries. Finally, well aware of the importance of the sea lines of communication to Europe, the Soviet Union will continue to try to develop the means to interdict them.

Forces on the Chinese Border and for Use in North-east Asia

Approximately a quarter of Soviet ground forces and tactical air forces are stationed along the Chinese border, and the USSR maintains a major naval force in the Pacific. These forces are unlikely to diminish during the 1980s but they may not grow much, despite long-standing Soviet concerns about China and developing concerns about possibly closer ties between China and the United States or Japan. After the fairly rapid build-up that began in the middle 1960s (and levelled out in the early 1970s), the main effort has been devoted to improving the basic military position through construction of defensive zones and the modernization of equipment, especially for air and naval forces. In addition, the Soviet Union is likely to continue to develop nuclear capabilities against China. This may well involve deployment of the SS-20 and the modernization of the frontal aviation and long-range air force units in the area. There will probably be an emphasis on improved warning

from air-defence systems around key Asian and Pacific installations.

The Baikal–Amur–Magistral railroad, scheduled to be completed by the mid-1980s, will increase the depth of Soviet positions, ease communication problems and permit an increased readiness level of existing forces along the Chinese border. Improved transport should improve the ability of Soviet forces to sustain operations and should make those forces less dependent on prepositioned stocks. The introduction of newer heavy-lift helicopters could also significantly enhance Soviet military capabilities, given the problems of transport in the area.

The Soviet Union will probably increase sea control and power projection forces. Here, as in the NATO area, she is likely to improve her amphibious and air assault capabilities to seize straits and conduct other amphibious operations.

Power-Projection Forces

As noted, the Soviet Union will probably continue to develop her still embryonic military power-projection capabilities. In the 1980s we will see her naval forces deployed around the world, eventually with a credible sea-based tactical air component, with air-cushion vehicles and other upgraded amphibious and naval infantry components, together with a mobile logistics component. She will expand the quasi-naval role of her merchant fleet, which already includes a number of specialized roll-on/roll-off ships with ramps, that allow the use of less developed harbour areas, reinforced decks and other provisions that make them ideal for the transport and rapid loading and unloading of wheeled and tracked vehicles.

The Soviet Union will also try to obtain access to ports and airfields in third-world countries as part of a systematic attempt to create an improved support system for distant operation. In time we may even see her deploy detachments of *Backfire* aircraft, in a manner similar to her current deployment of ASW patrol aircraft, to deny the use of certain sea and air spaces to the West.

She already has a substantial airborne force with specialized equipment. What role these forces may play in the future in the power-projection area is unclear. They seem likely to be used as part of a combined arms philosophy of power projection. For the moment maritime components provide the political leverage and most of the transport for military supplies when needed, but strategic lift aircraft have already played a significant role and can be expected to continue to grow in numbers and to participate more prominently in distant operations in the future.

In general, the Soviet Union is likely to become bolder. This boldness may manifest itself in the actions she takes to provide herself with more direct lines of communication to the Middle East and to Africa. She may first try increasing pressure on adjacent nations to allow the transit or overflight of aircraft. She will probably make greater use of Cuba and other allies to support her clients in local conflicts.

The big question is in what circumstances the Soviet Union would be willing to commit her own forces in combat at a distance. She would now be, and will continue to be, quite vulnerable if it were to come to actual conflict with the United States or the West at some distance. Areas of weakness are, for example, protection of her own battle groups, logistics forces and airlift forces. As mentioned earlier, it seems more likely that Soviet use of these forces will be political in nature – perhaps in an attempt to pre-empt a crisis. This may lead to a strong emphasis on small forces that can be marshalled quickly.

Major Uncertainties
Internal Developments
The major uncertainty would appear to be the severity of the Soviet economic problem and the nature of the competition for resources that may develop in the mid-1980s. The continuing decrease in the rate of growth of Soviet GNP, the increasing defence burden and demographic and energy problems are assumed to be components of a gradually emerging dilemma that the Soviet Union may have to resolve. However, because several negative trends are converging and may reinforce one another, the economic problems of the Soviet Union in the 1980s and 1990s may be much more severe and more resistant to solution than anyone can forecast at the moment. If that were to be so, it could force upon the Soviet Union a major reassessment of her policies. She may have to face the need to divert resources from the military sector to improve the prospects for the long-term economic development of her society. The raising of such fundamental problems of priorities and values would undoubtedly develop into an intense political struggle within the Soviet Union. Clearly, this could lead to a very different course for the 1980s from that predictable at present. We cannot be sure even how severe the problems will be, let alone how the Soviet Union would react to them.

Unexpected Reactions
As the Soviet Union becomes bolder in pushing out into the Third World, and perhaps in involving her own forces more openly, there is the possibility of a major confrontation some time in the 1980s. Even now, a number of nations are reacting to Soviet initiative overseas. A confrontation, perhaps as intense as that of the Cuban missile crisis of 1962, could have a major impact on expected trends. If the situation turned out badly from the Soviet point of view, circumstances could lead to a reassessment of how rapidly she could pursue interventions in the Third World and perhaps of the nature of the forces she would try to develop. Depending on its outcome, such a confrontation might lead to increased military expenditure in the West and in the Soviet Union. On the other hand, a major East European crisis might arise, perhaps like the Hungarian or Czech crises of the past. Should the Soviet Union find herself required to reassert control over an Eastern European country by military force, the effects could be substantial. Her views concerning her need for forces opposite NATO might change, and she might increase them as she did following the Czech crisis. She might begin to doubt the reliability of other Warsaw Pact forces and frustrate the harmonious development of the Warsaw Pact nations.

Changes in the External Environment
There are three possible changes in the external environment that the previous discussion has not adequately reflected. The first of these is the emergence of regional powers which, during the course of the 1980s, will develop significant military capabilities. These regional developments may make the intervention of the Soviet Union outside her borders more likely and may increase the need for visible power-projection

capabilities to offset this somewhat more hostile environment.

A second, though related, development is the wider distribution of sophisticated weapons in the Third World. Trends in military technology generally have been in the direction of giving smaller units significantly more fire-power. This may make both intervention and the general use of military force somewhat more difficult or risky.

A third and extremely unpredictable factor is the future Japanese defence effort. Japan has one of the most powerful and productive economies in the world, but she has had very limited and defensive military forces. Recently Japan has become increasingly concerned about the development of Soviet military strength in the Far East and has taken more notice of specific Soviet force developments and exercises. She might wish to maintain her current situation, keeping her defensive forces very limited, but if she should decide that that was unwise in the light of Soviet activity, she could develop large and very capable military forces. Japan might also play a critical role in the future development of China's military forces, given her strong technological base. Any major shift in Japan's policy with respect to her defence effort would soon alter significantly the military situation in the Far East. Soviet naval forces in particular would no longer appear adequate, and access to and from the Sea of Japan would seem less assured. The technological level of the military competition in that region could be revolutionized.

Conclusion

Projections for the 1980s are, in large part, a continuation of current trends and momentum. This seems reasonable in view of the rather predictable nature of developments in the Soviet Union up till now, but predictions could well be upset by major perturbations in the domestic or international environment. These might include the severity of a confluence of problems of demography, economic productivity and investment, and their interaction with an already massive allocation of resources to defence. External developments quite independent of the actions of the Soviet Union might also upset current trends, as would any substantial Western challenge to Soviet initiatives and policies.

In the absence of such major and inherently unpredictable stimuli, we can expect to see a Soviet military force of increasing sophistication and strength but of a size comparable with that of today. The higher costs of acquiring, operating and supporting that technologically more advanced force may lead to organizational and manpower adjustments, but the composition of military force will remain much as it is today, except for the continuing emergence of power-projection forces.

Sources of Soviet Power:
Economy, Population, Resources

GEORGES SOKOLOFF

In 1980 the Soviet Union will generate 3,000 million kw-hr of electricity; her mechanical industries will produce, in volume terms, five times as much as their American rivals; the abundance of goods and the reasonable behaviour of the consumers will have removed any consumption difficulties; thanks to their own demographic dynamism, as well as the seductive power of the Soviet economic model for third-world countries, socialist people will constitute a very large majority of the world's population. Capitalism will thus be beaten without bloodshed.

These prophecies, advanced by the veteran Communist economist Strumilin,[1] are more than just an anecdote. They are a reminder of an important evolution in opinion which occurred in the USSR twenty years ago about the best means for her to dominate the world. It was no longer a question of aiming to triumph by the shining light of revolutionary ideals, or merely by the intimidating power of military-industrial capacity, but by developing a central position in the world economy. This challenge to the West in the realm of non-military power would not be a totally free choice. Once accomplished, it would enable the Soviet Union to envisage intervention in world affairs with a range of means much more flexible than naked military pressure.

Today this idea must itself be re-examined. Work undertaken in the West on the economic future of the USSR gives a better impression of the basis of her power.[2] Although the programme for the construction of Communism has not been officially abandoned by the Party, this Western work reaches much the same conclusions on many points as the predictions of the Soviet planners themselves. In fact, taking into account her present position and the unencouraging prospects opened up by a prematurely slowed growth, the USSR does not, and probably will not, have the means to become an economic super-power.

The Present State of the Soviet Economy

Using estimates which, in the last analysis, satisfy the demands of the expert least as well as distorting the testimony of Soviet economic realities, the 1976 gross national product (GNP) was approximately $710 billion.[3] This figure undoubtedly classifies the Soviet Union as the second economic power in the world, a classification which is confirmed by several other indicators. The total labour force is, at present, over 140 million, of which more than 50 million are employed in industry and construction and 10 million have completed courses of higher education. While spending considerable efforts to develop her resources – to the point of having become the world's most important producer of several – the Soviet Union has notably developed her processing industry (92 per cent of industrial outlays) and has devoted an increasing proportion of her industrial investments (one-third in 1976) both to the mechanical and the chemical sectors.

In fact, however, the USSR remains a semi-developed economy. Dividing the GNP by population (GNP per capita = $2,760: nineteenth in Europe), by work force or by surface area gives a better indication of the low standard of living and productivity of labour and the difficulties associated with the efficient exploitation of the land. In the richest zones the products on offer to the consumer are of 'utilitarian' types; elsewhere serious shortages, especially after years with bad harvests, are the rule. The structure of foreign trade with the West recalls that of a developing country. This impression is confirmed by the rapid rise of the foreign debt in convertible currencies since the leadership decided to open up the economy to mitigate the qualitative and quantitative inadequacies of her existing capital stock.

To complete this evaluation, and partly to explain it, it is necessary to take into account the drain on national resources represented by the search for military parity with the United States, whose GNP has been consistently double that of the Soviet Union. This drain on resources represents about one-eighth of the Soviet GNP. To indicate more clearly what such a rate means, military stocks represent about one-third of the mechanical products going to final demand,[4] a serious handicap for the weakest element of Soviet investment capacity – machines and equipment. There is also the impact (on consumption) of maintaining an army of 4 million men as well as spending the lion's share of total research and development funds on defence; the services use an important proportion of the intermediary products (one-fifth of metallurgic products, one-sixth of chemical products and of energy resources) and of the Soviet factors of production. And all this is even more serious as, from the qualitative point of view, the services absorb what is best in the country, whether it be men, machines or materials.[5]

A Fragmented Economic Power
The sources of non-military power available to the Soviet Union are not the products of her economic weight in the world, for this would mean that all Soviet decisions concerning domestic, economic or foreign-trade policy would have international repercussions, usable by the USSR to affirm her hold on her international environment. This is patently not the case. In fact, such power as she has seems more like a collection of trumps, separately identifiable but of uneven value in the regions where the USSR strives to act.

Within COMECON she mainly uses the vastness of her mineral resources and basic industrial products[6] as a means of control. Similarly, the comparatively enormous capacity of the Soviet market for her COMECON partners gives the USSR the option of influencing their choice of specialization.[7] With regard to the Third World, the Soviet Union can also use her powers as buyer and seller, although for different groups of products. We know that the volume of Soviet aid to the Third World is not very large, but it is prominent because it is concentrated in few countries and on conspicuous public-sector industrial projects. The Soviet Union has thus been able to contribute visibly towards the development of heavy industry in India and Egypt, towards Syrian and Iraqi industries and towards the extraction of Afghan and Iranian natural gas.[8] In addition to undertaking to buy back a proportion of the production initiated, she also buys large quantities of certain raw materials (Malaysian rubber, Bolivian tin, Moroccan phosphates and 'tropical' foods).

There were some in the West who feared that the development of East–West trade would lead to a dependence on Soviet supplies analogous to that in Eastern Europe. Even taking into account isolated cases – such as the relative importance for Italy of Soviet gas supplies – observations tend to lead to opposite conclusions. One-eighth of new Soviet investment in machinery depends on Western supplies. Yet this dependency can be turned to good effect, especially when the West's economic sluggishness makes export markets for her capital-goods industries more scarce and slows down her banking activities. The unequal conditions of access to her markets can be used by the USSR, even when she is in no way responsible for these inequalities, to create conflicts of interest between the Western countries. We therefore see her trying to profit from the crisis in her relations with the United States by turning towards Western Europe, even encouraging it to become an independent political entity.[9] Her position as COMECON's largest borrower (with a total debt of approximately $50 billion at the end of 1977) gives the Soviet Union, as it does to all debtors, a certain hold over the Western financial system. Finally, her purchases of Western capital goods have placed her in a position of strength in certain well defined areas: for example, through the establishment of a large naval freight capacity and the export of fertilizers.

The Use of Economic 'Trumps'
The fragmentary, unequal and sometimes paradoxical nature of these sources of economic power draw particular attention to the more or less judicious use that is made of them. In this context there are two main lines of thought.

According to the first – which is the older and more often used – the Soviet Union has used her trumps in accepting, on occasions, an economic loss to prevent a greater political loss. This is how the Soviet acceptance of the pricing policy within COMECON, in the name of the 'Bucharest Principle', is interpreted.[10] (The 'Bucharest Principle', or pricing policy, derives from the Ninth COMECON Council Session of June 1958, at which the Soviet Union agreed not to take advantage of world price fluctuations in selling raw materials to East European countries. For many years, therefore, she has been selling materials to these countries at prices below those of the world market in order to gain some political capital.) The advantageous credit conditions offered by the USSR to developing countries are also interpreted in this way, as are certain aspects of Soviet commercial policy towards the West – especially the 'political bonus' given to France to the detriment of the Federal Republic of Germany in the second half of the 1960s. This is a fundamental constant of the economic policy of the USSR, for she is better equipped than free-market societies to carry out a cost/benefit analysis giving priority to political criteria.[11] In any case, charges of 'political dumping' seem to stem from the feeling that the USSR's economic trumps, bargained at their real price, would not have been sufficiently attractive to secure the political interests of the countries concerned.

The second line of thought, which conflicts with the first, argues that the Soviet Union desires to make her trump cards economically profitable. This was given concrete form by the adoption in 1975 of new guidelines for determining prices within COMECON which were definitely more favourable to the development of Soviet terms of trade. It can also be seen in the modification of credit terms to the Third World (once $2\frac{1}{2}$–3 per cent over twelve years but, since 1966, for certain undertakings, higher interest rates and shorter terms – five to ten years, with a first payment of 10–15 per cent). As to the criteria used to choose between Western suppliers, the Soviet Union always clearly prefers technological capacity, financial strength and stable labour relations. Following a cost/benefit analysis, one would tend to explain this evolution by a marked raising of the marginal cost of economic resources in the USSR, which has tended to increase considerably the opportunity cost of using them for 'political' considerations. Any analysis of the Soviet prospects for economic growth in the 1980s shows that there will be an unprecedented growth in the marginal cost of resources.

The Conditions of Economic Growth in the 1980s

Mr Brezhnev, Admiral Turner and other experts of all nationalities have reached an astonishing consensus about the future productive resource dynamics of the USSR. This is even somewhat worrying when one realizes that one is dealing with medium- to long-term economic projections in a country noted for its tradition of secrecy.

An analysis of the USSR's demographic prospects, especially well studied by M. Feshbach,[12] provides one of the cornerstones for these projections. This analysis has a double claim to usefulness. On the one hand, a large population is one of the distinguishing features of a great power. The Soviet population will increase by about the same number – 25 million – between 1980 and 1990 as it did in the previous decade, but the proportion of Slavs will decrease, due to the faster growth of the Central Asian populations. And the fall in the birth rate of the 1960s will have particularly strong repercussions on the Soviet population of working age. One would expect this part of the population to grow at no more than 0.5 per cent per year during the 1980s as against 1.8 per cent since the beginning of the 1970s. The fact that most of the expected growth will be in Central Asia complicates matters, in as much as this region tends to be less developed, and its population, for sociological reasons, does not seem to wish to migrate to the industrial zones. The global economic impact of this demographic trend must certainly not be exaggerated. According to the elasticities most often used to calculate the USSR's aggregate production functions, a variation of 1 per cent in the number of hours worked (which can be a different parameter to the population of working age) leads to a change of 0.6–0.7 per cent in GNP. Nevertheless, if the growth of the latter were to be cut by only 1 per cent, because of the relative scarcity of available labour, it would be a cause for serious concern for the Soviet leadership.

It is even more alarming since the main source of Soviet growth – the increase in capital stock –

is itself causing serious problems. In the USSR, the capital stock must increase by about 3 per cent to obtain a 1 per cent growth in GNP. Under these conditions only a truly enormous investment effort could compensate for the loss of growth due to the relative scarcity of labour. Such an effort does not appear feasible. First it will not be possible to increase the total rate of accumulation without further endangering the prospects for consumption. Second – although this hypothesis is open to discussion – it will not be possible to achieve large-scale substitution of productive capital-goods production for that of military equipment. Third, the experience of recent years has shown that increases in the rate of investment, notably in modern industries, is accompanied by large increases in convertible currency debts. Furthermore, there is the problem posed by the availability of raw materials. Most of these are still abundant, but their location, very far from the main centres of economic activity, considerably increases their cost.

The Military Burden

These considerations explain why Central Intelligence Agency (CIA) analysts[13] and other Western experts[14] estimate an average annual growth of total inputs to the Soviet economy of the order of 2½–3 per cent during the 1980s. But as already noted, this projection is partially dependent on the hypothesis advanced for determining future trends in military hardware spending.

The CIA assumes that the future growth rate of military spending in the Soviet Union will be set at 4.5 per cent per annum, that is, at a higher rate than the growth in GNP. It is true that many analyses have shown that 'too great' a reduction in the growth of armaments (below 2 per cent per annum) would benefit neither the consumer nor the Soviet growth rate,[15] because the resulting excess growth would be absorbed by the additional investment needed to maintain a very high rate of growth of the capital stock. But all studies stress that the maintenance of a high growth rate of military spending would seriously compromise the Soviet Union's economic outlook.

Why do Western projections associate a small increase in the input to the economy with a Soviet GNP growth rate hardly greater than 3 per cent per annum? This assumes a very small contribution by productivity to total growth.

Productivity growth has regularly declined in the USSR, to the point of actually being negative between 1971 and 1975. This decline is explained partly by the exhaustion of the traditional productivity gains (especially intersectorial transfers of productive factors), partly by the particularly violent impact on growth in recent years of the 1975 harvest failure and, more important, partly by the maintenance of a demobilizing economic system. Such conservatism is damaging to itself because, at the macrostructural level, the authorities apparently wish to have a more even-handed economic policy, especially as regards the consumer, the agricultural world and the country's innovative capacity. But the authorities also intend to exert a forceful control over the effects of this policy. The degree of centralization of each decision remains very great and nothing is being done to replace the rigid rules of an administered economy with a real economic mechanism. As a result, good intentions do not, in practice, work the necessary changes.

Reforms could change this situation profoundly and, in particular, could help to loosen the constraints which burden the resources of the Soviet Union. From what we know of the lack of intensity of work and the totally artificial nature of full employment in the USSR, we can be sure that the 150 million workers she will have, on average, in the 1980s will be, according to Western norms, an excessive work force. Similarly, capital resources would appear less stretched if there could be some reduction in those innumerable wastages of means and time which at present are part of each stage of the investment cycle.[16]

The self-evident necessity for these reforms does not mean, however, that they will be adopted. Recent trends in Soviet pricing policy do not indicate a will to adjust to market relationships.[17] The attempt by Professor Valovozh to revive a discussion about reform, based on a sharp critique of the present system,[18] produced no response. Basically, the impression remains that the present *modus vivendi* has satisfied not only the business managers and the bureaucratic process, but the population itself as well. The latter has been able to accommodate itself to a formalist regime of 'natural incentives' by which the rate of growth of nominal incomes has remained greater than that of the 'official' consumption fund, in as much as the resurgence of black-market activities, tolerated by the authorities, has enabled it to use its excess roubles according to its wishes.

The permanence of a heavy military burden and of a rigid economic system naturally remain working hypotheses. Modifying these hypotheses, we could usefully build alternative scenarios of future conditions for Soviet economic growth. The realism of such scenarios could be based on one of the rare certainties we have about the political future of the country: the reign of Mr Brezhnev is drawing to a close. As all preceding Soviet leaders since the Revolution, he will probably be criticized for his 'subjectivism'.[19] Such criticism could embrace an excessive commitment to the West and the lack of internal economic reforms, in that Soviet dependence on the West's industrial enterprises appears to be the ransom that must be paid by a planning system which is incapable of giving the USSR an original development programme.

Nonetheless, there are additional reasons which make real changes improbable. The internal debates, instead of producing alternative policies, may simply further divide the Politburo into 'reformers', 'hawks' and 'centrists'. In this case, 'wait and see' policies would probably be implemented. Furthermore, if the pressure that is being exerted on the USSR by the present American Administration were to continue, it would deprive the holders of such liberal ideas as exist of the atmosphere of security they will need for some time if they are to consolidate themselves. Finally, 'pessimistic' hypotheses appear most compatible with the ways in which the USSR might be led to use her future power.

Future Sources of Economic Power
One point emerges clearly from the previous analysis. In the 1980s the Soviet Union will not be able to appear to be an economic super-power even if the state of affairs in the West were not to improve. On the contrary, the development gap between the USSR and the main Western powers will stabilize, leaving the USSR at an intermediate level. This situation will mean that the consumption volume in the USSR will not be able to grow at a rate greater than 2.5 per cent per annum.

As at present, the Soviet Union will then only have a series of trumps and not a more complete form of power. However, as some of these trumps represent non-reproductive resources, and as their value depends on variations in the international economic and political situation, their structure is liable to change. Hence gold could become a real instrument of power for the Soviet Union, especially if the political situation in South Africa were to deteriorate sharply.[20] Siberian resources of non-ferrous metals, timber, coal and natural gas will represent, despite the cost of extraction, a supply of growing interest, especially for countries such as Japan. We can also expect an increased role for certain Soviet products or services: an increase in maritime freight capacity; increased interest on the part of certain third-world countries (because of their unemployment problems) in the labour-intensive technologies offered by the USSR; and an increase in Soviet export capacity in products resulting from the compensation agreements negotiated with the West (natural gas, wood pulp, basic chemical products and non-ferrous metals).

If the importance of certain trumps increases, that of others will decrease sharply. This is the case with oil. The problem of oil has been given great prominence by the CIA reports published in 1977, but its seriousness was already apparent from a reading of Soviet sources: there were warnings by the previous Minister for the petroleum industry, V. Shashin, in May 1976,[21] recently confirmed by his successor, N. Mal'cev;[22] the weaknesses of geological prospecting were denounced by F. Salmanov;[23] and there was confirmation by three experts from the petroleum industry[24] of the swift increase in water content and extraction costs between now and 1980. Predictions are difficult but the best that can be expected is that in 1985 the USSR will produce about 630 million tonnes and will be able to export a maximum of 30 million tonnes. Certainly the Soviet Union's domestic needs will still be met, but the general restructuring of the different energy components which will then be necessary would probably weigh heavily on the East European economies, whose petroleum deficit could reach 150 million tonnes in 1985.[25] Even as a supplier of alternative energy sources, and with her importance as a market, the USSR would then undoubtedly lose a part of her physical hold over her COMECON partners.

Problems of Profitability

Not only will the nature of her trumps change but the Soviet Union will probably wish to play them differently. 'Political' considerations would still guide certain decisions. For example, the USSR's socialist partners will pay for their supplies at world prices but not in convertible currencies, and certain developing countries will continue to benefit from aid under favourable conditions as a reward for becoming members of COMECON. However, in general, the USSR will probably seek to maximize the economic profitability of resources which will be costing her more and more to extract.

It is clear that any increased political insecurity in those parts of the world which sell the same resources as the Soviet Union can only serve her economic interests. South African gold, platinum and diamonds are a case in point, as is copper from Africa (Zambia, Zaire) and from Latin America (Chile, Peru). If growth of Soviet activity in the Southern Hemisphere seems probable, it is not only because this region of the world contains resources which are competing with those of the USSR. The opening of new markets for her heavy industries and her ability to control sea lanes are conditions for increasing the value of her freight services. Also, when the USSR tries to compensate for her loss of petroleum power by seeking outside contributions from Iran, Iraq and the Middle East in general, these areas will more than ever be the main targets of Soviet foreign policy.

Evidently these predictions carry the seeds of numerous sources of friction with the West, and it is appropriate to ask if the future 'reciprocal advantages' of detente and of East–West co-operation will be sufficient to balance these damaging developments. From this point of view, there is no doubt that the Soviet Union's need for investment goods will continue, even if only because the role of new investment as a factor of domestic growth will be more important than ever to her.

On the other hand, there are numerous uncertainties with regard to the USSR's capacity to balance her 'industrializing imports'. Future demand in Western markets is still unpredictable. The conditions for putting into effect compensa-

tion accords might be more difficult than expected.[26] Although a more favourable trend in the USSR's cereal production after 1985 is feasible, it is also likely that petrol will become more expensive and no longer a source of convertible currencies. Nor is it certain that the imbalances in the USSR's current account can be financed in an orderly way. Cheap Western credits with public backing will probably become more scarce. The banks' base rates are increasing once again. Consequently, the USSR may well limit her imports to proportions which Western bankers and exporters have recently experienced. It is already apparent that the Western world is unconvinced by the Soviet message that detente and co-operation are a priority compared with which the USSR's actions in the Third World are relatively unimportant.

The number of risks and hazards that the future world holds for the USSR justify the hypotheses we have adopted about future trends. They explain why she keeps 'in reserve' at least part of her economic system, allowing her, should the occasion arise, to make political use of certain sources of economic power – as opposed to needing to make them profitable. They explain, particularly, the maintenance of an enormous defence effort as a means of intimidating the West, as a police force within the socialist camp and as a support for intervention – through the export of arms – in the Third World.

Conclusion

The Soviet Union continues to need, in order to maintain her power abroad, the very conditions which limit her domestic growth. Furthermore, it is likely that this need is being emphasized by the Soviet pressure groups that profit most from it. Whatever the case it is evidently very difficult for the USSR to tear herself away from a form of power the exigencies of which – the possible recourse to force and to politically motivated dumping – limit her internal development, to enable her to reach a level at which her weight in international affairs would be based essentially on the wealth of her economy.

That the Soviet Union faces grave economic problems in the 1980s seems fairly certain. What is far less certain is what, if anything, she can or will do to mitigate her economic difficulties. Her self-imposed limits to action define quite narrowly her range of alternatives. Perhaps the central question is whether she will be forced to moderate her foreign and internal policy in order to continue to secure the economic benefits of detente. And that, of course, will depend upon the price demanded by the West. We can see now that demands for moderation over human rights are unlikely to influence Moscow, for movement in a liberal direction would seem to be too high a price to pay for some rather marginal economic benefits. Nevertheless, Soviet economic vulnerability undoubtedly gives the West a degree of leverage which can be used to moderate Soviet behaviour – particularly in those areas of the world which are of less than central importance for Soviet security. Whether the West can concert economic policy so as to make something of that potential for leverage remains to be seen.

NOTES

[1] S. Strumilin, 'Nash mir cherez 20 let', Moscow, 1964.

[2] See, in particular, 'Soviet Economy in a New Perspective', a compendium of papers submitted to the Joint Economic Committee of the US Congress, Washington, October 1976. This source is cited below as 'JEC, 1976'.

[3] According to the World Bank's estimates. For a discussion of the different methods of evaluating the USSR's GNP in dollars, see G. Sokoloff and G. Wild, 'Un bilan des comparaisons Est–Ouest de niveaux de développement', *Economies et Sociétés*, Cahiers G, No. 35, 1978.

[4] The calculations of S. Cohn ('Estimation of Military Durables Procurement Expenditures from Machinery Production and Sales Data', Stanford Research Institute, June 1977) give the same results on this as my estimates.

[5] 'Allocation of Resources in the Soviet Union and China, 1977. Hearings before the Subcommittee on Priorities and Economy in Government of Joint Economic Committee. . . .', Part 3, p. 19.

[6] See the table published for 1976 in *East–West Markets*, 10 July 1978, Vol. 6, No. 14, p. 8.

[7] See G. Sokoloff, 'Deux stratégies d'intégration internationale: socialisme et capitalisme', *Economie Appliquée*, Vol. XXIV, No. 4, 1971, pp. 559–603.

[8] O. Cooper, 'Soviet Economic Aid to the Third World', JEC, 1976, pp. 189–96.

[9] Results of the meeting between the representatives of the Fondation Nationale des Sciences Politiques (Paris) and of the IMEMO in Moscow, 19–22 June 1978.

[10] P. Marer, 'Has Eastern Europe become a Liability for the Soviet Union ? The Economic Aspect', Conference on the International Politics of Eastern Europe, Columbia University, March 1975.

[11] See A. Nove, *The Soviet Economic System* (London: Allen and Unwin, 1977), chap. XIV.

[12] M. Fesbach and S. Rapawy, 'Soviet Population and Manpower Trends and Policies', JEC, 1976, pp. 113–54.

[13] 'Soviet Economic Problems and Prospects', July 1977.

[14] H. Hunter, M. Earle and R. Foster, 'Assessment of Alternative Long Range Soviet Growth Strategies', JEC, 1976, pp. 197–215; G. Wild, 'L'URSS en 1985 – Elements de réflexion', *Economies et Sociétés*, Cahiers G, No. 36 (to be published).

[15] L. Calmfors and J. Rylander, 'Economic Restrictions on Soviet Defense Expenditure – A Model Approach'; H. Bergendorff and P. Strangert, 'Projections of Soviet Economic Growth and Defense Spending', JEC, 1976, pp. 377–430.

[16] V. Krasovskizh, 'Investicionnyzh process i ego sovershenstvovanie', *Eko* (Novosibirsk), 1975, No. 1, pp. 16–31.

[17] M. Bornstein, 'Soviet Price Policy in the 1970s', JEC, 1976, pp. 17–66.

[18] D. Valovozh, 'Sovershenstvuzha khozzhazhstvennyzh mekhanizm', *Pravda*, 10, 11, 12 November 1977.

[19] See G. Sokoloff, *L'Economie obéissante – Décisions politiques et Vie économique en URSS* (Paris: 1976).

[20] S. Schoppe, 'Myth and Reality of the Soviet Gold Policy', *Intereconomics* 1, 2, 1978 (Hamburg: HWWA – Institut für Wirtschaftsforschung).

[21] V. Shashin, 'Gorizonty neftzhanozh industrii', *Ekonomiceskazha gazeta*, No. 22, 1976, p. 4.)

[22] N. Mal'cev, 'V tret'em godu pzhatiletki – novye ruberzhy', *Neftzhanoe khozhazhstvo* (Moscow), 1978, No. 4, pp. 3, 9.

[23] F. Salmanov, 'Opirazhas' na prognozy', *Pravda*, 19 February 1976.

[24] V. Grazhfer, S. Levin and L. Kolosova, 'Vazhnoe napravlenie ekonomicheskozh raboty v otrasli', *Neftzhanoe khozhazhstvo*, 1977, No. 7, pp. 5–8.

[25] Groupe d'Etudes Prospectives Internationales, 'Situation et perspectives du bilan énergétique de l'URSS et de l'Est européan', *Le Courrier des Pays de l'Est*, March 1978, No. 216, Paris, La Documentation Française.

[26] L. Brainard, 'Financing Soviet Capital Needs in the 1980s', in *Prospects for Soviet Growth in the Eighties and the Role of Foreign Trade* (Brussels: Economic Affairs Directorate, NATO).

Recruitment Patterns for the Leadership

JOHN ERICKSON

Today both the Soviet and the non-Soviet world have a common interest in one pressing problem which involves not so much the vagaries of detente as the eventual resolution of the Kremlin succession issue, and it is here that the pattern of recruitment to the leadership may be most visible. The succession problem has plagued successive Soviet regimes, but for all the labyrinthine Muscovite intrigue and palace plots, certain rules have emerged – arbitrary affairs, to be sure, but something of a guide as to how things might be conducted.

What stands out in the present circumstances – as if in deliberate defiance of the rules – is the reluctance (or the refusal) of Brezhnev publicly to indicate his successor: Stalin stood out most prominently as a successor to Lenin; Stalin himself took the opportunity provided by the 19th Congress to give Malenkov that prominence which showed him off as heir-apparent; Khrushchev allowed himself the luxury of several successors, including Kirichenko and Kozlov, but it was the last 'crown prince', Brezhnev, who acted to displace his master. Perhaps Leonid Brezhnev has not forgotten the ambitions of 'crown princes': certainly he deliberately ignored the occasion of the 25th Party Congress (February 1976) to show off any new leader, from which one can only assume that Brezhnev intends to carry on as long as he is able – and it can be speculated that retirement (in a special Soviet sense) is ruled out, since Brezhnev could not relinquish his post as General Secretary and still retain a measure of real influence over Soviet policy. To institutionalize such an innovation would mean significant change at the top, which the Politburo and the Central Committee would not be willing to endorse, for it could set an embarrassing precedent. Thus we can assume that the present succession crisis (or process) in the USSR is not quite following the rules and will, therefore, exhibit some unique characteristics. Much depends, of course, on the state of Brezhnev's health: barring total collapse, there is, ironically, a reason why certain elements in the Politburo and the Party may keep Brezhnev propped up in office, for it would enable these groups not only to consolidate their own power but also to expand their own constituencies.

Any real contender for power must control the Party organization, which is Kirilenko's present forte (and was Brezhnev's own path to power over Khrushchev). It is this which at once limits the list of possible contenders, especially among the younger men, for the key post of General Secretary of the Party. Under present circumstances it is almost inconceivable – given the ramifications of the nationalities problem – that a non-Russian would be acceptable: in addition to increased Party and KGB control of the nationalities, the key posts of Second Secretaries in the Union Republic Central Committees are being steadily 'russified', thus checking any non-Russian predominance.[1] (The Politburo will no doubt continue to be weighted in favour of Russians in a 3:1 ratio.)

The first Secretaries of the Republic and Regional (*Obkom*) Party Committees are the real king-makers in the Soviet system. The Regional Secretaries were of enormous significance in Stalin's rise to power, and they helped Khrushchev on his way to the top (they also speeded his downfall in 1964, largely because of the havoc his policies caused amongst their ranks). Having established some two-thirds of the present Regional Secretaries in office,[2] Brezhnev can claim to have a secure and loyal power base here, even if there is some limited cause for dissatisfaction in the lower rate of replacement of cadres practised under Brezhnev – a new man might promote changes in the Party leadership as a whole and thus open up new opportunities. It is also worth noting (also in the context of Brezhnev's general line of recruitment to the Party) that these Regional Secretaries have largely an *industrial* background (as opposed to Khrushchev's stress on agriculture).

Thus, we come to see in the succession problem not merely a nominal change in names and men, but a whole displacement in the system. There are, of course, coalitions of interests and combinations of purpose which impinge on the entire scene – the main division within the ruling group being between those who embrace technocratic solutions and others who see the primacy of Party control as the main issue, with a persistent struggle taking place over these issues at a level just below the Politburo and the Secretariat.

Barring the immediate collapse of his health, Brezhnev can probably count on as many men anxious for him to stay – for the short-term, at least – as would have him go: in terms of actual control of the Party organization, that *sine qua non*, Kirilenko has obvious advantages but age conspires against him. A short-term caretaker government could combine Kirilenko with Suslov to hold the line, but the succession problem would still remain. Among the younger men there is no one of obvious pre-eminence, so that we might otherwise predict another version of collective leadership after Brezhnev, allowing time for a younger man to force his way through, mobilize the First Secretaries, re-order the 'cadres policy' in his own favour and possibly deflect a rival in the direction of the premiership. If anything, he would probably open the Politburo to some greater institutional/bureaucratic representation – the present arrangement in Party–State terms is 8:7 (8 for the Party) – if only because he would need this institutional support. In any event, it would not be easy to reverse the institutional promotions made by Brezhnev in 1973.

We can now reappraise some of the rules pertaining to the organization of the top leadership in the Soviet Union. It would appear that none can escape the requirement to control the Party organization or to develop his own 'cadres policy' – with respect to the First Secretaries in particular. Nor can he reverse the wider institutional representation on the Politburo initiated by Brezhnev – indeed, he may well expand this process, thus creating a special 'bailiwick' of his own. It would also seem that an established rule both now and for the future is that the General Secretary should gather to himself most significant offices. Policy will also be generally constrained by the present institutional arrangements and by the same need to compromise, to balance the coalitions represented within the Politburo itself, the Central Committee and the bureaucracies.

The Role of the Military

It goes without saying that one of the singular features of the Brezhnev regime has been its special relationship with the military. The present convolutions associated with the succession problem cannot be divorced from changes in the Soviet High Command, which has been experiencing its own succession problem and generation gap. In general, with the death of Marshal Grechko a whole generation of Soviet military experience and expertise came to an end; while the appointment of Ustinov meant that there need be no flurry within the Politburo itself, that a certain managerial element had been introduced formally at the highest level and that this man – in view of his age – need not necessarily be binding for too long on any successor regime. Equally (and here the speed of the appointment is significant) the choice may well have represented Brezhnev's partiality for having men about him with whom he was familiar, not unlike Grechko himself. Now aged 70, Ustinov can carry on for some time and could finally be elevated to some honorific position, not excluding the premiership, in any reshuffle, but the eventual departure of Ustinov – the so-called civilian (which, in fact, he is not)[3] – will cause problems for the selection of a future 'civilian' Defence Minister. In general, it appears that this is not a precedent for the severing of the institutional link between the military and the military-industrial complex by 'civilizing' the leadership of the Defence Ministry: the crucial change would be a dissolution of the Politburo majority presently in favour of the massive Soviet arms programme and proponent of an approach to arms-limitation talks which amounts to little more than an attempt to hobble the enemy.

Three factors have generally affected (and will continue to affect) the higher levels of the Soviet military command: the impact of the 'military-technical revolution', the expansion of the Soviet armed forces over the past decade and the military implications of overall Soviet policies – including detente – both for the present and for the future. Of all these, the growing sophistication of weaponry and the impact of technology have worked most specifically to force a certain rejuvenation – younger officers with technical backgrounds – on the senior command levels, a process counter-balanced by an opposite tendency encouraged by the political leadership (and best exemplified in the Grechko–Brezhnev relationship) to retain military men known to them and whose style is very familiar. The result has been not only to sustain senior officers who are over-age but also to keep these same officers in particular posts for lengthy periods of time; Deputy Defence Ministers (arms and services commanders) have been in office for a time-span ranging between ten and seven years, and Admiral of the Fleet of the Soviet Union Gorshkov has outdone all with his astonishing tenure (more than twenty-two years) as naval C-in-C and as a Deputy Defence Minister. The Soviet High Command thus emerges with an average age of 63, and its general profile bears a curious similarity to that of the political leadership – there is a group of younger men waiting and working to break into key positions (see table, pp. 37–38).

What do we mean by 'High Command' and 'key positions'? In round numerical terms, there are about fifty positions which can be said to compose the 'High Command' (either by rank or by importance of the post itself). While those who hold key positions include the Minister of Defence, the First Deputy and Deputy Defence Ministers, the Chief of the General Staff of the Soviet Armed Forces and operational arms commanders (six of them, including one in charge of Civil Defence), the group of senior officers within the 'High Command' group can be broadened to take in the commanders of Groups of Forces abroad and of fleets and flotillas and military districts – to which must be added all first deputy commanders, not to mention chiefs of political administrations. The High Command is filled from a pool of some 350–400 officers (first deputy commanders and chiefs of staff), a figure which could be somewhat expanded by counting in the senior level of the military-educational system.

The General Staff will probably increase in importance in the coming decade, exercising its command and operational functions and its military–managerial competence. Its rejuvenation, carried out by Kulikov (now C-in-C, Warsaw Pact), has resulted in the dropping of the average age of senior echelons of the Staff to the mid-50s. The General Staff will expand both its competence and its personnel in the next decade and will undoubtedly occupy a key position in the future development of Soviet military policies.

The Main Political Administration (MPA) must also undergo some change in its leading echelons, though again this will probably be postponed for as long as possible. General Yepishev, Chief of the MPA, has held this post since 1962 and is now 70 years old. A likely possibility is that he will be succeeded in formal style by Colonel-General Sredin, the First Deputy Chief, unless new political masters have other preferences. Much the same kind of waiting game is being played with Political Directorates of the Navy, the Ground Forces and the Air Force, so that we can expect a grand reshuffle in most of the major posts in the none too distant future. The basic connection between political control and security must be maintained by any future regime at it is currently cultivated by the present leadership. The responsibilities of the Political Administration will grow throughout the next decade as the problem of the relationship between technical progress and political reliability comes to the fore, propelled by the impact of demographic changes which may oblige the military search for 'technology-intensive' solutions as opposed to labour-intensive practices. This may be difficult for the Party to accept.

A decade ago a case could be made for the Soviet military being somewhat short of talented and experienced officers to fill senior posts. That situation has now been rectified. A pool of able officers has been developed in the Groups of Forces abroad and in the major and strategically important Military Districts (MDs). It is worth noting that officers are also advancing from command of élite formations (in the Group of Soviet Forces in Germany or in the interior) to important MD posts, thus establishing and reinforcing a command/promotion line for men displaying the requisite characteristics – loyalty to the Party, professional ability, discipline combined with initiative and a creative approach to their duties. This style, praised by Brezhnev, is very likely to appeal to his successors as establishing criteria both for patronage and for promotion.

Party patronage of military promotion has been used and will continue to be used to ensure the kind of stability favoured by the Party leadership, be this with men or institutions: the uncertainties of detente and the implications of continued technological progress will reinforce this symbiosis, but while professional competence and technical expertise will advance younger men, promotion will still require underwriting by the Party. The days of relationships fashioned by wartime friendships and associations are now practically over, so that any military–political compact will not carry the personal imprint of the association of say, Brezhnev and Grechko. The Party and its new leadership will almost certainly continue to give high priority to defence programmes, but they will probably resist the military's claim to a greater managerial role (preferring their own supervisors) and will also watch with caution the move towards technology-intensive solutions in military organization. At the same time, a new leadership will also require some stability in senior appointments where new weapons or new branches are involved – here it may override immediate military preferences. In short, we are likely to see little basic change in the pattern of military promotion.

Rules for Accession

We can now summarize those rules which appear to govern accession to the top leadership and to high command in the Soviet system. Paradoxically, Brezhnev has obeyed the rules by breaching them: for example, he probably learned from Khrushchev that it is well-nigh fatal to nominate a successor. He has also realized that younger rivals must be kept as much as possible out of the public eye (internal and external), lest they build up their own image (as Brezhnev did himself). As for the much vaunted

collective leadership, while it lasted longer than most Western experts predicted, it did finally fall victim to the political ambitions of one man – Brezhnev. Following the rules almost to the letter, Brezhnev first adjusted the Party apparatus at First Secretary level, and he not only built up his own power base but also brought into existence something akin to his own faction, the 'Dnepropetrovsk group', a mixed group owing much to Brezhnev in terms of patronage, protection or (not least important) wartime friendships. Brezhnev then went on to use the 25th Party Congress to implement his primacy, which was signalled by his elevation to head of the Politburo and the use of the term *vozhd* (leader) in connection with his office. Thus, retracing Brezhnev's steps, we see (1) an astute, even cynical and certainly opportunistic use of his position as heir-apparent; (2) the creation of a faction all his own linking those men to himself as leader; (3) the very able and deft manipulation of the Party organization – perhaps the key element in the power business; and (4) the calculated disbursement of patronage – to which we must add, in the case of Brezhnev, a very singular association with the military designed to bring the 'leader' the bonus of 'authority by association' (however grotesque the historical distortions, the myth being more important than the fact).

The military itself has benefited from this compact involving both the role of the Party and the *persona* of Brezhnev himself. However, the technical demands of the military build-up have made professionalism more important than political patronage. This trend must surely continue. In any event, a successor regime must live not only with the existing weapons procurement plans, but also with a substantial number of senior commanders in key positions, officers young enough to hold their posts for some considerable period. What will be worth watching will be the manner in which the military manages its own feuds and internal differences – for example, the fate of the 'Kulikov group' and Kulikov himself, for that matter, as well as the issue of 'politics versus technology' and the whole management of the Soviet military effort. As in the political establishment, there are younger men stamping about impatiently and watching for an opportunity to break into the highest echelons. What will unite them, however, will be the promotion and protection of the super-power status of the USSR, the implementation of a Soviet version of her own international *droit de seigneur*, deepening doubts about China and an unyielding nationalist fervour. Curiously enough, the 1980s in the Soviet Union could come to resemble the 1890s of Imperial Russian days.

NOTES

[1] For a detailed study, see John H. Miller, 'Cadres Policy in Nationality Areas – Recruitment of CPSU First and Second Secretaries in Non-Russian Republics of the USSR', *Soviet Studies*, January 1977, pp. 3–36.

[2] See T. H. Rigby, *Die Gebietssekretare der RSFSR. Die Brezhnev-Generation* (1964–1976), published by Bundesinstitut für ostwiss und internat. Studien (Report 28, 1977), 55 pp. Also his important study, 'Soviet Communist Party Membership under Brezhnev', *Soviet Studies*, July 1976, pp. 317–37.

[3] While Ustinov is frequently cited as a 'civilian', he was after all for many years a colonel-general (technical branch) and rather than talking about 'civilian' leadership of the Defence Ministry, we should emphasize the Party element and the institution of direct Party control.

[4] In a recent interview (*International Herald Tribune*, 10 July 1978) Andrei Amalrik reiterated his view that the Soviet Union was heading for catastrophic crisis and recalled the situation in the 1900s: he contrasted the advanced structure of Soviet society and 'the immovable and antiquated structure of Soviet power'. I still think that there is a case for looking at some of the historical coincidences, particularly in the role of the military and the General Staff.

The Soviet Military Leadership

Name	Post	Rank	Age/Time in post
The 'High Command': Defence Ministers and First Deputy Defence Ministers			
D. F. Ustinov	Defence Minister	Marshal of the Soviet Union (MSU)	70; 2 years
V. G. Kulikov	1st Dep. Def. Min., C-in-C/Warsaw Pact	MSU	57; 20 months
N. V. Ogarkov	1st Dep. Def. Min., Chief of the General Staff		60; 20 months
S. L. Sokolov	1st Dep. Def. Min.	MSU (since February 1978)	67; 10 years
Deputy Defence Ministers			
V. F. Tolubko	C-in-C Strategic Missile Forces	Army General	64; 6 years
I. G. Pavlovskii	C-in-C Ground Forces	Army General	69; 11 years
A. I. Koldunov	C-in-C Air Defence Command	Air Marshal (presumably replaces MSU Batitskii)	54; just appointed
P. S. Kutakhov	C-in-C Soviet Air Force	Air Chief Marshal	64; 9 years
S. G. Gorshkov	C-in-C Navy	Admiral of Fleet of Soviet Union	68; C-in-C since 1956; Dep. Def. Min. since 1962
K. S. Moskalenko	Chief Inspector/Def. Min.	MSU	76; 16 years
S. K. Kurkotkin	Chief/Rear Services	Army General	61; 6 years
A. V. Gelovani	Chief/Billeting and Construction	Marshal of Engineers	63; 4 years
A. T. Altunin	Chief/Civil Defence	Army General	57; 6 years
N. N. Alekseyev	Dep. Min. Weapons Production	Colonel-General	61; 8 years
(An additional Deputy Defence Minister has recently been appointed, by rank a colonel-general.)			
Main Political Administration (MPA)			
A. A. Yepishev	Chief/MPA	Army General	70; 16 years

83

Name	Post	Date of promotion	Age/Time in post
	Army Generals (Full General)		
A. T. Altunin	Chief/Civil Defence	1977	57; 6 years
Yu. V. Andropov	Chairman/KGB	1976	64; 11 years
P. I. Batov	Chairman/Veterans Committee	1955	82; 8 years
P. A. Belik	GOC/Trans-Baikal MD	1969	69; 12 years
S. P. Vasyagin	Chief/Ground Forces Political Administration	1976	68; 11 years
I. A. Gerasimov	GOC/Kiev MD	1977	57; 3 years
V. L. Govorov	GOC/Moscow MD	1977	54; 6 years
A. I. Gribkov	Chief of Staff/Warsaw Pact	1976	59; 2 years
E. F. Ivanovskii	C-in-C/GSFG	1972	60; 6 years
P. I. Ivashutin	Deputy Chief/General Staff	1971	69; 15 years
S. K. Kurkotkin	Chief/Rear Services	1972	61; 6 years
N. G. Lyashchenko	GOC/Central Asian MD	1968	68; 9 years
A. M. Mayorov	GOC/Baltic MD	1977	58; 6 years
E. E. Mal'tsev	Chief/Mil.-Pol. Academy	1973	68; 7 years
V. F. Margelov	Cdr/Airborne Forces	1967	70; 17 years
I. G. Pavlovskii	C-in-C/Ground Forces	1967	69; 11 years
V. I. Petrov	1st Dep. Cdr/Ground Forces	1972	61; 2 years
V. F. Tolubko	C-in-C/Strategic Missile Forces	1970	64; 6 years
I. M. Tretyak	GOC/Far Eastern MD	1976	55; 2 years
V. I. Varennikov	GOC/Carpathian MD	1978	54; 5 years
I. E. Shavrov	Head/General Staff Academy	1973	62; 5 years
I. N. Shkadov	Chief/Main Admin. Cadres/Defence Min.	1975	63; 6 years
	Senior Admirals		
S. G. Gorshkov	C-in-C Navy	1967 (to Admiral of the Fleet of the Soviet Union)	68; 22 years
N. I. Smirnov	1st Dep. Cdr/Navy	1973	61; 4 years
G. M. Yegorov	Chief of Naval Staff	1973	60; 1 year

Decision-Making in Soviet Defence Policies

DAVID HOLLOWAY

No analysis of the prospects of Soviet power in the 1980s would be complete without a look at the way in which defence policy is made, for it is through the policy-making process that the Soviet Union determines the size and shape of her armed forces and decides how military power will be used. An examination of how policy is made will not tell us what the substance of policy will be, but it may help us to understand how the Soviet Union will react to the problems of the 1980s. This paper will look at the structure of the policy-making process, at the pressures and influences that come into play and at the way in which Soviet security concerns are formulated. It will ask whether what we know about the decision-making process makes it possible to determine which Western policies might influence Soviet decisions in the direction of restraint, co-operation and arms control.

When looking at Soviet defence decision-making it is important to bear in mind the role of the military factor in Soviet history. When the Soviet leaders in the late 1920s embraced the goal of 'catching up and overtaking' the advanced capitalist powers, they proceeded to channel resources into heavy industry to provide the basis for economic growth and military power. A vast and powerful Party–State bureaucracy enforced the priorities of the leaders, and a wide rift was created between regime and people. One of the ways in which Stalin tried to bridge this rift was by encouraging a form of Soviet nationalism in which the Russian element was dominant. It was during the war (the Great Patriotic War) that the regime most appealed to this source of its legitimacy, and it was then, in spite of the opposition that did occur, that regime and people were most closely united in a common purpose. Since 1945 the war itself has formed the basis of military-patriotic propaganda. The intensity of this campaign, and the genuine feeling behind it, are evident even to the casual observer. It has been an important feature of the Brezhnev years, and Mr Brezhnev has himself made a contribution to it with his own memoirs.[1]

General though these considerations are, they form an essential backdrop to any discussion of Soviet defence decision-making. The strength of 'military patriotism' does not mean widespread support for war, but it does underpin a system of decision-making that gives priority to military matters; it points to the significance of the armed forces as a symbol of national power and integrity; it suggests a general belief that Soviet security requires military strength and that there is no contradiction between Soviet military power and a more peaceful world; finally, it indicates a conviction that it is in Moscow, and not elsewhere, that Soviet security interests should be decided.

The Formal Organization of Defence Policy-Making

The Politburo is the most authoritative policy-making body in the Soviet Union. It is there that the main lines of Soviet policy are determined, the major resource allocation decisions taken and the most difficult issues resolved. The Politburo meets once a week; it has also met in special session on several occasions to consider American arms-control proposals. Its role in foreign and defence policy has been strengthened by the inclusion of the Ministers of Defence and Foreign Affairs and the Head of the KGB as full members since 1973.[2]

There exists also a Defence Council which, under the 1977 Constitution, is a state, and not

85

a Party, body. This, like the Politburo, is chaired by Mr Brezhnev (who is also Supreme Commander-in-Chief of the Armed Forces) and has wide responsibilities for the armed forces and for defence policy. Reports of its composition suggest that it is small, consisting of some leading Politburo members, along with the Party Secretary responsible for the defence industry. The Minister of Defence appears to be the only representative of the armed forces on the Council (although the extent to which he *represents* them is an open question); the Chief of the General Staff and the other First Deputy Ministers may also be members, however, and others will be called to attend when necessary. The precise relationship of the Defence Council and the Politburo is not clear. It may handle detailed matters of policy for which the Politburo has no time, while leaving the major issues to that forum. Alternatively, it may consider all major issues and make recommendations to the Politburo, in which case it is likely to be an important body and an effective instrument for ensuring Mr Brezhnev's domination of defence policy within the Party leadership. The constitutional status of the Council, and Mr Brezhnev's new position as Chairman of the Presidium of the Supreme Soviet (which decides on the composition of the Council), suggests that the latter role is more likely. In any event, it is the most important body for high-level politico-military consultation and decision-making.

The Politburo's work is supported by the Central Committee apparatus and the personal staff of the General Secretary. The Central Committee has three departments which deal with defence matters: the Main Political Administration (which is also an important branch of the Ministry of Defence) is concerned primarily with the morale and political state of the armed forces; the Administrative Organs Department deals mainly with personnel matters; the Department of the Defence Industry has responsibility for military production. It is important to note, however, that there is no Central Committee Department that matches the Ministry of Defence or the General Staff over questions of military doctrine or military operations as the International Affairs Department 'shadows' the Ministry of Foreign Affairs. The Defence Council may have a secretariat, but there is no evidence to suggest that it has great influence or embodies any particular military expertise.

The Central Committee apparatus is not very large and certainly does not match the government bureaucracy in size. But what it lacks in size it makes up for in authority and influence. It prepares the policy decisions of the Politburo and can call on any institution or individual in the Soviet Union for advice and help. It is largely by providing expertise and staff work for the Central Committee that the policy-orientated Institutes of the Academy of Sciences (for example, the Institute of World Economy and International Relations and the Institute of the USA and Canada) have been able to play a role in policy-making. They can write analyses of political, economic and military developments in the areas they study, point to new problems and issues that may come to face the Soviet leaders and serve as the source of new policy ideas. These Institutes may play a role in arms-control policy-making by providing analyses of the other side's policy, but they do not appear to take part in the detailed formulation of Soviet defence policy – for example, decisions concerning weapons acquisition or the use of military power – for this is not their responsibility, and they lack access to the necessary information.

The role of the Council of Ministers in defence policy is confined mainly to the planning and management of military research and development (R&D) and production, in line with the general policy of the Politburo. Since the Ministers of Defence and Foreign Affairs are members of the Politburo, it is unlikely that major issues of policy are discussed in the Council of Ministers, which appears now to be concerned largely with social and economic policy. One of the Council's Deputy Chairmen (L. V. Smirnov) heads the Military-Industrial Commission which oversees the weapons-acquisition process, but even his work may be directed by the Central Committee Secretary responsible for the defence industry, and the Commission probably serves as an executive arm of the Defence Council. Production and R&D are carried out chiefly in the research institutes, design bureaux and factories of various production ministries (in particular, the nine ministries in the defence industry group). The defence sector enjoys special priority in the economy, and this helps it to perform more effectively than civilian industry. The operation of the defence sector imposes its own pattern of design and development on Soviet weapons policies.

The armed forces naturally play a major role in the formulation of defence policy. They draw up operational plans, gather and assess intelligence information, produce procurement plans and orders and play a part in planning and managing R&D and production. The procurement plans have to be co-ordinated with other agencies such as the Military-Industrial Commission, *Gosplan* and *Gossnab* (the State Supply Commission); they also have to be approved at a higher level by the Defence Council or the Politburo. The High Command in recent years has acquired considerable technical and managerial competence to enable it to perform this side of its work. The exact division of responsibilities between the General Staff and the main administrations of the Ministry of Defence is not always clear (naturally, they must work closely together), but the General Staff does have particular responsibility for command and control and for operational and doctrinal matters, while the Ministry focuses more on administration. The appointment as Minister of Ustinov, whose career has been in defence production rather than in the military profession, may strengthen this distinction. It is the General Staff that is the main repository of military professionalism in the Soviet Union. It is there that future military operations are prepared for and the requirements of the armed forces worked out. It is not unknown for individual branches and arms of service to lobby the political leadership, but the main channel of communication between the High Command and the Party leaders appears to be through the Minister and the Chief of the General Staff. In the Ministry of Defence the Collegium (consisting of the Minister and his Deputies) co-ordinates the activities of the different elements of the armed forces. It may have considerable power in the day-to-day running of the military establishments.

The present arrangements for defence decision-making appear to have been created in the late 1960s, but more information about them has become available in the last two or three years, as Mr Brezhnev's position has grown even stronger than before. In the defence policy-making process it is the Party leaders who hold the dominant positions, and there is nothing to suggest that civilian political supremacy is threatened. The Party leaders have various sources of advice and analysis in matters of foreign policy – the Ministry of Foreign Affairs, the Central Committee apparatus, the KGB and the Academy Institutes. In military matters, however, the armed forces play a major role in decision-making by virtue of their monopoly of professional expertise. With the extension of Soviet military power throughout the world, and the involvement of the Soviet Union in arms-control negotiations, the military are being drawn more often into the policy-making process. In these areas the General Staff will provide advice on negotiating positions and on the feasibility of using military power in particular areas of the world. The role of the military in arms-control negotiations is clearly important. The general policy of creating the capability to use military power abroad will certainly be decided by the Politburo, which will draw on the various institutions named above in making its decisions. It is unlikely that, in particular instances, the military will be asked to comment on the desirability of the general foreign policy goals, except in so far as these affect Soviet military policy – for example, if basing rights in the Indian Ocean are sought, or if the prospects for military success seem problematic.

Although we know something about the formal arrangements for defence decision-making, informal alliances and personal networks are much more difficult to examine. Past history suggests that these are equally important, even if Mr Brezhnev has paid more attention to formal procedures than did either Stalin or Khrushchev. Moreover, the system of decision-making is more flexible than the outline given here might suggest because the Party leaders can call on individuals and agencies for alternative advice; for example, the KGB – the traditional enemy of the armed forces – might be another source of intelligence assessment (though there is no evidence of this). Further, scientists have played a part in arms and arms-control policy-making. Thus Academician Artsimovich had an important role in the negotiations for the Test Ban Treaty of 1963, while Academician Shchukin, who has been a member of the SALT delegation, has been able to provide the leaders with reports and advice that are not tied to the institutional perspectives of the Ministries of Defence and Foreign Affairs.

Pressures and Influences

The formal structure of the defence decision-making process is not very different from that which existed under Stalin, but the informal process has changed in important ways. Stalin dominated, in a ruthless fashion, the Party–State bureaucracy which his policies had helped to create. His authority in military matters was unquestioned, and he intervened in a detailed way in all aspects of defence policy. He took advice, of course, but he could ignore it when he wished. Khrushchev's leadership was naturally different, for even when he was at his most powerful, his position did not compare with that of Stalin. He was not able to dominate the Party–State bureaucracy in the same way, and his attempts to ignore the views and interests of the various elements of that bureaucracy led him into political difficulties. When he fell from power it was opposition not so much to his policy goals as to his methods of pursuing them that formed the basis of the coalition that removed him.

The Brezhnev Politburo has adopted a style of policy-making that is much more responsive to the advice of the different elements in the Party–State bureaucracy. Most observers agree that there has been a diffusion of power at the centre and that this has had important consequences for policy-making. In the Soviet Union these changes have been described in terms of a shift towards a more scientific form of leadership – an approach that recognizes the claims of professional expertise and special competence. In the Politburo itself an attempt is apparently made to reach decisions on the basis of full agreement. In other words, the support of the Party leadership and the relevant bureaucracies is sought for policy decisions.

It would be a mistake to idealize this style of leadership and to suppose that conflict and disagreement have been eliminated entirely. But even where a policy is controversial, the effort is made to assuage doubts and fears by some compensating measure: thus in the policy of detente we find arms control pursued along with high levels of procurement, defence spending raised alongside an attempt to regenerate the economy by importing foreign technology, better relations sought with the West but repression at home in an attempt to prevent any political contamination from this.

This new approach to policy-making has been called 'institutional pluralism' or 'pluralism of the centre'. Like all pluralisms, however, it is very far from perfect, in the sense that some groups have a prestige and weight which others lack, while some are excluded completely from the political process: hence the paradox, characteristic of the Brezhnev years, that greater policy debate (within clear limits) has been possible even while cultural and intellectual freedom has been severely curtailed. With the diffusion of power at the centre, some groups and institutions have been well placed to increase their influence. The armed forces have had an advantageous position. They enjoy general prestige as institutions that embody national power and integrity – a prestige enhanced by the extensive military-patriotic education. Second, the high priority given to defence remains embedded in the system of planning and administering the economy, as well as in Soviet political culture. Third, the General Staff and the Ministry of Defence are institutions of undoubted competence and reputation which enjoy a monopoly of expertise in the relevant field. They are able to protect that monopoly by holding secret the information necessary to make informed judgments about current policy. Moreover, they are able to couch their arguments either in the technical language of systems analysis or in Marxist–Leninist terms – both of which count as 'scientific' discourse in the Soviet Union. Finally, in the political conflicts of the post-Stalin period the military have shown themselves to be a powerful ally, whom no cautious political leader would antagonize unnecessarily.

One other factor requires fuller mention if we are to understand the relationships between the different groups in defence policy-making. In Soviet terms, military doctrine consists of two parts. The first is the political element, which determines the political goals and character of war, and the end to which military power is to be used; this is the prerogative of the political leadership. The second is the military-technical element, which (in line with Party policy) is concerned with how a future war is to be waged, with the equipment of the armed forces and with the maintenance of combat readiness; these questions are a military, and in particular a

General Staff, responsibility. The political element is the primary one, as has been evidenced in the desire to avoid war and achieve arms control on the basis of some kind of equality with the West. But this approach to military doctrine allows considerable scope for military influence on the size and structure of the armed forces. In the late 1960s the doctrinal debates of that decade were settled in an open-ended way, which provided a framework within which all elements of the armed forces could press their claims. The Party leaders accepted this settlement and thus left themselves open to military pressure.

It is now possible to point to some general features of the defence policy-making process under Mr Brezhnev. The Party leadership is the dominant force in the process and sets the objectives of policy. The armed forces appear to have considerable influence on the methods used to obtain these objectives. In assessing military requirements the Party leaders must rely on the General Staff, for there appears to be no other institution competent or well enough informed to provide alternative advice. The Brezhnev style of policy-making has been inflexible because the support of the relevant expert groups and the agreement of the Politburo are sought and once they are obtained, the policy will not be changed readily. It is, moreover, a style of decision-making that can lead to internal contradictions precisely because it is responsive to domestic pressures. In general, it is a style of policy-making that does not lead to dramatic twists and turns of policy, and yet by small steps it has helped to bring about large changes in East–West military relations, to the advantage of the Soviet Union.

Ever since the 24th Party Congress in 1971 it has been clear that, though the Politburo has adopted a consensual style of policy-making, Mr Brezhnev has been the dominant figure in foreign and defence policy. Since 1976, however, what can only be described as the 'militarization of Brezhnev' has taken place: it has become known that he is Chairman of the Defence Council and Supreme Commander-in-Chief; he has been made a Marshal of the Soviet Union and has received a number of major military decorations; his military career has been publicized; he has appointed as Minister of Defence a close associate who is not a professional soldier. Personal vanity alone cannot explain these developments. They point to a closer identity between the Party leadership and Soviet military power. They signify, if not an increase in Mr Brezhnev's institutional power, then at least greater authority in military affairs. They are likely to give him more flexibility and room for manoeuvre in defence policy, although they have come, strangely enough, at a time when his health is failing.

All this represents a shift in relationships in the defence policy-making process, but it is not clear to what end the new flexibility might be used. There are signs of a greater assertion of Party primacy over the armed forces; Mr Brezhnev has stated that the Soviet goal is not military superiority but equality and parity (and such statements must now be treated as authoritative elements of Soviet military doctrine);[3] there has been a new approach at the Vienna talks and an evident desire for a SALT II agreement. The significance of these moves is not self-evident. If equality is sought with all potential enemies, is there not room for a continuing military build-up? Will not the General Staff's assessment of 'equality' look like 'superiority' to other governments? Is an attempt being made to shift military resources from the central relationship with the West to other areas (China, Africa)? Finally, it should be noted that the greater flexibility which Mr Brezhnev seems to have acquired in defence policy-making may not be transferable to a successor, for much of his authority is personal rather than institutional. The professional authority of the armed forces, on the other hand, does not depend on an individual and will remain a permanent factor in defence policy-making.

Unlike other periods of Soviet history, the Brezhnev years have seen good and co-operative politico-military relations. Mr Brezhnev has proved a shrewd and capable political leader. The Party and military leaders appear to have shared common assumptions about the requirements of defence policy, and resources have been made available for a steady military build-up. There have, of course, been debates and arguments about military doctrine and policy, but these do not seem to have placed the political leaders on one side and the military on the other. Under these favourable conditions the power of the armed forces has not posed a serious threat to Party supremacy. One cannot assume, however, that politico-military relations will necessarily remain so good. They might change for the worse if a new leadership embarked on a political course which shifted resources away from the military effort.

Western Influence on Soviet Defence Policy
Most of Soviet defence policy is directed against the Western powers as potential enemies. But it is not clear how far Western governments can use their policies to elicit desired responses from the Soviet Union – for example, restraint in the use of military power, readiness to conclude arms-control agreements or the reduction of military spending. The Soviet policy-making system is designed to protect the high-priority area of defence from social pressures and economic shortcomings in the Soviet Union. The same arrangements which insulate defence policy against domestic pressures also make it very difficult for foreign governments to intervene in the policy-making process to put pressure on the Soviet Union. In a complex international environment, where political alignments are shifting, military power seems to be regarded by the Soviet leaders as a stable and reliable instrument which it would be foolish to put at the mercy of foreign pressures.

The impermeability and the closed nature of Soviet policy-making make it generally difficult for Western governments to influence Soviet defence policy in desired directions. More specific factors can also be pointed to. In the first place, Soviet policy is not merely a response to what the West does but is a product of Soviet history, institutions and domestic power relationships. Consequently, many (perhaps most) of the factors influencing any policy are not amenable to Western pressure. When the Soviet Union responds to Western actions she does not necessarily respond as the West would like.

Second, the Soviet policy-making process appears to be inflexible, so that policies, once launched, may be difficult to change. This, along with the secrecy which surrounds defence policy-making, makes it difficult for the West to exert influence on the process in any very precise way. It is true that one can point to specific instances in which American decisions have triggered Soviet weapons developments – for example, atomic bomb development, the MiG-25 (a response to the B-70 which was not deployed) and perhaps MIRV as well. Despite this, there are problems associated with the idea of using Western restraint as a way of eliciting specific desired responses from the Soviet Union (though it is likely that a MIRV test ban could have been negotiated): the secrecy surrounding Soviet military R&D makes it hard to make such proposals at an early stage, and when a weapon has become visible its development may already have acquired considerable momentum. Besides, it may be difficult to balance the value of restraint on either side. Western governments were not impressed by Mr Brezhnev's willingness to forgo deployment of the neutron bomb if the United States did likewise. They had hoped that the Soviet Union would at least slow down deployment of the SS-20 missile, but this hope was not fulfilled.

Third, any attempt to put overt pressure on the Soviet Union to change her policies could arouse Soviet nationalism and super-power *amour propre* and thus merely stiffen resistance to outside influences. In his memoirs Mr Brezhnev has an interesting passage about the American decision to embargo certain exports to the Soviet Union:

> The "Cold War" began. It reigned for long years, essentially for two decades. This was not the first and, unfortunately, not the last occasion on which the capitalist powers, setting their hopes on our difficulties, tried to dictate their will to us, to interfere in our internal affairs. The calculation was simple: it makes no difference, they said, the Soviet Union will ask for these machines, this steel plate, the Communists have nowhere to turn to, they will come cap in hand, they will get down on their knees . . . And what, did we perish? Retreat? Stop our movement? No! The foreign wise men miscalculated in their policy, and it is useful to recall this today inasmuch as it is both instructive and topical.[4]

This undoubtedly represents a very powerful element in the Soviet political tradition.

Many of the reasons for scepticism over the possibility of influencing Soviet policy spring from the inability of Western governments to co-ordinate and control their own policies in a precise way, or even to decide precisely what is desired from the Soviet Union. But those elements of the Soviet decision-making process outlined in this paper also suggest a need for caution: there is no formula for gaining influence over Soviet defence policy. Of course, the degree to which the Soviet Union will respond to Western actions in the desired way depends in part on the issues at stake and in part on the way in which influence is exercised. There is a difference between trying to influence Soviet weapons development or defence spending, which is likely to be very difficult, and trying to restrain the use of military power beyond the Soviet borders, where the normal instruments of foreign policy can be used. There is also a difference between negotiations on specific issues and the attempt to use one instrument of pressure – for example, trade – to change the general line of Soviet defence policy, which is likely to end in failure. The only practicable approach appears to be to try to structure, in a consistent way and over a sustained period, the choices which the Soviet Union faces and to keep open the avenues leading to restraint and co-operation. In this way it might be possible to influence the 'institutional pluralism' of the Soviet political system. Western policies which do not themselves show a readiness for restraint and co-operation are unlikely to encourage these qualities in Soviet policy, for they will merely strengthen the hand of those in the Soviet Union who want to accumulate more military power and employ it for political purposes.

All of this raises the question of whether the Soviet Union is able to apply to her defence policy the kind of political calculation that seems to be required in the current state of East–West relations – for example, in assessing the implications of using military power far from the Soviet borders, or in bringing arms-control considerations to bear on weapons-procurement decisions. In making a decision about the use of Soviet military power abroad, the Soviet leaders, besides calling for military advice, can seek recommendations and analyses of the political context from other bodies. In making procurement decisions, however, it seems unlikely that any advice other than military, scientific and industrial recommendations is sought, given the secrecy which surrounds these questions. Consequently, assessment of the political, diplomatic and arms-control implications of new weapons

would seem to be provided mainly by the armed forces themselves.[5] This may have positive military advantages in reducing political pressures on defence policy. It may also have political disadvantages in the repercussions that development may elicit in relations with other governments. This compartmentalization of policy-making makes it less likely that the Soviet Union will accommodate her defence policy to her political relations with other powers, and it thus reduces the opportunity for those powers to influence Soviet defence policy.

Conclusion

Specific predictions are not possible, but some general issues can be raised about Soviet defence policy-making in the 1980s. First, the Party leadership will remain dominant, but unless there is a drastic recentralization of power or a much greater degree of democratization, military influence will remain strong in defence policy-making and the armed forces will continue to be a powerful element in the Soviet state. The significance of this military influence is hard to assess. There is no evidence that the High Command has foreign policy objectives that are different from those of the present Politburo. It appears to support the policy of trying to stabilize the strategic relationship with the United States. Nor is there any sign that the High Command is pushing for a risky or adventurous policy based on the use of military force abroad. Perhaps one can say only that the General Staff will make cautious and conservative estimates of their own requirements for the missions they have to perform and the wars they might have to fight.

Second, as long as the present leadership remains in charge, major shifts in policy are unlikely, although there is evidence that Mr Brezhnev has been increasing his own authority in defence policy-making. The succession question has not been resolved, however, and this suggests that Mr Brezhnev's disappearance from the scene will be followed by a hiatus until a new leader establishes his authority. The 1977 Constitution may make it easier for the successor to establish himself (if he is made both General Secretary of the Central Committee and Chairman of the Presidium of the Supreme Soviet) but, as has been affirmed above, much of Mr Brezhnev's authority is personal rather than institutional and will not easily be transferred. Past experience suggests that power becomes more diffused during a succession crisis and also that the armed forces are well placed to take advantage of the opportunity to increase their influence. At the same time, however, a succession crisis would provide an opportunity for the reordering of priorities and the advancement of new political strategies. A new leadership might decide to focus attention on domestic economic and social problems, or it might pursue a more militant foreign policy. The new generation of leaders will not have been marked so strongly by the war: this might give them a different attitude towards military power, though it might also lessen their authority *vis-à-vis* the armed forces.

Third, if the Soviet Union faces serious economic problems in the 1980s, it is possible that strong pressure for a shift of resources away from the military effort will arise within the Party–State bureaucracy. Because of the way in which the Soviet system has developed, however, there will be those who are opposed to a re-ordering of priorities. Moreover, the SALT negotiations testify to international recognition that, in terms of military power at least, the Soviet Union has achieved her historic mission of 'catching up' with the West. It is very unlikely that any Soviet leadership would (or could) willingly adopt policies that jeopardized its relationship of military parity or equality with the advanced capitalist powers. Consequently, the international situation is likely to have an important bearing on the choices which a new leadership makes.

Finally, the possibility that the West could influence Soviet defence policy is remote, although it might grow during a succession crisis. Accommodation and co-operation on some matters are, of course, possible, but the Soviet Union is unlikely to respond favourably to pressure for major changes in her defence policy. If the West seeks restraint, co-operation and effective arms control from the Soviet Union, then it must adopt these policies itself and at least provide for the possibility that the Soviet Union may pursue them too.

NOTES

[1] L. I. Brezhnev, *Malaya Zemlya* (Moscow: Politizdat, 1978).

[2] In this paper I have been able to draw on a number of very useful studies which have been published in recent years, among them: M. Mackintosh, 'The Soviet Military: Influences on Foreign Policy', *Problems of Communism*, Sept.-Oct. 1973; R. L. Garthoff, 'SALT and the Soviet Military', *Problems of Communism*, Jan.-Feb. 1975; T. W. Wolfe, *The SALT Experience: Its Impact on US and Soviet Strategic Policy and Decision-Making* (Santa Monica, Calif., Rand, 1975); R-1686-PR; K. A. Myers and D. Simes, *Soviet Decision-Making, Strategic Policy and SALT* (Washington DC; Georgetown University Center for Strategic Studies, 1974); A. Alexander, *Decision-making in Soviet Weapons Procurement* Adelphi Papers Nos. 147/8 (London: IISS, 1978.)

[3] See, for example, the authoritative article on military doctrine in *Sovetskaya Voennaya Entsiklopedia*, Vol. 3 (Moscow: Voenizdat, 1977), pp. 225–9, which quotes Mr Brezhnev's speech of 19 January 1977 in which he said that superiority in armaments is not the Soviet Union's objective.

[4] Extracts from L. I. Brezhnev, *Vozrozhdenie* appear in *Novyi Mir* (Moscow, 1978), no. 5, p. 6.

[5] Lt.-Col. V. M. Bondarenko writes that among the important tasks that only military research institutions can perform is 'the evaluation of the latest scientific achievements . . . from the point of view of their possible application in military affairs, taking account of the scientific, economic, military, political (including diplomatic) prospects of such a step'. *Sovremennaya Nauka i Voennoe Delo* (Moscow: Voenizdat, 1976), p. 41.

Soviet Security Concerns in the 1980s

WILLIAM HYLAND

Technically, the 1980s begin in sixteen months. But history does not divide itself neatly into discrete decades. Nothing of major significance is destined to occur in January 1980; indeed, the first landmark for the 1980s, in Soviet terms, could be the Party Congress, scheduled to take place in 1981. The odds are that there will be a top-leadership change before then, and this could be the first post-Brezhnev Congress. Projections probing well into the next decade are hazardous, if not foolish: only historians are able to identify the characteristics of various decades. Even the Soviet Planning Commission (*Gosplan*) and the Pentagon make only five-year plans.

What follows, therefore, tries to build on a few 'facts', beginning with the Soviet leadership and the domestic economic situation and moving into the vagaries of regional security and the effect of the military balance.

Internal Politics

Sovietologists generally must strike a balance between the 'objective' factors that shape Soviet policies and the impact of power politics within the top leadership. Some would argue that it does not matter very much who the General Secretary of the Party is in the 1980s; even if we could name the individual, we would still not know much about his policy. Soviet history, however, lends some weight to the importance of the play of politics and personalities – after all, Stalin and Khrushchev (and, to a lesser extent, Brezhnev) have left their imprint. We can only guess at the identity of individuals who might survive; nevertheless, some insight may be gained from rough calculations. For example, barring an enormous political upheaval or a wholesale purge of the Politburo (admittedly

major assumptions), and using a rule of thumb that 72 is the age limit for Politburo members, then at the 27th Party Congress in 1987 the leadership could conceivably still include about nine or ten members of the present top hierarchy (that is, the Politburo, candidates and secretariat). Their average age would be about 69 and they would include Andropov, Grishin, Mazurov, Solomontsev as 'elder statesmen' – all aged 72; the 'youngsters' would be Masherov and Shcherbitsky at 68, Romanov at 63 and Dolgikh at 61.

The point of this artificial exercise is that there is at least some chance that a few of the men who will be making Soviet policy in the 1980s will have some links with the Brezhnev era and even with the Khrushchev period – in other words, there is likely to be an element of continuity. Ironically, however, Sovietologists of the mid-1980s could be making the same prediction they are today, namely that the Politburo of the 27th Party Congress is ageing and due for wholesale replacement.

To the extent that the current oligarchic character of the top leadership persists, there will be bureaucratic inclination to persist with tested policies, or at least to change them only modestly and gradually. In this scenario of considerable continuity, the chances of a revolution from above will recede. This could mean that the Soviet leadership of the 1980s will reflect some of the characteristics of their mentors of the 1970s and 1960s: they could be a rather conservative, prudent lot, appreciative of the power of the Soviet Union and committed to expanding it, but wary of running excessive risks. One authority, Robert Conquest, recently wrote that the 'younger generation of *apparatchik*, the men around 40–45, are even more dogmatic and more dangerous, in their total myopia about the dogma and the system'.

There are obviously alternative scenarios. Two may be worth mentioning because of their potential impact on foreign policy:

– Conceivably, there could be growing pressure to 'get the country moving'; a sort of reaction against the conservatism of the 1970s; a quest for more innovative domestic policies, particularly economic reform. The question is: would a regime engaged in major domestic changes be more or less likely to see its security problems in a new light? Would the leaders be more adventuresome or more prudent? One would guess that the tendency would be towards seeking more stability abroad.

– Also conceivable is a series of mini-crises, precipitated in part by a disorderly succession process; in this case, a general disintegration could occur, from which one man would have to emerge almost out of necessity. The possibility of a return to one-man rule unfortunately still does not tell us much about policy: assuming, however, that one man consolidates his position by gaining support in key political sectors, then an alliance of the traditionally most powerful forces (the KGB, the armed forces and the political cadres) would be necessary – in other words a conservative coalition.

All of this may simply be a way of stating a probability: a 'liberal' Soviet regime composed of personalities that tend to the reformist mode seems the *least likely* outcome. In this light, changes in Soviet security policy seem less likely to result from a change in the mental make-up or political outlook of the top command than from the influence of external forces.

Economic Necessities

An examination of Soviet security in the 1980s should begin with the domestic base. It is, after all, the prime purpose of the CPSU to stay in power and, according to all the Holy Writ of Party Congresses, to ensure the 'peaceful' building of Communism. Most projections, however, suggest that 'building Communism' in the 1980s is going to be far more complicated, or at least a much slower, process than the Soviet Union might desire.

According to the CIA, rapid economic growth of the past decade has enabled the Soviet Union to catch up with the United States militarily; steadily to expand her industrial base; and to meet at least minimal consumer expectations. But according to CIA projections for the next decade, reduced growth 'will make her pursuit of these objectives much more difficult and pose hard choices for the leadership, which can have a major impact on Soviet relations with Eastern Europe and the West'. Without debating all the assumptions and estimates involved in this study, several possibilities should be mentioned as factors affecting Soviet security:

– A cut-back in oil deliveries to Eastern Europe would force the East European states to turn to the West to make up oil shortfalls and, most important, would burden them with import bills that would affect their ability to purchase industrial materials and equipment.

– Almost out of necessity, the Eastern European states would be drawn towards increased trade with the West and acceptance of international organizations such as the World Bank and the IMF.

– National defence, expenditure on which seems likely to continue to grow, will, nevertheless, increasingly be a target for reductions; as the CIA study puts it, 'ways to reduce the growth of defense expenditures could become increasingly pressing for some elements of the Soviet leadership'.

– Finally, as Soviet ability to pay for imports from the industrial West declines in the early and mid-1980s, the USSR may well seek long-term credits, especially for the development of the oil and gas industries, and much of the needed technology will have to come from the United States.[1]

To put it crudely, Soviet economic vulnerability may increase. The new political leadership will have to grapple with such explosive questions as how far Eastern Europe could be permitted to drift into significant dependence on the West, whether defence investment could be curtailed and what political price would have to be paid for Western credits and technology.

Thus a new leadership could emerge in the 1980s that was not significantly different in character from the present one, but it will have to face some painful economic choices which will have consequences for foreign policy that a conservative regime will resist.

The foregoing is highly conjectural. If the CIA can foresee these economic problems, the Soviet leaders cannot be oblivious to them. Remedial action could be taken. The most important point, perhaps, is that the 1980s will not be an easy decade for the USSR, at least as far as the management of her domestic economy is concerned. But that probably could have been said at any time since the Revolution. In general, policy pressures will tend to promote a political atmosphere that permits greater opportunity for economic intercourse, especially with the Western countries.

European Security

This tendency, arising out of economic realities, would be consistent with what has been the main trend of post-war policy in Europe: the consolidation of the territorial and political *status quo*. It is instructive to re-read the statements of the Soviet leaders on the topic of Germany in the 1960s and to compare them with today's more comfortable appraisals. At the 23rd Party Congress in March 1966 Brezhnev said:

Today West German imperialism is the United States' chief ally in Europe in aggravating world tension. West Germany is increasingly becoming a seat of the war danger, where revenge-seeking passions are running high . . . The policy pursued by the Federal Republic of Germany is being increasingly determined by the same monopolies that brought Hitler to power.

The Rhineland politicians fancy that once they get the atomic bomb, frontier posts will topple and they will be able to achieve their cherished desire of carving up the map of Europe again and taking revenge for defeat in the Second World War.

One of the most ominous factors endangering peace is the bilateral military alliance that is taking shape between the ruling circles of the United States and the Federal Republic of Germany. This factor remains an objective of our unflagging attention.

More recently, in an offhand remark in Minsk, he is reported to have said:

The improved political climate in Europe is one of the most important peaceful gains of *the last decade*. This could be felt especially during our recent visit to the Federal Republic of Germany.

There is hardly any country in Europe with which there would be as many obstacles, both objective and subjective, in the way of establishing relations, and where every step would be as complicated. Today, however, the relations between the USSR and the FRG – without shutting our eyes to the negative moments – have become an important element of stability in Europe and in relaxing tension on the European continent.

This is simply an illustration of the fact that at present the Soviet Union has cause to be satisfied that her European policy has been a reasonably successful one and that there is very little reason to change it.

In short, economic security and political security would seem to be mutually reinforcing; a stable relationship with Germany and France should lead to economic benefits that the Soviet Union may well need for domestic reasons. The longer-term effect of a European detente is more problematical.

A protracted period of stability between East and West in Europe might consolidate the spheres of influence. Soviet optimists may even hope that a European detente will produce a political atmosphere in which anti-Communism will be seriously weakened and Communist participation in governments will come to be regarded as an acceptable process. But there are two areas in which the Soviet Union could have grounds for apprehension: first, the issue of the European military balance; and, second, the question of the political-ideological impact of any dilution of Soviet authority in Eastern Europe.

The Soviet Union has supported the *status quo* in Central Europe because the military balance provides an underpinning that gives Soviet diplomacy in Europe added weight. But it is also possible that she is provoking a European reaction to her military preponderance. The Western defence record is not encouraging, despite repeated pledges to increase the common effort. But, leaving aside purely conventional defences, there is looming on the horizon the question of a European nuclear capability, under American auspices, designed to counter Soviet theatre forces either by cruise missiles or medium-range ballistic missiles. No Soviet leadership, however, could simply accept the possibility that West Germany could be converted into a base for launching deep attacks against the interior of the Soviet Union. This may explain renewed interest in some form of limited disengagement in Central Europe, as reflected in new Soviet MBFR proposals. Should these, by some outside chance, lead to some agreement, it would probably mean that a bargain could be struck, as a result of which, for the first time since the war, some Soviet forces would march eastward and leave Central and Eastern Europe in return for a limit on longer-range nuclear forces in West Europe. One can only raise the question of the psychological and political impact of this process on both East and West Europe, once it had begun.

And this leads to the second area of potential apprehension: the dilution of Soviet authority in Eastern Europe. It is one of the minor ironies of history that as the Soviet Union seemed at long last to attain her coveted goal, that of the ratification of the *status quo* in Europe at Helsinki, forces were being unleashed that challenged the settlement. The demands for 'human rights', freedom of movement, etc., which the West interprets to be the true meaning of Helsinki, raise a fundamental challenge to the USSR. The Soviet Union has no intention of permitting East European states to be infected by the 'spirit of Helsinki' to such a degree that they feel that they can carve out greater autonomy within the Soviet sphere: she has already demonstrated at Belgrade that she can hamper the process. But she is also stuck with it, amd the chances are that the idea of pan-European co-operation will grow and may be given an occasional impetus through the European Security and Co-operation Conferences.

This fear of the dilution of authority would probably also increase if, as a result of political evolution in Western Europe, hybrid regimes arose that were imbued with a sort of Carrillo-ism. A simultaneous weakening of political, economic and ideological barriers in Europe would be a nightmare for the Soviet Union – but there is some chance that such a trend could gain ground in the 1980s. (The obverse of this process would be the weakening of Western links, especially in the security area, which would raise the question of which side would benefit from a blurring of the East–West division.)

Asian Security
The real Soviet nightmare, however, is the two-front threat. Since the death of Mao, Chinese policy has swung sharply towards a more pragmatic line. The main thrust of this policy has been to check the USSR through various diplomatic combinations: (a) a *rapprochement* between China and the EEC in economic relations; (b) a political *rapprochement* with key European countries, with the aim of securing military supply sources in Europe; (c) a clear breakthrough with Japan, reflected in the new treaty, as well as potential economic collaboration; and (d) some strengthening of economic ties with the United States.

Of particular concern to the USSR is the prospect that China will gradually modernize her military establishment with European, American and Japanese assistance. At present the Soviet Union, as a result of a major effort, has established a military position along the Chinese frontier which is probably satisfactory for defensive purposes. According to United States Government studies: spending for Soviet forces aligned against China has accounted for about 10 per cent of the total Soviet defence effort over the past decade; the number of divisions doubled between 1967 and 1972; there has been a five-fold increase in frontal aviation in the last ten years; since 1975 more modern versions of aircraft have been deployed in the Far East; and the level of spending in 1977 in constant roubles was triple the 1967 level.

China has made no comparable effort, which gives the Soviet Union some clear present advantages. If China now embarks on modernization, in conventional military terms the balance should shift in her favour – and this could occur in a period when she is certain to develop some more significant strategic capabilities against the Soviet interior. In this same period some increase in Japanese re-armament is almost inevitable. And it seems likely that the Sino–Soviet Treaty of Friendship will lapse formally in 1980.

It would be surprising if the Soviet Union watched all of this occur with passivity; the general Soviet reaction is already forcefully stated in formal diplomatic notes warning of the consequences of the Sino–Japanese treaty: 'It was also noted that in the case of the conclusion of a treaty with provisions directed against the USSR, the Soviet side would be compelled to make certain conclusions and introduce certain correctives into its policy towards Japan.'[2]

Her reaction to Japan, however, illustrates the dilemma facing the Soviet Union. Japan supplies over $3 billion in official credits to the USSR and Eastern Europe. She is the major source of technology and capital for the exploitation of Soviet resources in the Far East and Siberia. A long-term deterioration of relations with Japan *and* China would seem the most foolish Soviet diplomacy. But weaning Japan away from her present course would require territorial concessions, which would have a backlash effect in any negotiations over the Sino–Soviet border. The Soviet Union has steadfastly refused to make the concessions that might possibly divert Japan from her Chinese alignment. Two possibilities seem open to the Soviet Union. First, a serious effort to find some accommodation with China. Despite the strident anti-Soviet policy of the new Chinese leaders, there is the intriguing possibility that they are sufficiently pragmatic to consider some bargain with the Soviet Union. In particular, if China concludes that the United States is a weak reed in the triangular competition, she would have to consider some effort calculated to appease the Soviet Union. Indeed, one can speculate that the various incidents and manoeuvring of this past year – in Indochina, in the border incidents, in Brezhnev's Far East tour and the accompanying military demonstrations – are all manifestations of a political dialogue that has been conducted in private.

Assuming, however, that accommodation fails, then the military option may become a more serious one for the Soviet leaders. After all, the Soviet Union remembers that the battle of Khalkin Gol bought her a respite in the Far East in circumstances that may be quite similar to the 'encirclement' of the 1980s. The tactics, risks, goals, etc., of the military option can be debated, but given the geo-political realities of a quadruple alliance directed against the USSR, it would be unwise to discount the possibility of drastic Soviet measures designed to disrupt or wreck such a coalition. The humiliation of China would go a long way towards relieving the USSR of some of her security problems; the political impact would be massive, not only in Asia but also in Europe.

The Military Balance

It is customary to begin rather than end a discussion of Soviet security with the various military equations. One reason for deferring this issue until the end of the discussion is to stress that Soviet security is not solely a question of military hardware but is equally a question of geo-politics. The military outlook can be divided into two distinct periods: the present through the early 1980s, and the remainder of the decade.

In this first period the trends seem clearly favourable to the USSR in terms of strategic nuclear weapons and conventional forces. The vulnerability of the American land-based ICBM has been emphasized at great length and in alarming terms. It appears that this period will peak about 1982–4. The major question is whether this margin of strategic advantage (which is by no means agreed on by all the experts) will give the Soviet leaders new confidence that the 'correlation' of forces has turned decisively. If so, then we may witness a period of growing Soviet assertiveness. The dangers are obvious: a direct confrontation in an era of apparent Soviet advantage would face the West with stark choices. At the very least, one would expect strong Soviet political pressures in Europe and in Asia to prevent the formation of a quadruple alliance. Moreover, Soviet strategy is already showing some signs of a thrust towards the Persian Gulf and the Arabian peninsula, where European and Japanese sources of energy are located. It can be argued, therefore, that we are already witnessing the political consequences of a shift in the overall military balance.

In the second period the outlook is hazier. It is difficult to believe that the United States will permit the present trends in strategic and theatre capabilities to continue without a counter-programme. A great defence debate in the United States is likely to be precipitated either by the signing of a SALT II agreement or by its failure. Out of this debate will almost certainly come a clearer picture of American defence priorities for the 1980s. The discussion that is taking place in the United States over esoteric programmes such as multiple aim points simply reflects the growing American awareness that strategic competition with the USSR will not be

97

seriously affected by arms control. The outcome of the debate is guesswork, but two trends can be identified. First, some short-term, stop-gap measures are likely – cruise missiles for the bomber force, a light air defence and a 'new' medium-range bomber, possibly some form of ICBM mobility, and a renewed interest in hard-point anti-ballistic missile defence. Second, in the period from about 1984–5 onwards new programmes may offer the prospect of a shift in the balance towards the West – a new large ICBM in a less vulnerable system, a second generation of submarine-launched missiles, a new ballistic missile submarine, air-launched cruise missile carriers, and possible land- and sea-based long-range cruise missiles. Finally, it is worth noting that the redressing of the strategic balance will coincide with a period of major economic strains in the USSR, the probable expiry of a SALT II agreement, the inauguration of a new American President, the 27th Congress of the CPSU and the Five-Year Plan of 1986.

Very roughly speaking, it would appear that the optimal period for Soviet security policy will be the next five years or so; after that the trends may be less favourable. The overwhelming question, therefore, is whether the Soviet Union will try to take advantage of this optimal period to insure against some of the problems that will beset her in the late 1980s.

NOTES

[1] For a CIA discussion of these issues, see *Soviet Economic Problems and Prospects*, ER 77–10436U, April 1977.

[2] Soviet statement, 19 June 1978.

Economic Resources and Dependencies

HEINRICH MACHOWSKI

All statements concerning the future develop-
ment of the economy of the Soviet Union are
more uncertain than ever before; forecasting has
become a sort of economic futurology. This is
only partly due to the lack of adequate informa-
tion (the economic statistics relating to the
USSR have not improved very much in quality
or in quantity, despite the commitment the Soviet
Government made in the final agreement of the
Conference for Security and Co-operation in
Europe (CSCE)). It is much more because we are
uncertain how the Soviet economic leaders will
react towards the altered conditions of growth in
their country and to the obvious obsolescence of
national economic planning. The imminent
change of leadership will increase that uncer-
tainty. Simple extrapolation of the prevailing
trends in development may be pointless.

In this context it is especially significant that
the Soviet Government has not yet announced
any revision of the aims it set for the period from
1976 through 1980, although such a correction
would seem to be absolutely necessary, since it
must be clear by now not only that a whole series
of detailed targets are unlikely to be attained
but that even the basic proportions of this
medium-term plan can hardly survive.

Labour
The shortage of labour is among the most
crucial changes in the bases of growth of the
Soviet economy which are already obvious now
but which will have their full effect in the 1980s.
On the one hand, the demand for labour is
traditionally high, and this is accentuated by
rather large employment reserves in existing
industrial enterprises, which is one of the most
striking contradictions and one of the most
serious failures of the Soviet economic system.

On the other hand, labour is proving more
difficult to recruit due to several factors: the
decline of the growth of population overall; the
displacement of the crucial points of growth into
Central Asia, Kazakhstan and Transcaucasus;
exhaustion of the 'classic' reserves of population
(those working in agriculture and in household
economy); and prolongation of education and
training ('investment in human resources').

The labour force, which is supposed to increase
annually by 1.5 per cent during the current Five-
Year Plan (1976–80), will in fact only increase by
0.9 per cent during the next Five-Year Plan
(1981–5) and by 0.5 per cent between 1986 and
1990. For the first time the working population
in the 'Russian' Republics is expected to decrease
from 1981 to 1985, so that growth will depend on
the development in Central Asia and in the Trans-
caucasus. The drafting into productive indus-
tries of young able-bodied people from areas
which are far away from the most important
industrial centres of the country (Asian 'migrant
workers') will cause considerable problems, not
only because of language and culture. The
employment of young people with an agricul-
tural background who have no experience of
industrial labour and who have no labour class-
consciousness can only have a negative effect on
average labour productivity.

Agriculture
Only in one field has the Soviet Union announced
tangible economic policy aims for the years after
1980. During the course of its 1978 July Plenum,
the CPSU Central Committee decided that the
development of the agricultural-industrial com-
plex of the Soviet Union was to be accelerated.
The grain production of the 1981–5 plan is
intended to reach a yearly average of between

99

238 and 243 million tons, as against 182 million tons in the 1971–5 plan and 220 million tons in the 1976–80 plan. Meat production, which came to barely 15 million tons in 1977, is to increase to 19.5 million tons by the end of 1985. At the same time, the Soviet economic leaders have stipulated that farm production should be increased by 1990 to 1,000 kg of grain per inhabitant (estimated population by 1990: 292 million).

West German agriculture experts believe that this production would be sufficient to bring the USSR up to a nutritional standard which would, quantitatively as well as qualitatively, come up to the present nutritional standards of the United States. But Soviet agriculture is at present nowhere near this output level; the annual average grain production during 1971–5 was only 732 kg per inhabitant; it ought to be 837 kg according to the aims of the Soviet Union for the 1976–80 period and this is now hardly being achieved. For the period of the 1981–5 plan, the Soviet Union is resolved to produce 881 kg of grain per inhabitant. In order to guarantee this (as well as all other agricultural policy goals), agriculture is to receive 27 per cent of all investment funds of the eleventh Five-Year Plan (this represents the present agricultural share of all productive and non-productive investments). By means of these measures 'mechanization' and 'chemicalization' of agriculture shall be continued, accompanied by more capital and more qualified personnel.

It is by no means surprising that the Soviet economic leadership makes every effort to overcome the traditional problems of agricultural shortfalls and instability. Agriculture still contributes about a fifth to overall economic production, and almost 30 per cent of the total labour force is employed in agriculture. Furthermore, 20 per cent of the total industrial workforce is employed in the foods and beverages industry, and the output of this industry depends to a very large extent on the results of the harvests. The Soviet Union had to import grain worth $7.5 billion from the OECD countries between 1972 and 1976; this amount represents about 70 per cent of her cumulative trade deficit *vis-à-vis* these countries – in other words, grain imports represent a considerable burden on the Soviet balance of payments. It seems unlikely that the USSR will succeed in transforming agriculture from a growth constraint into a growth reservoir by 1985.

Energy

Politically and economically, crude oil will represent the most important raw material of the Soviet economy in the years after 1980. As far as the future development of Soviet oil production is concerned, Western experts do not agree amongst themselves. The CIA estimates that the USSR will fail, by a fair margin, to reach her planned target of extracting 630 million tons of crude oil by 1980 because Soviet oil production is expected to stagnate at the end of the 1970s and to decrease at the beginning of the 1980s at the latest. The amount of crude oil extracted (according to the CIA) will probably only be 400 to 500 million tons in 1985 (as against 520 million tons in 1976). The most important consequences which would follow from this rather unjustifiably pessimistic CIA estimate are the following: in the future the USSR will have to import considerable quantities of crude oil from the OPEC countries at an annual cost of approximately $10 billion, which would not only seriously affect her balance of payments position but would make it difficult for her to repay the credits extended to her by the West; and the smaller COMECON (CMEA) countries, which now receive 90 per cent of their petroleum imports from the USSR, would have to use far more of their foreign exchange holdings for oil imports from OPEC countries because the USSR could not meet their needs.

The Soviet Crude Oil Balance (millions of tons)

	1975	1980	1985
Extraction	491	632	770
Imports	6	8	10
Total quantity	497	640	780
Total exports	93	132	138
of which:			
to COMECON countries	67	92	114
to the rest of the world	26	40	24

The USSR and the other COMECON countries might have to import 175 million tons of oil from the OPEC countries so that the world oil supply may come under even greater pressure

100

than hitherto and world market prices will consequently go up.

Assuming that the Soviet economic leadership will make every effort to avoid these consequences, the Berlin-based German Institute for Economic Research comes to the conclusion that an actual decrease in Soviet oil production could be avoided by the supply of sufficient investment funds; however, even then the rate of growth of crude oil extraction will decrease considerably.

No matter which turn the future development of the Soviet oil economy takes, the energy costs of the Soviet economy will increase considerably during the years to come and this in turn will have an adverse effect upon the growth of productivity.

Economic Organization

In searching for new ways of accelerating productivity, the overall economic organization of the USSR might be changed. There have recently been a number of critical comments on the weak points of the Soviet economic system in the Soviet economic press. The most pointed criticism came from a competent voice, that of Professor Walowozh, Deputy Editor and head of the economics section of Soviet *Pravda*. His criticism focuses on the present weaknesses of the Soviet economic system and, in particular, on the use of gross production figures for planning purposes. This can, he argues, lead to inefficiency and a gross waste of precious resources. He accuses the system of not applying the Marxist law of the 'economy of time', which is the criterion for the efficiency of any society, and its use of scarce resources, labour and capital. He concludes that the Soviet economy suffers from considerable losses through inefficiency. His criticism is undoubtedly one of the strongest yet made by a Soviet official.

On the other hand, the traditional system of central planning has always been an effective instrument for the application of power by Party leaders. If a conflict arises between the 'control by the Party' and 'efficiency requirements', the former will usually win. For this and other reasons (such as the 'vested interests' of the Party and state bureaucracies, an ideologically motivated refusal to accept the market mechanism and the lack of a comprehensive concept for reform), we cannot expect fundamental reform

of the Soviet economic system to take place. There will certainly be some limited corrections to the system (the founding of industrial and production associations, new plan indicators and mathematical planning methods, for example) but the success of these measures is likely to remain limited.

Since the beginning of the 1970s the Soviet Union has been implementing a policy of growth which is more orientated towards foreign trade than ever before in her economic history. At the 25th Party Congress in February 1976, foreign trade was declared a key sector of the Soviet economic policy. With a macro-economic export ratio of 7 per cent, the Soviet economy's foreign trade linkage is nevertheless rather small, and in this connection the most direct comparison is with the American economy. Trade with the Western world now represents about 30 per cent of all Soviet foreign trade; in 1970 it was only about 20 per cent. This demonstrates that Western trade can have no great influence on Soviet economic growth. For instance, according to some American estimates, the USSR invested $321 billion of fixed capital in 1975, at a time when the actual annual increment of Soviet hard-currency debt averaged only $1.2 billion. This is also true for the technology imports from the Western world. There are certainly some sectors in which the imports from the West are of crucial significance for the Soviet economy (for example, oil technology), but the diffusion of new foreign technologies in the USSR encounters the same obstacles as impede more general technological innovations. Foreign trade in general, and the trade with the Western world in particular, can only make a very limited contribution to the solution of the productivity problem. This problem is one that can only be solved by means of domestic measures.

The Growth Prospects

Against this background, we can summarize the Soviet Union's growth prospects in the first half of the 1980s. It would be much too strong to say that these conclusions amount to predictions; they are rather results based on logic. The overall economic labour productivity is expected to increase annually by a maximum of 3 per cent during the 1981–5 plan, as against 3.5 per cent from 1976–80. In terms of the national product (as defined in Soviet methodology which, in the

Western sense, is incomplete in that it omits a variety of services), the overall economic production of the USSR could expand by 4 per cent annually in the next Five-Year Plan. It is presumed to be expanding by 4.5 per cent from 1976 to 1980.

The Soviet Union will need an export surplus in the coming years in order to finance the debt service for the credits received from the Western world and/or to finance the granting of commodity credits to the smaller COMECON countries and the Third World. If the produced and utilized national products – the difference lies mainly in the balance of exports and imports – expand until 1980, in accordance with the growth rates planned for 1978 (4.5 per cent and 3.4 per cent respectively), the export surplus in 1980 will amount to some 4.5 per cent of overall economic production. On the other hand, if we assume that the export surplus will be only 2 per cent of the produced national product in 1985, the domestic spending on goods and services in the eleventh Five-Year Plan is likely to increase at an annual rate of 4.5 per cent. But, in contrast to 1976–80, the accumulation will have to expand at a higher annual average (6.5 to 7 per cent) at the expense of private and public consumption, because the need for capital will continue to increase substantially, due primarily to the displacement of the economy to the East, the unfavourable age structure of fixed assets, the necessary catching-up of agriculture and the needs of transportation and the social infra-structure. Thus, only a 3.5 per cent growth rate annually is left for consumption. No matter how the Soviet leadership divides this margin up between private and public consumption, the rate of increase of the standard of living of the Soviet population will have to diminish as against the 1976–80 plan.

Although the growth prospect is not at all favourable for the Soviet Union, such a prospect could hardly be considered calamitous by a leadership that can contemplate with some satisfaction the economic vicissitudes of the West in the aftermath of its worst post-war recession. The main economic policy goal for the Soviet leadership should therefore be to prevent things from getting worse.

Ideology in the Soviet View of International Affairs

HANNES ADOMEIT

The 'End of Ideology'

Many Western specialists on Soviet affairs are likely to react to any discussion of the role of Soviet ideology in foreign policy with a sense of *déjà vu* and boredom and the comment that there is nothing more to say about a problem that has been discussed *ad infinitum* and 'solved'. Ideology, they say, may have explained something of Soviet foreign policy in the early period (that is, before Stalin came to power) but there has been a long evolutionary process, as a result of which 'national' or 'state' interests of the USSR have superseded the ideological dimension of Soviet politics. Brest-Litovsk, the proclamation of the New Economic Policy (NEP), entry into the League of Nations, the Hitler–Stalin pact, the 20th Party Congress and the Sino–Soviet split are taken as landmarks supposedly demonstrating the increasingly marked contradiction between 'national' or 'state' interests and ideology.

This perceived contradiction is seen as being reinforced by another. 'Ideology' is usually associated with 'irrationality', 'recklessness' with 'adventurism', but these concepts are contrasted sharply with 'pragmatism', 'opportunism' and 'realism'. As a consequence, ideology as a factor influencing Soviet policy is being eroded in the mind of the Western analyst as he is faced with instances when Soviet representatives display diplomatic skill, act as shrewd and calculating businessmen or pay considerable attention to military power as an instrument of furthering state interests.

Behind this alleged contradiction between ideology and pragmatism lies the view that the ideological content of foreign policy is equivalent to the degree of Soviet support for world revolution, more specifically, the extent to which the Soviet Union is willing to employ military force on behalf of local Communists in various areas of the world. As a result, ideology in Soviet foreign policy is being eroded in the opinion of Western analysts as the Soviet leaders apparently close their eyes to the oppression of local Communists while engaging in co-operation with the oppressors at the state level (as in many countries of the Arab world), as they stand by with folded arms as Marxist regimes are crushed (as in Chile) or fail to exploit alleged or real opportunities for deepening the 'crisis of capitalism' (as in the wake of the oil crisis after 1973).

These two contradictions add up to a third one (the main contradiction, as seen by Western analysts), namely that between *Rechtfertigungsideologie* and *Antriebsideologie*, the argument being that the Soviet state is indeed an 'ideology in power', but that ideology is merely providing 'legitimacy' (*Rechtfertigung*) for action; that is, it can no longer be regarded as a guide to action and as furnishing 'motivation' (*Antrieb*). Proof of this thesis is derived from the – undoubtedly valid – observation that Marxist–Leninist doctrine has served to justify all sorts of policies. At the inter-Party level it has been used to justify support for schemes of 'historical compromise' and national union (Italy), adventurous disregard of 'mathematical majorities' (the Portuguese Communist Party in 1975) and hesitation with regard to popular-front tactics (France). At the state level it is being used to legitimize policies of co-operation with the United States and of confrontation in the case of China.

It is not these facts that are in dispute but their interpretation. This paper attempts to show that the triad of assumed contradictions does not rest on solid ground and that different constructs are needed for analysing the probable role of ideology in Soviet foreign policy in the 1980s. It suggests that it is premature to speak of the 'end of ideology' in Soviet foreign policy and argues that what has taken place so far is no more than a transformation in various functions of ideology.

Ideology versus National Interests

If it is true that the Soviet state is an 'ideology in power', it follows that the contradiction between 'ideological' and 'state' or 'national' interests is more apparent than real. The reconciliation of the apparent contradiction was provided long ago by Stalin in the following terms:

> An internationalist is ready to defend the USSR without wavering, unconditionally; for the USSR is the base of the world revolutionary movement, and this world revolutionary movement cannot be defended and promoted unless the USSR is defended [and supported].[1]

The essence of this doctrinal assertion is the idea that what serves to enhance Soviet power internationally increases simultaneously the prospects of world revolution. In practice, 'world revolution' reads 'world socialism', which reads 'the Soviet Union and the fraternal socialist countries' and those 'progressive forces' (primarily pro-Moscow Communist Parties) allied with that camp.

It would be very comforting indeed if one could reject the identification of Soviet state interests with progress in the world revolutionary movement as cynical, arrogant, pretentious, completely out of touch with reality and hence nothing to do with the foreign policy of the Soviet leadership. However, it is not wise to do so. Dynamic inter-relationships between Soviet support for 'revolutionary transformations' abroad, the occasional success of such transformations and the consequent benefits for Soviet power and foreign policy persist. Cuba is perhaps the best example of such an inter-relationship. Castro's conversion from a brand of liberalism to Marxism–Leninism would have provided the USSR with an extensive strategic-nuclear advantage in 1962 if Khrushchev's idea of a *fait accompli* had worked out, as he had anticipated it would. More recently, Cuba was instrumental in putting the Marxist–Leninist MPLA into power in Angola and pulling the chestnuts out of the fire for Mengistu's regime in Ethiopia, thereby compensating for the setback the USSR had suffered in Somalia.

Vietnam is another important example. The 'significant changes in the correlation of forces in favour of world socialism' (that is, first and foremost through the growth of Soviet military power) provided North Vietnam with the weapons and political backing to deter the United States from escalating the air and naval war beyond certain limits, carrying the ground war to the north and later enabling Hanoi to defeat the South Vietnamese forces. In turn, a reunified and militarily even more formidable Vietnam agreed, at the 32nd Council meeting in Bucharest (late June 1978), to become a full member of COMECON. Backed by a treaty of co-operation and friendship with the USSR and by Soviet political support, she took the risk of invading Cambodia, thereby serving her own purposes (realizing Ho Chi Minh's dream of a Vietnamese-controlled Indochina) as well as securing a Soviet objective (to liquidate Chinese influence wherever possible).

Needless to say, the Soviet Union does incur some costs, including about $6 million a day in direct and indirect subsidies to the Cuban economy, the costs of arms shipments and logistical support for Cuban armed forces, and suffers from certain negative repercussions of East–West detente. And as for the Vietnamese ventures, it is safe to assume that the USSR enticed Hanoi to align itself more closely with 'world socialism' and to join COMECON with promises of substantial economic and military aid, and persuaded Vietnam to embark on the invasion of Cambodia by promising to control the risks *vis-à-vis* China. But the bearing of these costs and risks shows that the revolutionary, anti-colonial and 'anti-imperialist' image successfully projected by Cuba and (before the conquest of Phnom Penh) also by Vietnam, and the demonstration of 'proletarian internationalism in action', are worth a great deal to the Soviet Union. The USSR evidently hopes that part of the revolutionary image of Cuba, Vietnam and the 'national liberation movements' will rub off and cast a bright colouring of selfless mission and international solidarity over the drab Soviet reality of depression at home and imperialism abroad. This is of some importance. Moves in the international arena that might otherwise appear unacceptable (direct military interventions in Eastern Europe, for example, and interventions by proxy in Africa and Asia or inflammatory broadcasts for the purpose of exacerbating instabilities and undermining Western influence in areas of the Third World) appear less offensive when they are legitimized and justified not in terms of Soviet national interests but in the name of a universalist ideology.

To a great extent, then, revolutionary conviction has given way to a manipulation of images, and world revolution has been transformed from a goal into a technique. The main question that arises from this is whether this technique has generally been effective.

On the one hand, Communism has largely been unsuccessful in the Arab world (certainly in Egypt) – but also in countries where relatively good relations exist(ed) between the Soviet Union and particular regimes at the state level (for example, Syria, Iraq and Libya). It is also quite apparent that the main impetus behind the violent protest movement that forced the Shah of Iran to leave the country did not originate with Moscow-inspired revolutionaries but with nationalist and fundamentalist religious forces. This underlines a more general phenomenon. There are various brands of radicalism and socialism in the Third World, but many of them, from the Soviet point of view, are 'reactionary', 'unprincipled' or 'unscientific' in ideological outlook. Even in countries like India, where the scope of socio-economic transformation has been wide and co-operation in foreign policy excellent, Soviet ideological and cultural penetration has been extremely limited.

On the other hand, these deficiencies must be contrasted with the advantages of the Soviet Union's influence over the policies of Cuba and Vietnam (as mentioned above), her strong position in Mongolia, the recent emergence of regimes with a more straightforward pro-Soviet or Marxist-Leninist orientation, including Machel's regime in Mozambique, Neto's in Angola, Ismail's in South Yemen (formerly Aden) and Taraki's in Afghanistan, and the opportunities that are provided by instability in a number of countries in the developing world.

The Soviet Union's record of using 'world revolution' as a tool of foreign policy, therefore, is ambiguous. Its likely effectiveness in the future remains to be examined (see below). It is possible to say at this point, however, that the position of the Soviet Union in world affairs would not be as powerful as it is if she had not used this tool and if she had not supported it by a skilful 'dual policy' (the phrase is that of E. H. Carr – see note 5), pursuing businesslike relations at the state level under the slogans of 'peaceful co-existence', 'non-interference in internal affairs', and so on, while at the same time attempting to utilize Communist parties and allied 'progressive forces' to achieve changes in the systems and foreign policies of the countries concerned.

The often cynical manipulation of ideology and 'progressive forces' alike may also reveal much of the perceptions of the Soviet leadership, in particular the view that 'revolutionary transformations' are first and foremost a blow to 'imperalist' influence and control – in Cuba and potentially elsewhere in Latin America; in Vietnam, Laos, Cambodia and elsewhere in Asia; in Angola and in other African countries; potentially in Portugal in 1975; also perhaps in the future in France, Italy or Greece. Not every revolutionary or pseudo-revolutionary transformation *per se* can be regarded as strengthening the power of the Soviet state, nor in all cases is it possible to say that a Western loss is automatically a Soviet gain. This is the 'objective' state of affairs. Yet it appears that the Soviet leadership is untiring in its optimistic view that if the correlation is not direct and immediate now, it will ultimately turn out to be so.

What is at issue, therefore, is the matter of Russian state power not *supplanting* Soviet ideology but *supplementing* it.[2] Just as ideology constitutes a form of power that can be used to exert influence, power in turn can be used to spread ideology. (In practice, the growth in Soviet naval and long-range airlift capabilities has been used precisely for that purpose.) It is erroneous to construct an irreconcilable antagonism between 'the Soviet national interest' and ideology: 'the national interest' is not something that is immutable or self-evident but it is subject to almost limitless manipulation and reinterpretation. Rather than one clearly defined national interest, there is instead a whole spectrum of interests, which themselves may have ideological dimensions to a greater or lesser extent. As summarized by Vernon Aspaturian, 'Soviet ideology itself defines "national interest", "power", and "world revolution" in such a way as to make them virtually indistinguishable and inseparable as the three sides of an equilateral triangle'.[3]

Ideology versus Pragmatism

To speak of Soviet ideology is to speak of Leninism, which is largely an adaptation of Marxism to a Soviet social, economic and political setting, providing a set of policy pre-scriptions and operational principles. The essence of these principles lies in the firm belief that the ends justify the means, and that man-oeuvring and flexibility are necessary attributes of politics at home and abroad. Seen from this perspective, opportunism or pragmatism can indeed be a reflection of ideologically conscious policy rather than a contradiction of it. As the editor of *Izvestiya* put it sixty years ago, at a time when ideology was of undoubted relevance to policy-making, 'We are convinced that the most consistent socialist policy can be reconciled with the sternest realism and most level-headed practicality.'[4]

It is precisely to conform with the dictates of stern realism and level-headed practicality that the Soviet Union will not be found rushing into military intervention or breaking off diplomatic, economic and other ties every time local Com-munist parties suffer from suppression by regimes with which the USSR maintains reason-ably good relations. (A recent opportunity for doing just that was provided by the Ba'ath regime in Iraq when, in the wake of the coup in Afghani-stan, it proceeded to hang twenty-one Communist Party members for having formed illegal cells in the Iraqi armed forces.) The reasons for not doing so are obvious. On the one hand, inter-vention on behalf of weak Communist parties could be very costly and counter-productive, and the rupture of relations would probably not change the fate of the Communists in question anyway. On the other hand, the maintenance of relations on the state level can safeguard some degree of influence over the internal policies of the regime. This is known to have happened in Egypt under Nasser, but it has also occurred in Syria and Iraq, where Soviet diplomats interceded on behalf of local Party comrades to mitigate their fate, to let them enter into the dominant party (for example, the Arab Socialist Union in Egypt) or into coalition governments (Syria and Iraq). Undoubtedly, this is the classic 'dual policy' still in operation.

As for the conflict of pragmatism versus ideology in Soviet relations with the developed 'capitalist' countries, matters today do not seem to be very different from those at the beginning of the 1920s, when the Soviet Union was about to embark on economic co-operation with the West in order to relieve 'temporary' economic difficulties. Lenin wrote:

> We must be clever enough, by relying on the peculiarities of the capitalist world and ex-ploiting the greed of the capitalists for raw materials, to extract from it such advantages as will strengthen our position – however strange this may appear – among the capitalists.[5]

Then, as now, the primary form of exchange was to be Western technology for Soviet raw materials. The purpose of economic exchange, then and now, was not to integrate the USSR into the Western-dominated world economy but to exploit that economy to the Soviet Union's own advantage. The methods used by the Soviet leadership were to utilize 'intra-imperialist' and 'inter-imperialist' contradictions to extract maxi-mum advantage. And then, as now, the effective-ness of this policy was limited because of the serious deficiencies of Soviet agriculture (neces-sitating the import of grain in addition to tech-nology), the difficulty of assimilating technology imports and spreading them throughout the economy and Western distrust of Soviet intentions.

Whereas there has been considerable con-tinuity in Soviet economic relations with the West, there have been changes with regard to formalized dogma and probably genuine per-ception as well. This concerns principally the long-expected and often-predicted 'collapse of capitalism' which will result from an ever-deepening crisis. It is doubtful whether the Soviet leaders still operate under the assumption that such collapse is imminent, and in fact at the 25th CPSU Congress Brezhnev felt obliged to clarify that it was 'far from the minds of Com-munists to predict an "automatic collapse" of capitalism' and that capitalism still had 'con-siderable reserves'.[6]

But it is equally doubtful whether they see the present economic difficulties in the West and Japan as anything other than the manifestation of irreconcilable contradictions inherent in the capitalist world economy. The main controversial issue in the Politburo seems to be the extent to which it is possible and desirable to intensify severe economic crises in the West, both from the outside and from the inside (using local Communist parties), and to what extent such policies would prove counter-productive by bringing to an end the benefits currently derived by the USSR from economic exchanges and even possibly by provoking a right-wing or Fascist backlash.

It is the latter – 'pragmatist' – orientation that appears to command the support of a majority among the Soviet leaders and their specialist advisers. Not surprisingly, Georgi Arbatov, the head of the Institute for the Study of the USA and Canada at the USSR Academy of Sciences (and said to be one of Brezhnev's chief advisers on East–West relations), is on record as warning against trying to give history and the apparently shaky edifice of capitalism a push during severe economic crises because of what had happened in the 1930s – the Great Depression, Hitler and World War II.[7] It is more surprising that exactly the same point has been made by Boris Ponomarev, a candidate member of the Politburo, whose sphere of responsibility in the Central Committee includes relations with Communist parties in the capitalist countries and who, along with Suslov and Konstantin Zarodov, editor-in-chief of *Problems of Peace and Socialism*, has been regarded as ideologically orthodox and a 'hardliner'. In fact, he went further in saying, 'In the nuclear age the strengthening of Fascism and, even more, the seizure of state power by it, would be even more dangerous for mankind than on the eve of World War II'.[8]

But in the final analysis, no matter whether it concerns policies *vis-à-vis* the developing industrialized countries or policies in the Third World, it is not inappropriate to say that the pragmatism of Soviet foreign policy is not pragmatism *per se* but pragmatism in the service of objectives. These objectives in turn are defined, among other things, by ideology. Faced with the problem of the surprising adaptability and dynamism of capitalism and the erosion of the traditional tools of Soviet influence in the West (that is, the reduction of control over the Communist parties), the optimal state of affairs, from the Soviet leadership's point of view, would be a long-term, creeping crisis in the world

capitalist economic system that would be severe enough to *force* its individual members to export to the USSR, slow down their tempo of economic growth and allow the USSR to catch up.

The conflict of pragmatism versus ideology in foreign policy finds its counterpart on the domestic political level in the conflict of 'Red' versus 'expert'. It is undeniable that a considerable degree of professionalization has taken place in the middle echelons of the foreign-policy establishments. Experts of the various international relations institutes under the auspices of the USSR Academy of Sciences and of the Moscow State Institute of International Relations – a category of experts whom Horelick has called the *institutchiki* – have probably more access to the top leadership today than ever before in Soviet history. So far, however, it appears that professionalization has served only to increase the overall *effectiveness* of Soviet foreign policy without having altered its basic priorities and goals.[9]

It is difficult to say whether this will change with the inevitable passing of the present gerontocracy and the emergence of a new leadership. But when speculating about the future one should not forget that the Party *apparatchiki* have never had any problems in maintaining preeminence over the *institutchiki* or any other brand of experts (including, one might want to add, the military professionals). In previous succession struggles it was always the contender in control of the Party apparatus who succeeded in rising to pre-eminence: this was true for the transition from Lenin to Stalin, from Stalin to Khrushchev and from Khrushchev to Brezhnev. Thus, any assessment of the relevance of ideology and the likely role of experts in the foreign-policy-making process hinges crucially on the evolution of the Party. It is also inextricably bound up with the problem of legitimacy of rule.

Legitimacy versus Motivation
Legitimacy of rule in the USSR is not based solely on achievement. Ideological principles – more often than not, Leninist rather than Marxist – are used to justify basic features of the 'mature socialist society', including the predominance of the Party (the 'vanguard of the working class') over all social and political forces, the restriction of all autonomous aspirations and

the rejection of 'bourgeois' notions of liberalism, pluralism and democracy. Individual rights and freedoms are not regarded as 'inalienable', value-free or neutral but are subordinated to the *bonum commune* of the society as a whole – a view that has been codified unambiguously in the 1977 Constitution in provisions requiring the citizen 'to safeguard the interests of the Soviet state, to contribute to the strengthening of its might and prestige' (Art. 62) and 'to be intolerant of anti-social behaviour, [and] to contribute in every way to the maintenance of public order' (Art. 65).

Perhaps, as argued by Robert Wesson,[10] Marxism might have been effectively (if not overtly) left behind as the new state settled down after the Revolution, and might have been replaced by a straightforward faith in patriotism, Russianism and loyalty to the new leadership, were it not for the fact that the new Soviet state undertook to govern a multi-national domain. Because of its international appeal, Marxism made it possible to gather discontented Poles, Georgians, Jews and Russians into a single militant organization before the Revolution, and it facilitated the reassertion of control over the non-Russian minorities after the Revolution. It became indispensable as Soviet forces asserted hegemony over nations of Eastern Europe.

If it is true that ideology plays a role in the European sphere of Soviet influence, it must of necessity affect Soviet attitudes and policies with regard to the Berlin problem and the German problem (West Berlin, West Germany and the Western Allies). Ideology must also impinge on European security and the scope of East–West relations in political, trade and cultural affairs, not only in Europe but also on a global scale. Because of Soviet concern about ideological security, it is even bound to make itself felt in connection with issues such as mutual reductions of armed forces and armaments in Central Europe. Finally, as the conventional and strategic balance can only be seen in conjunction, it does affect SALT.

All this was true even before the era of the Carter Administration, with its emphasis on human rights, its demands for observance of the provisions of the Helsinki Final Act and its demonstrative gestures of support for Soviet dissidents; when the Administration took office it was inevitable that the inter-relationship of issues would come into sharp focus. For years Soviet spokesmen have been taking every opportunity to point out that relaxation of tensions at the political and military level do not, and cannot, mean relaxation of the struggle at the ideological level. There has been no change in this respect. What has changed is the fact that the ideological gauntlet has been seized by the opponent, first by the American Senate (for example, the Jackson–Vanik amendment) and then by the Administration itself.

So if ideology plays an important legitimizing role, is it one of *ex post facto* 'justification' of policy but not of *ex ante* 'motivation'? This distinction looks neat in theory but is not very persuasive in practice. This is perhaps best shown by an analogy. For a tribal medicine man, the sacred myths and rituals involving the alleged healing properties of snake skins, goat's blood and monkeys' tails are undoubtedly a source of 'legitimacy' for the power he exerts. This is so irrespective of whether or not he is a complete cynic. Nevertheless, the myths, rituals and taboos can assume important 'motivating' functions under two conditions. The first is a belief on the part of the medicine man that his power will be increased if he can spread the myths to other tribes. The second is the appearance of internal or external critics who dare call his assumed healing powers a deplorable hoax or a deliberate deception; this is likely to call forth his vigorous retaliation.

Both of these conditions exist in Soviet foreign policy. The Soviet tribal chiefs hope to spread Marxism–Leninism to the national liberation movements of the Third World. And it is painfully obvious to the Soviet medicine men that the Soviet type of ideology and the Soviet type of system in Eastern Europe is vigorously under attack, not only from President Carter and the Western bourgeois theoreticians (Brzezinski being perhaps the most notorious of them all in Soviet eyes), with their concepts of 'convergence' and 'bridge-building', but also from the 'Eurocommunist comrades', in particular comrades Carrillo, Marchais and Berlinguer, and – even more important – from China.

The Chinese political and ideological challenge during the rule of Mao Tse-tung was essentially from the 'Left'. It consisted of an effort to portray China as the more revolutionary and the more internationally class-conscious of the two

Communist rivals and in an attempt to depict the Soviet Union as having succumbed to *embourgeoisement*. For as long as this policy lasted it was not particularly successful, not least because revolutionary rhetoric stood in such marked contrast to actual caution and restraint in Chinese foreign policy. However, Teng Hsiao-ping's move away from revolutionary rhetoric and 'self-reliance' to a programme of modernization, his appeals to his countrymen to learn from the industrialized countries and his calls for placing 'curbs on the polar bear' by establishing close co-operation between the United States, Western Europe, Japan and China add up to a much more serious challenge from the 'Right'.

Predictably, the Soviet leaders have not reacted and cannot react to these developments by acknowledging that they have been cynics all along and that Marxism–Leninism has been a deplorable hoax; they are obliged to react with vigorous attempts to restore ideological orthodoxy wherever possible and with strenuous efforts to maintain a pivotal position in the 'changing archipelago' of national Communisms (Arrigo Levi). In this way, the quest for legitimacy of power and 'mere' justification of policy are being transformed into motivation for policy.

The Changing Role of Soviet Ideology

To sum up, an evolutionary process has taken place, in the course of which an important transformation has occurred in the role or 'functions' of Soviet ideology. The humanist, emancipatory content of Marxism has given way to a bureaucratized and stereotyped ritualism in the service of an authoritarian state. Revolutionary idealism and missionary zeal have virtually disappeared in the Soviet Union and have yielded to a greater emphasis on legitimacy and justification of policy. However, much of the impetus behind the age-old 'dual policy' still remains intact. Increases in Soviet state power are seen by the Soviet leadership as providing more effective opportunities to produce 'revolutionary transformations' abroad; these transformations in turn raise hopes in Moscow that they will lead to an increase in Soviet influence. Thus in the future, as in the past, political, military, economic and other forms of influence will continue to be seen and acted upon in conjunction with ideological instruments.

Perhaps even more important than this (but less quantifiable and measurable) is the *psychological* dimension of ideology, the deep motivations of the Soviet leaders, including their fundamental beliefs and values, their subjective perceptions of history and politics and their assumptions about the nature of conflict. It would be fair to say that their belief, derived from Marxism–Leninism, that domestic and international politics is unrelenting struggle and that he who falls behind consistently is condemned to be thrown on the 'rubbish heap of history', explains much of the Soviet quest for military-strategic parity with (and, if possible, superiority over) the adversary super-power. It also explains much of the remarkable dynamism of Soviet policy abroad that stands in such stark contrast to the retrenchment and repression at home.

If it is correct that the psychological factors accounting for this policy are deeply rooted in the ideological heritage and in the history of Bolshevik Party struggles, and if it is also true that the role of the Party – notwithstanding the greater input of experts into the foreign-policy-making process – is unlikely to diminish with the passing of the present gerontocracy, the character of Soviet foreign policy in the coming years will continue to be that not of a *status quo* orientated power but of a power determined to effect (to use the appropriate terminology) a 'fundamental transformation of the world correlation of forces in favour of socialism'.

The political determination may be present but there are tremendous problems of implementation. Challenges to the Soviet system and to leadership of the CPSU in the international Communist movement – whether from dissidents in the USSR herself, from nationalism and liberalism in Eastern Europe, 'anti-hegemonism' in China, 'Eurocommunism' in Western Europe or the human-rights campaign of the Carter Administration and the follow-up conferences to the CSCE – have all combined to put the Soviet Union on the defensive.

As if further proof were needed, the conferences of European Communist parties in East Berlin in 1976 and on 'real socialism' in Sofia at the end of 1978 demonstrated once again the hollowness of Soviet assertions of 'proletarian internationalism' in action and exposed the deep divisions in international Communism. The problem goes much deeper than the 'sounding of a discordant note' by individual parties or the failure of the CPSU to secure a condemnation of China.[11] Mutual recriminations and ill-concealed hostility are part of a larger trend – the declining effectiveness of Marxist – Leninist ideology as an instrument of Soviet policy.

This is true for the Soviet Union herself, where central Party control clashes with the need for economic reform and efficiency. It applies to Eastern Europe, where autonomous aspirations and anti-Soviet (as well as anti-Russian) sentiments continue to smoulder dangerously under the surface. It is valid for the industrialized countries, where many intellectuals have turned their backs on Marxism and whole Communist parties have rejected Leninism. And despite 'revolutionary transformations', instabilities and the changing fortunes of Soviet influence and control, it is also true of the developing world: the process of anti-Western ('anti-imperialist') decolonization is gradually coming to an end; nationalism rejects the exchange of one form of imperialism for another; and modernization, with increasing differentiation of economic processes, tends to reduce the attractiveness of the USSR as a model of development.

So why retain an instrument that is rapidly turning from an asset into a liability? The Soviet leaders evidently face an acute dilemma. To yield to the temptations of outright nationalism and a 'right-wing alternative'[12] would deprive Soviet expansionism of its prime justification and sense of purpose. It would be unpalatable as a rationale of Soviet control in Eastern Europe. And it would fuel the conflicts within the USSR between Russians and non-Russian nationalities. As the power of the institutions (the Party, the armed forces, the courts, the police, the KGB, etc.) and the policies of the leadership are justified in ideological terms, and as immense sacrifices have been demanded in their name, from the Soviet leaders' point of view to abandon ideology would mean to pull the rug away from under their own feet. Because of this, even seemingly unimportant 'historical' problems (say, whether or not to rehabilitate Bukharin) take on explosive political importance. It has been argued that Soviet policy after Brezhnev could become more stridently nationalistic. This is quite conceivable. But if it does, ideology will not be excluded as an instrument of policy – indeed, it appears that greater emphasis will have to be placed on ideological orthodoxy.

NOTES

[1] Speech at the Joint Plenum of the Central Committee and the Central Control Commission of the CPSU(B), 1 August 1927, in I.V. Stalin, *Sochineniya*, Vol. 10 (Moscow Gosudarstvennoe Izdatel'stvo Politicheskoi Literatury, 1949), p. 45.

[2] This is a point made by Alexander Yanov, *Detente After Brezhnev: The Domestic Roots of Soviet Foreign Policy*, Policy Papers on International Affairs (Berkeley, Calif.: University of California, 1977), pp. 48, 59.

[3] Vernon Aspaturian, *Process and Power in Soviet Foreign Policy* (Boston: Little, Brown, 1971), p. 333.

[4] Yu. Steklov, *Izvestiya*, 15 March 1918.

[5] *Leninskii sbornik*, Vol. 30 (Moscow, 1932), p. 169, as quoted by E. H. Carr, *The Bolshevik Revolution, 1917–1923*, Vol. III, pt. V, *Soviet Russia and the World* (Harmondsworth: Penguin Books, 1966), p. 277.

[6] *Pravda*, 25 February 1976.

[7] Arbatov in discussions with a group of visitors from West Germany, as reported by Theo Sommer, Editor-in-Chief of *Die Zeit*, in *Newsweek*, 24 February 1975.

[8] Ponomarev's warnings against trying to give history a push were made at a gathering where illusions about the 'collapse of capitalism' usually find an easy breeding ground, namely, at the January 1975 conference of

'ideological workers' in the Soviet armed forces: 'Vsearmeiskoe soveshchanie ideologicheskikh rabotnikov: rech' kandidat v chleny Politbiuro TsK KPSS, sekretarya TsK KPSS B.N. Ponomareva', *Krasnaya zvezda*, 29 January 1975.

[9] This problem is examined in more detail in my 'Consensus versus Conflict: The Dimension of Foreign Policy', in Seweryn Bialer (ed.), *The Domestic Determinants of Soviet Foreign Policy* (forthcoming) and in Hannes Adomeit and Robert Boardman (eds.), *Foreign Policy Making in Communist Countries* (Farnborough: Teakfield, 1978 and New York: Praeger, 1979).

[10] Robert G. Wesson, 'Soviet Ideology: The Necessity of Marxism', *Soviet Studies*, July 1969, p. 69.

[11] The Romanian delegate at the conference in Sofia was attacked precisely for this, for 'sounding a discordant note', *Pravda*, 15 December 1978. More than seventy Communist parties had sent delegations, twenty-one of which were represented by their Party leaders. Theme of the conference: 'The Building of Socialism and Communism and World Development'.

[12] Possibilities for a 'right-wing alternative' to the policies of the present leadership are examined by Yanov, *op. cit.*, especially pp. 43–73.

Soviet Power and Policies in the Third World: East Asia

SIDNEY BEARMAN

It has been aptly said that all history is in some sense the history of the present. Each generation reorganizes the known facts of the past in the light of its own philosophical assumptions, its own passions and anxieties. Similarly, all estimates of the future, and particularly a future as close to us as the 1980s, are extrapolations from the present. The best that can be done is to identify the key trends as they have evolved from the recent past, as seen through the prism of the present, and project them onward, hoping that no unforeseen upheavals threaten our neat symmetries.

If the Soviet Union did but seem to have a 'master-plan' for East Asia,* the task of assessing the prospects for Soviet policies and power there in the 1980s would be vastly simplified. Soviet policies in the area, however, have been more reactive and opportunistic than creative and steady. They have also tended to be more negative than positive; that is, their underlying motivating force has been to attempt to counter the spread of power and influence, first of the United States and then of China, rather than a cohesive effort to expand the Soviet Union's own influence. Indeed, until recently, East Asia was an area of secondary importance to Soviet policy-makers.

The reasons for this are not difficult to see. Firstly, while the major land mass of the Soviet Union lies in Asia, European Russia has had the vast majority of the population, the heaviest concentration of industrial development, most of the productive agricultural land, and the most

completely developed transport system within the Soviet boundaries. The centre of Russian, and then Soviet, life had always lain very much in European Russia, the area west of the Urals. Although the country lay at the eastern extremity of Europe, and many Europeans thought, and still think, of it and its population as somewhat 'oriental', when Russia looked abroad for cultural and technological inputs, she looked westwards to Europe.

Secondly, the major security problems for Russia and the Soviet Union have historically come from the west. It is true that in early history the Mongolian hordes swept across the steppes from the east, and there is a residual fear of China for this reason; it is true, too, that at the turn of the century, and again at the beginning of World War II, the Japanese threatened the Soviet Union's eastern territories. But this was always a secondary threat; the major security problem stemmed from the west; in the recent past from Germany, before and during World War II, and from the United States and Europe after that. After the war, China, which shares a 4,000-mile border with the Soviet Union, was a Communist ally, the Korean border was secured by the North Korean Communist regime, also an ally, and Japan had turned from militarism to the pursuit of economic power. Until the development of Sino-Soviet differences into direct conflict and confrontation in the middle and late 1960s the Soviet Union had little to fear from the east.

Thirdly, the Soviet Union has had limited economic and political interests and assets in East Asia. The Soviet Union and Asian countries are not natural trading partners. Japan, for the first twenty years after World War II, was

---

*East Asia, as used in this Paper, includes the countries of North-east Asia (China, North and South Korea, Japan and Taiwan) and those of South-east Asia (Vietnam, Laos, Cambodia/Kampuchea, Thailand, Burma, Malaysia, the Philippines and Indonesia).

mainly interested in integrating her economy with the major industrialized nations of the capitalist West. And the brief period of Sino-Soviet economic co-operation, including the increased trade of the 1950s and the development of joint economic ventures, ended in 1960 with the Chinese challenge to Soviet political positions. Soviet support for revolutionary parties in Asia was equally bereft of success, since for the most part these parties turned to China for their inspiration and support. The major Soviet investment in Indonesia in the early 1960s, for example, was a failure even before the army's seizure of power in 1965. Both Sukarno and the Indonesian Communist Party, although heavily supported by the Soviet Union, had become orientated towards China, and Chinese influence had become paramount at the expense of Soviet influence.

By the middle of the 1960s changes in the Soviet Union's internal situation, in the international sphere, and in Asia were set in motion; they accelerated during the 1970s to produce by the end of the decade a completely new environment in which Soviet policies now have to operate. Each of the three areas mentioned was affected. First, the Soviet Union's eyes have turned towards her own Far East as an important frontier for economic development. Large-scale economic investment plans have been drawn up for the exploitation of the vast mineral riches of Siberia. Secondly, Soviet security concerns have also shifted eastward. As a result of the gradual accommodations reached with the United States and Western Europe, Moscow's sense of a threat from the West has been lessened. The borders of Eastern Europe have been accepted by the West, the primacy of Soviet interests in Eastern Europe is explicitly acknowledged, and the constant increase in her military power has given the Soviet Union a new sense of confidence that an attack from the West is an unlikely contingency. At the same time, however, a threat to Soviet security has arisen in East Asia. The bitter Sino-Soviet conflict, the possibility of an anti-Soviet coalition developing between the United States, China and Japan and China's plans to modernize her forces with the help of Western nations have given rise to acute concern in Moscow. Thirdly, developments in Indochina since 1975 have resulted in increased Vietnamese dependence on the Soviet Union in the political,

economic and defence spheres. As a result, Moscow has acquired a position on the Asian mainland from which to project her political influence, and the possibility of naval and air bases from which to project her military power. The first two of these developments have radically changed Soviet perceptions of the centrality of Far Eastern affairs, and the third has created a new opportunity for the Soviet Union to affect those affairs.

Soviet Siberia
Until recently the Soviet economy could rely on the more easily accessible areas of the European USSR for the coal, iron ore, oil, gas and other minerals that it needed for growth and development. These are now being fully exploited, and in some cases are in danger of depletion. To assure certain supplies and future growth, Soviet economic planners have turned to the huge natural riches of the Soviet Far East.

In this harsh and inhospitable region are found over 80 per cent of the Soviet Union's total reserves of primary energy. The Tenth Five Year Plan, covering the years 1976 to 1980, reflected the importance of this fact. Siberia was to provide all of the planned increases in oil production, with its output planned to rise from 148 million tons (about 30 per cent of the national output) in 1975 to 300–310 million tons in 1980, representing about half of the projected national production of 620–640 million tons at the end of the plan period. National output of natural gas was planned to rise from 289 billion cubic metres in 1975 to 400–435 billion cubic metres in 1980, with Siberia providing the bulk of the increase by raising output from 38 billion cubic metres (13 per cent of the total) in 1975 to 125–255 billion cubic metres (28–39 per cent) in 1980. The plan called for a rise in national coal production from 701 million tons in 1975 to 790–810 million tons in 1980, with four-fifths of the increase coming from Siberia.

In addition, there are in the Soviet Far East vast deposits of non-ferrous metals, gold, asbestos, fluorite and magnesite, together with lesser deposits of copper, tin and tungsten, and a large potential for the development of hydro-electric power. Almost all the increases by the mining industries called for in the current Five-Year Plan are to come from these reserves. It has become clear that none of these projected

112

increases will in fact be achieved in the time-frame allotted, but there can be no doubt that there will be a steady effort and considerable investment in the coming decades.

Work is now progressing rapidly to overcome one of the major inhibitions to the development of the Soviet Far East, that of transport. The Baikal–Amur Mainline railway (BAM), a second trans-Siberian link, will reportedly be completed by its target date of the mid-1980s, and various sections appear to be ahead of schedule. Its completion will add considerably to the economic development of the area, enhanceMoscow's aim of further populating Siberia and provide greater security than the existing trans-Siberian railroad, which runs uncomfortably close to the Chinese border.

Further economic development of the Soviet Far East can only lead to increased Soviet interest in improved trade relations with East Asia, in particular with Japan. During the 1960s trade between the Soviet Union and Japan increased rapidly, with the USSR exporting timber, coal, mineral ores and fish, and Japan supplying machinery and some consumer goods. In the early 1970s it appeared that trade would continue to expand steadily. By 1975 the total two-way volume was $2,795 million; in 1976 it increased by 22 per cent to $3,422 million, and the volume of trade had more than doubled since 1973. However, while there has been continued growth in Soviet-Japanese trade since 1976, the rate has slowed considerably. There are intertwined economic and political reasons for this slowing of trade, reasons which will continue into the 1980s.

A large part of the growth in trade between the two countries had been dependent on the considerable Japanese investment in Siberian development. Since 1966, when economic co-operation for Siberia was discussed in the first joint meeting of the national economic committees of the USSR and Japan, seven joint development projects in Siberia have been undertaken, for which Japan has provided credits worth $1,470 million. Counting other export financing, the total amount of credits provided by Japan up to 1977 was $2,400 million. But discussions about the largest of the proposed investment projects, the development of the Tyumen oil fields and the export to Japan of the expected oil production, have stalled.

Originally, the plan called for the construction of a pipeline linking Tyumen with Nakhodka, but the Soviet Union cancelled this and asked instead for help in constructing the BAM railway, raised the amount of Japanese investment to more than $3 billion and stiffened her terms, making the whole package much less attractive for Japan. In addition, concern arose on the Japanese side over the growing Soviet foreign debt, and particularly over the amount of credit Japan had already advanced.

Adding to these economic problems were the heightened tensions in political relations between Japan and the Soviet Union, tensions which, can only adversely affect the promotion of economic co-operation and trade. Difficulties have been caused by the defection of a Soviet pilot with his MiG-25 aircraft in 1976 and by the increasing Soviet restriction of Japanese fishing rights in the seas between the Soviet Union and Japan (and by the brutal treatment of Japanese fishermen caught contravening the unequal regulations). These problems, together with heavy-handed Soviet pressure on Japan as she negotiated for a peace treaty with China, and Moscow's continued insistence in the face of strong Japanese irredentist sentiment on retaining the four Kurile islands acquired at the end of World War II, have combined to pollute the political atmosphere so much that it is difficult for Japanese businessmen, banks, and enterprises to move forward in co-operative ventures.

Nevertheless, the trend for the future is clear. A slow and gradual improvement in the economic well-being of the Soviet Far East is under way. The Soviet Union is determined to improve the economic life of its Far Eastern components, and if necessary will go ahead on the basis of her own investment resources, although the planned levels will take far longer to reach without outside capital investment. Her interest in trade with East Asia will grow as development in Siberia grows, and the cost of transport across Siberia makes it economically far more sensible to export to East Asia than to ship the same goods to European Russia. For example, it is almost twice as far from the Soviet Far East to West Siberia as it is from Yakutsk to Japan. The Soviet Union could gain by exporting her Far Eastern oil to Japan and replacing it with oil bought from the Middle East – and such a three-way trade would also benefit Japan, who must now buy most of her oil from the Middle East and ship it over long distances. The Soviet Union has launched large-scale improvements to the ports of Nakhodka and Wrangel Bay in order to give herself added opportunities for moving goods in and out of the Far East.

With this shift in attention to the Far East, the USSR's concern about her security in this area will increase. Central to that concern is the problem raised by Chinese hostility, the potential growth of Chinese military power, and the possibility, as the USSR sees it, of a three-power anti-Soviet coalition (China, Japan and the United States) which could create a critical threat for her.

Soviet Asian Security Policies
In the immediate post-war period, Soviet strategic concerns in East Asia were at the least to forestall the further development of American dominance of the area, and at best to remove US influence entirely. In 1950 Soviet policy makers must have derived considerable satisfaction from the East Asian scene. Both China and North Korea, the two North-east Asian countries sharing borders with the Soviet Union, were controlled by Communist regimes, and China had a Mutual Security Treaty with the Soviet Union. The United States was re-drawing her defence perimeter in Asia away from the mainland and centring it on the strategic islands of Japan, the Philippines and the Ryukus; American troops had already been withdrawn from the Korean peninsula.

Stalin's miscalculation in supporting North Korea's abortive attempt to unify the peninsula by force changed the calculus of power in the region but not the policy. American forces returned to South Korea, Japan came to rely more heavily on US military support, the Seventh Fleet was strengthened and Taiwan secured from Chinese efforts to recover it. But Soviet policy, with less potential for success, was still dedicated to weakening the American position in Asia.

This policy was complicated by the overt outbreak of Sino-Soviet political and ideological hostility in the early 1960s. The Soviet Union first tried to force a change in Chinese political competition by exerting economic pressure, hoping, however, that their mutual concern with the threat from American 'imperialism' would be sufficient to assure common security interests. But by the late 1960s even this hope had evaporated. The exchange of polemics had escalated to include direct personal attacks by each country on the other and its leaders; Chinese accusations that the Soviet Union had withdrawn promised assistance on nuclear weapons development and had demanded payment for the arms supplied to China during the Korean war had been aired; intense competition for influence in Vietnam had developed, with China going so far as to refuse to transport Soviet military help across China to the beleaguered Vietnamese Communists; the Soviet Union had supplied India with military equipment, including the MiG-21, which she had refused to give China, and during the 1962 war between India and China had supported India diplomatically and given her additional military equipment. For these and many other reasons the hostility between the Soviet Union and China had hardened beyond any possibility of early amelioration, the political and ideological struggle had escalated to military probing along the once peaceful border, and containment of China, both militarily and politically, had moved to the forefront of Soviet Asian policy.

The record of the build-up of Soviet land-based forces in the Soviet Far East since 1964 suggests that the initial phases were intended more to produce political pressure on China, to induce a change in her policies than as a reaction to a real military threat from China. In 1960 the Soviet Union had 12 divisions in the Far East near the border; as Sino-Soviet difficulties surfaced this force was increased slowly, reaching 17 divisions in 1965 and 21 in 1969. This build-up of forces, coupled with the Soviet action against Czechoslovakia in 1968 and the announcement of the 'Brezhnev Doctrine', had the opposite effect on China from the one intended. Rather than being intimidated, the Chinese leaders responded with low-level probes across the disputed areas of the frontier, both on one of the Amur islands and in western Sinkiang. A combination of swift and powerful Soviet military reactions, which resulted in greater Chinese than Soviet losses, and scarcely veiled threats to launch a pre-emptive strike on Chinese nuclear facilities resulted in a Chinese agreement to enter into negotiations about the Sino-Soviet border problem – negotiations which ten years later are still in progress and which have as yet achieved no results.

The Chinese actions clearly raised Soviet fears on military as well as political grounds. From 1969 to 1972 the USSR increased the total of her troops on the border from 21 divisions to 44 or 45, including 3 in Mongolia. In addition, she has built a number of new airfields, brought in tactical nuclear weapons, constructed a series of permanent barracks areas for her troops, and now deploys about a quarter of her air force in the Far East. The military map of Asia has been completely altered. The Soviet Union is now clearly able to deal with any present threat from a militarily inferior China but the cost has been high. These Soviet actions were in large measure the motivating force behind China's efforts to improve her relations with the United States and Japan, to set in motion a modernization of her own military forces, including the creation of a nuclear strike force that provides a minimum but significant deterrent, and to threaten in the long run to create a real military threat to the USSR, rather than the present putative one.

The Search for Asian Allies

In conjunction with her efforts to constrain China militarily, the Soviet Union has attempted to isolate that country politically and to expand her own influence at Chinese expense. Until recently these efforts can be said to have met with little or no success. The difficulties bequeathed to the Soviet Union by historical and geographic factors have been compounded by poorly-conceived Soviet policies and a diplomatic style characterized by heavy-handed arrogance and disregard for Asian sensibilities.

In their dealings with Asian nations, Soviet leaders have attempted to portray themselves as leaders of an Asian nation, pointing to the huge Soviet land mass which lies in Asia to buttress their claims. Asian peoples and elites, however, have always refused to accept this self-definition. For them the Soviet Union is a European power, with interests and attitudes far from their own. As Russia, and later as the Soviet Union, she has appeared on the Asian scene like the other European powers, more often as antagonist than as protagonist. She has appeared to have predominance in mind, not friendship. They are therefore suspicious of the USSR's constant effort to proclaim herself one

of them; and Moscow's endless reiteration of this theme only makes them doubly suspicious.

The transparent nature of the 'collective security scheme' which Brezhnev first suggested in a speech in 1969 and the reaction accorded it by all Asian nations give point to these observations. Brezhnev's vague and ambiguous proposal came just after the Chinese attack on Chenpao Island in 1969, while the Soviet Union was building up her military forces on land to oppose China, and during a period when Britain was planning her withdrawal from the East and the United States was developing the Nixon Doctrine, which also contemplated a withdrawal of forces from mainland Asia. In these circumstances, the Brezhnev initiative was interpreted, correctly, as an effort to organize an anti-Chinese collective and to fill the presumed vacuum of power that might develop in Asia with Soviet political influence, backed by a growing and more powerful Soviet Pacific naval force.

Despite attempts over the next six years to re-define and refine the proposal to remove the stigma under which it was launched, Asian nations have been almost unanimous in carefully, if diplomatically, ignoring it. Having only recently succeeded in throwing off the colonial yoke imposed by European countries and acquiring national identities that are still fragile, most Asian nations have no interest in seeing Western powers replaced by the Soviet Union. Nor do most Asian nations wish to be seen to be joining in a clear anti-Chinese coalition; while wary of Chinese power, they are very much aware of that power. In the present circumstances, with Chinese policies dedicated to finding allies to oppose the spread of Soviet power, accommodation with China, rather than opposition, appears the most reasonable policy.

Efforts to find supporters for Soviet anti-Chinese policies have only met success in those countries whose hostility to China, based on Chinese support for enemies with which they have been at war, closely matches the Soviet Union's. Moscow gained a temporary ally in New Delhi by her support for India, first against China in 1959 and again in 1962, and then during the crisis that developed over East Pakistan in 1971, and the signature of the Soviet-Indian Friendship Treaty in 1971 is often cited by Soviet observers as a model for other

Asian nations to follow. As Chinese policies in South Asia changed during the 1970s, however, the strength of Soviet influence in India has waned. With the lessening of a clear threat from the Chinese, much of the impetus in the Soviet-rapprochement has evaporated.

More recently, however, the Soviet Union has found a new ally in Vietnam, and for much the same reasons. Vietnam's policies in Indochina, her clear intention since 1975 to bring Cambodia and Laos under her influence in some form of Greater Indochina, have brought her directly into conflict with China. The Vietnamese failure to find economic aid either in the West or from China in proportion to the country's needs has forced Hanoi to turn reluctantly to the Soviet Union and the Eastern European countries instead. Her growing dependence on this source was underscored by her joining the Council for Mutual Economic Assistance (COMECON) in June 1979 as a full member.

It was the outbreak of Vietnamese-Cambodian fighting, however, which moved Vietnam into heavy dependence on the Soviet Union. In the absence of Soviet diplomatic and military support for Vietnam, China would pose an acute physical security threat to the Vietnamese regime. An alliance with the Soviet Union, symbolized by the conclusion of a Mutual Security Treaty in November 1979, with a concomitant dilution of her independence was the price Vietnam was willing to pay for the freedom to pursue her ambitions in Indochina.

While the Soviet Union has acquired an Asian ally for her anti-Chinese policies, the price she has had to pay is also high. Vietnam is feared throughout South-east Asia as a potentially aggressive and expansionist power; Soviet support for Hanoi will badly tarnish Moscow's diplomatic efforts to present herself as a power with the best interests of Asian countries at heart. The costs of supporting Vietnam both economically and militarily are likely to be very high for some time to come; it has been estimated that they are running at about $1,000,000 per day. Soviet policies with regard to Vietnam are also helping to bring about the coalition of forces in Asia which the USSR most fears – a closer relationship between the United States, China and Japan. It is logical to assume that China's willingness to compromise on the demands that she had long insisted must be met

before relations with the United States could be normalized was related to her fear of the encirclement that the tightening of ties between Moscow and Hanoi represented.

Perhaps most importantly, the Soviet Union has in effect lost some measure of control over her own participation in events in the tense atmosphere that now exists in South-east Asia. There is a risk that she has become a hostage to developments in the Sino-Vietnamese dispute. Vietnam may well have been emboldened by Soviet support to the point where her actions will draw Moscow deeper into situations it would much prefer to avoid. While Moscow's preference is probably for the peaceful solution of the dispute, because any fighting may escalate quickly, the ability of Soviet leaders to orchestrate events has lessened and the odds on more serious confrontation have lengthened.

Into the 1980s

Reflected in the mirror of the present we can see the trends that will dominate Soviet participation in East Asia during the coming decade. The problems posed for Soviet policy-makers by economic and security developments in Asia have moved in from the periphery of Moscow's concerns, and the USSR can be expected to attempt to play an increasingly active role in Far Eastern Affairs. But the very considerable economic and political restraints that exist will continue to frustrate her designs. The Soviet Far East is an underdeveloped area, competing with other developing areas of Asia for investment and aid. Not only will the Soviet Union find it impossible to match the ability of the West, particularly the United States and Japan, to supply much needed economic aid to Asian countries, but she will be seeking aid herself.

The most logical course for the Soviet Union in her search for help to develop Soviet Siberia would be to reopen the stalled negotiations with Japan over joint exploitation and development of Siberia's riches. This would require a relaxation of the stringent requirements which have proved a stumbling block in the past. Japan might be willing to make some adjustments on her side, since her preferred course is to balance her policies between China and the Soviet Union. After the signing of the Sino-Japanese Friendship Treaty, with its anti-hegemony clause so detested by the Soviet Union, Japan would like to create an opportunity to demonstrate that her policies are not anti-Soviet.

Full normalization of Soviet-Japanese relations, leading to improvement in the economic sphere, however, is dependent on some solution to the question of the Northern Islands. This seems less likely than ever, given the Soviet Union's new, heightened concern for her security in the Far East, and given also her fear that returning these islands will create a precedent for the return of territory that China insists was 'stolen' from her by the 'unequal treaties' of previous centuries. In fact, the USSR has now begun to fortify some of the islands and garrison troops there. This, and the gradual but insistent build-up of the Soviet Pacific fleet, will quicken Japanese fears of Soviet intentions and encourage those in Japan who see an improvement of the Japanese military establishment as a necessary response.

While Japanese estimates of the size of the Soviet Far Eastern naval forces are somewhat higher than those of other observers, they are consistent with other estimates in charting the steady growth of Soviet naval power in Asian waters; their significance also lies in how Japan views the Soviet naval threat. The Japanese fears were expressed in the White Paper on Defence published in July 1977, where it was argued that 'the expanding military potential of the Soviet Union and the withdrawal of American ground forces from the Republic of Korea demand close attention. Particularly, Soviet naval expansion is affecting the West's control of the sea off the Russian coasts'. According to that White Paper, the Soviet Pacific Fleet had 10 cruisers, 80 destroyers and frigates, 125 submarines (50 of them nuclear-powered), 300 other warships and 240 auxiliaries. In 1979 the *Minsk*, a Kiev-class carrier, was added to the fleet.

One trend that has been clear over the past ten years has been the modernization of the Pacific Fleet to increase its mobility and endurance. These attributes will be heightened as a result of the acquisition of the use of forward logistic facilities at Danang and Cam Ranh Bay in Vietnam. The Soviet fleet will become more visible in the waters off the coast of South-east Asia as well as in the northern seas. At the height of the Sino-Vietnamese border war in early 1979, the Soviet Union sent a 14-ship task force headed by the Pacific Fleet's flagship, the missile-carrying cruiser *Sverdlovsk*, down to Vietnamese waters, and several of these ships are reported to have called into Cam Ranh Bay. In early May 1979 it was reported that a *Foxtrot*-class Soviet submarine had arrived at Cam Ranh Bay, the first report of a submarine using this facility. While Vietnam has repeatedly denied that she will turn over the Bay to the Soviet Union for use as a naval base, her willingness to allow Soviet use of the facility in return for Soviet military and economic aid makes a distinction more semantic than real.

It will not be easy, however, for the Soviet Union to translate this increasing naval power into political gains, any more than it was for her to translate the increased land power into political capital against China. In respect of Japan and the countries of South-east Asia, the enhanced Soviet naval presence will probably cause them to rely more on the US and her naval power to maintain the balance of forces in the Pacific. Only if the United States were to begin to reduce the force represented by the Seventh Fleet would these Asian powers move from maintaining correct relations with the Soviet Union to acknowledging that the Soviet Union's military power must be accommodated in political terms.

Soviet use of military might to bring pressure on her has similarly moved China to normalize her relations with the United States and to welcome the US military presence in Asia. Assuming that there is no radical change in the Chinese leadership in the next five years – and the indications are that the present pragmatic views will remain the predominant ones among Chinese policy-makers – Chinese accommodation to Soviet ideas on the direction developments in Asia should take seems unlikely. If anything, the Soviet support for Vietnam will make an improvement in Soviet-Chinese relations even more difficult.

Sino-Vietnamese hostility has had a direct impact on the Soviet-Chinese confrontation. The well-springs of the Sino-Soviet dispute are many and deep, and a reduction in tension between the two countries would require many compromises on both sides; such compromises can be visualized if the heightened military tension between the two powers could be reduced. This would in turn require some settlement of the very troublesome border issue, a reduction in the forces that now confront each other on the border, and some formula that satisfies the Chinese demand that the Soviet Union acknowledge that the Imperial Russian government had in the past seized Chinese territory. All this is far more difficult to visualize.

Although the Soviet Union would probably gain the most from an improvement in her relations with China, Soviet leaders probably now feel that there is a greater danger to be met from the south than before. If they had been able to bring themselves to thin out their forces along the border before Mao's death – or immediately after he died, when they stopped their polemical attacks for five months and made other probes to assess Chinese willingness to meet with them in meaningful talks – it is possible that some amelioration of the hostility might have occurred. Instead the Chinese leaders interpreted the Soviet refusal to deal positively with the border question as indicating no change in Moscow's attitudes towards China, and in consequence moved instead to try to form a *de facto* coalition of powers against the Soviet Union and reached out to the West for help in modernizing her forces. In addition, as part of the actions she took when preparing to attack Vietnam in early 1979, China moved at least two more divisions to her northern border with the Soviet Union to meet a possible Soviet action in support of Vietnam. In these circumstances, the USSR can only believe that no reduction in the level of her forces on the border is possible for the foreseeable future.

If Chinese hostility cannot be deflected, Soviet interest in the coming years is to find allies to help contain the growth of Chinese power. But the USSR's ability to do this is inhibited by the historical and economic realities in East Asia. Her successes have been limited to those situations in which she could exploit regional instabilities; but the provision of military aid in such cases tends to reinforce the fears other nations have of Soviet intentions. Support for Vietnam has already had this impact on the countries of South-east Asia, yet Moscow can be expected to continue to offer Vietnam such support in return for the foothold in South-east Asia that is thus afforded her.

The dilemma this poses for the Soviet Union

in Asia is indeed serious. The uneasy equilibrium that has existed for the past four or five years is being upset by the increased Soviet military and political presence, requiring a change in US policies to redress the balance and creating a situation in which Chinese, Japanese and American policies will, on this ground at least, run in parallel. The belated discovery by American intelligence that the North Korean forces are larger than had been thought has allowed President Carter to agree with the outspoken requests of Japan and South Korea, and with the clear but unspoken desires of China, and reverse his earlier decision to withdraw American ground troops from South Korea. While the troops are probably not essential to prevent a North Korean attack, this action will help rebuild US credibility in East Asia; the assurance that American power is not to be withdrawn from the area will be vital to any effort to maintain stability there.

While there will always be a risk of conflict in the Korean peninsula so long as there is no acceptance of the division of the country on either side, the greater danger to peace in Asia in the immediate future will centre on the conflict between China and Vietnam, with the Soviet Union trapped by her support for one and her hostility to the other. There are heavy restraints on a premeditated outbreak of hostilities in Korea. North Korea would need support from either the Soviet Union or China to be certain that an attack on the South, which would inevitably involve American troops, would have any chance of success; yet the Soviet Union has always been concerned to avoid such involvement of American force. China, now seeking American economic aid and trying to create a political relationship that will act as a restraint on the Soviet Union, will continue to exert her influence, an influence more significant than Moscow's, against a North Korean attack on South Korea. With American troops remaining in their blocking positions on the border, the chances of an incident escalating into full-scale war have again lessened, although that risk will remain until a political settlement can be reached.

The situation in South-east Asia, however, is very different. There, tensions exist without equivalent restraints. Each party in the dispute sees advantages in conflict, not in stability.

China will at the very least continue to supply the insurgent forces fighting against Vietnamese rule in Cambodia and Laos and may go further and attempt to teach Vietnam another 'lesson'. In this event, it may be far more difficult to keep any fighting localized, short, and controlled. Soviet prestige is now more deeply committed to support of Vietnam, and it is not difficult to visualize a rapid escalation of fighting which could involve Soviet and Chinese forces. While this would not be the Soviet preference, the USSR has, to a degree, lost control over future developments here through her ardent wooing of Vietnam. As in so many other areas of the world, the ability of the great powers to manipulate events to suit themselves has slipped somewhat from their grasp; whether a stable balance of power can be developed in East Asia is now more than ever a function of local and regional developments.

Index

120

DK
274
.P73
1980